# THE COMPASS OF
# FRIENDSHIP

*For my Dad and Mom, Jack and June Rawlins,*
*during their 65th year of marriage.*
*"I hope I've learned some*
*things they've been teaching."*

# THE COMPASS OF
# FRIENDSHIP

*Narratives, Identities, and Dialogues*

## WILLIAM K. RAWLINS
*Ohio University*

Los Angeles • London • New Delhi • Singapore

Copyright © 2009 by SAGE Publications, Inc.

All rights reserved. No part of this book may be reproduced or utilized in any form or by any means, electronic or mechanical, including photocopying, recording, or by any information storage and retrieval system, without permission in writing from the publisher.

*For information:*

 SAGE Publications, Inc.
2455 Teller Road
Thousand Oaks,
  California 91320
E-mail: order@sagepub.com

SAGE Publications India Pvt. Ltd.
B 1/I 1 Mohan Cooperative
  Industrial Area
Mathura Road, New Delhi 110 044
India

SAGE Publications Ltd.
1 Oliver's Yard
55 City Road
London EC1Y 1SP
United Kingdom

SAGE Publications
  Asia-Pacific Pte. Ltd.
33 Pekin Street #02-01
Far East Square
Singapore 048763

Printed in the United States of America

*Library of Congress Cataloging-in-Publication Data*

Rawlins, William K., 1952-
The compass of friendship: Narratives, identities, and dialogues/William K. Rawlins.
    p. cm.
Includes bibliographical references and index.
ISBN 978-1-4129-5296-5 (cloth)
ISBN 978-1-4129-5297-2 (pbk.)
    1. Interpersonal communication. 2. Friendship. 3. Interpersonal relations. I. Title.

HM1166.R39 2009
302.3'4—dc22                        2008017857

*Printed on acid-free paper*

08   09   10   11   12   10   9   8   7   6   5   4   3   2   1

| | |
|---|---|
| *Acquiring Editor:* | Todd R. Armstrong |
| *Editorial Assistant:* | Aja Baker |
| *Production Editor:* | Sarah K. Quesenberry |
| *Copy Editor:* | Teresa Wilson |
| *Proofreader:* | Sally Jaskold |
| *Indexer:* | Michael Ferreira |
| *Typesetter:* | C&M Digitals (P) Ltd. |
| *Cover Designer:* | Edgar Abarca |
| *Marketing Manager:* | Carmel Schrire |

# Contents

# Preface

What does it mean to speak and act as friends? How does friendship serve our well-being and identities as individuals and as members of various communities? To me these are fundamental questions. They call to mind the ethical spirit, practical flexibility, everyday enjoyment, and political significance of friendship. Accordingly, this book explores enduring ideals, concrete practices, and contextual demands of communicating as friends. It examines the potential contributions of friendship to the well-lived life across private and public contexts.

We can pursue friendship as a freestanding bond or as a dimension of other relationships. It intrigues me as a communication scholar that our friendships primarily continue to the extent that we meet the negotiated expectations of our relationships. Institutional, religious, and legal sanctions or familial bonds typically do not preserve friendships (Paine, 1969). Even if external forces compel interaction between persons, friendship cannot be coerced. Within the constraints of our social situations, our friendships are voluntary relations, which either party can unilaterally terminate. Sustaining friendships requires us to communicate in mutually worthwhile ways.

Despite their voluntary basis, material circumstances and cultural discourses condition our possibilities for friendships. This book argues that friendship offers edifying practices for addressing significant contingencies of social life. I begin with the dynamic tensions of similarity and difference composing our identities as selves and others. I further probe quandaries arising from our simultaneous needs for individual affirmation and belonging to groups. Throughout the book I emphasize the capacities of communicating in a spirit of friendship for making choices with others. I describe in depth how friends interweave dialogue and narrative in their communication. The book then demonstrates these conceptual advances across chapters devoted to actual conversation between friends, student discussions of cross-sex friendships, narratives of cross-race friendships, and the ethical and political potentials of friendships.

Using an array of stories and examples, I encourage readers to connect the issues at stake with their own lives. I hope readers will see their own identities and friendships as negotiated through storytelling and dialogues accomplished with others though subject to assorted constraints. I want to show how friendship presents us with moments of significant choice in shaping our selves, other persons, relationships, and communities. Thus, the book investigates the degree to which people have a say in shaping the events and quality of their lives with others.

The topic of friendship has steadily attracted greater interest both inside and outside of the academy over the past few decades. Even so, I know of no other book presently that addresses the configuration of issues examined here. The primary audience for this volume is persons seeking to understand resources and challenges of communicating as personal and political friends. I want the book to speak to a concerned, broadly educated, general reading public. I also believe professional scholars, teachers, and undergraduate and graduate students across a variety of fields such as communication, sociology, psychology, women's studies, human development, organizational studies, and education will find much of interest here. The book will be especially useful for scholars focusing on interpersonal and relational communication, social and personal relationships, friendship communication, dialogue studies, community building, and the social construction of identities. I write for a broad audience that spans disciplines with specific interests in friendships emphasizing face-to-face interactions. I acknowledge the widespread and proliferating use of communication technologies by persons who can afford and choose to employ them to supplement co-present interaction with friends and to develop virtual friendships. However, those practices for enacting friendships I leave to other scholars to study.

I would like to thank several people for their contributions to this work. First, I am always grateful for the opportunity to learn with undergraduate and graduate students. Undergraduates embody hope for me. Among other blessings, engaging with their candid insights over the last 15 years enlivens the treatment of cross-sex friendship in Chapter 5. Discussing questions and contentions with graduate students in my seminars on communication and friendship, dialogue and experience, and communication and narrative at Purdue University and at Ohio University has helped test and vivify ideas presented here. I appreciate Kenny Sibal's assistance with the references. I thank Karen and Chris for taping and sharing their conversation with me discussed in Chapter 4. I thank my friend, the late Cindy Marshall, for arranging their participation. I miss her thoughtful support, hearty laugh, and love of learning.

I thank Tom Berndt for his keen conversations and, as head of the Department of Psychological Sciences at Purdue, for providing me with office space to begin work on this book during my spring 2002 sabbatical. I thank Siv Fischbein and Cissi Olsson for inviting me to explore my ideas on friendship and learning at the Stockholm Institute of Education during October of 2006. I am grateful to Claudia Hale, Director of the School of Communication Studies at Ohio University, for providing time during the winter quarter of 2008 to complete the work.

I celebrate Margaret Seawell's encouragement early on to follow my lights in writing this book, Todd Armstrong's perceptive advice throughout the process, and Aja Baker's and Sarah Quesenberry's able assistance. I heartily thank the reviewers of this manuscript for their careful work and helpful comments: Austin S. Babrow (Ohio University), Arthur P. Bochner (University of South Florida), Jim DiSanza (Idaho State University), Elaine Bass Jenks (West Chester University), Christopher N. Poulos (University of North Carolina at Greensboro), Debra-L Sequeira (Seattle Pacific University), and Kathy Werking (University of Louisville).

I value the timely sentiments and beneficial insights of persons too numerous to mention who have talked with and supported me throughout the writing of this book. I am grateful to Dana Cloud for her generous and perceptive commentary on Chapter 5. I thank J. W. Smith for his valuable input on Chapter 6. I came to Athens to write this book, and I have much enjoyed the welcoming and collaborative environment I experience with my colleagues at Ohio University's School of Communication Studies. My friendship, teaching together, and zestful conversations with Greg Shepherd, Raymie McKerrow, Lynn Harter, and Scott Titsworth have continually provided spirited, scholarly interaction and, with Mary Shepherd, Gayle McKerrow, and Sandy Rawlins, many good times.

I especially thank Ed Shockley, my brothers Rocky, Ron, and Terry, and their families, J. R. and Laura Rawlins, Nancy Pollitt, and the memory of Jack Pollitt. I deeply appreciate the editorial skill, teaching acumen, and dedication to communication theory that Lainey Jenks contributed in carefully perusing this entire manuscript. It is a better book for her efforts.

I've written this book in the first home office I've ever had. This is because for many years I wanted to enjoy fully my time at home with Sandy, and our two children, Brian and Shelley, when they were younger and still lived with us. Now that they're out making their way in the world, I've appreciated Brian's encouragement and phone calls about "the new book." I've also enjoyed Shelley's support and her sharing readings with me. My wife, Sandy, outdid herself once more as my writing teacher. With consummate care she transformed my words from dense to danceable. She's a great bench coach who knows when to "take it to the house" and when to call time out and go for a walk. She shared grace, wisdom, and love with me during the times this book was written out on the ridge. It's time now to enjoy together some of the songs begun while writing this book.

—Bill Rawlins
Shade, Ohio

# 1

# Introduction

## *Living Friendship*

Freedom surely lives at the heart of friendships. I hope most of us can identify with Etta Mae's arrival at her old friend Mattie's home:

> She dumped her load on the sofa and swept off her sun-glasses. She breathed deeply of the freedom she found in Mattie's presence. Here she had no choice but to be herself. The carefully erected decoys she was constantly shuffling and changing to fit the situation were of no use here. Etta and Mattie went way back, a singular term that claimed co-knowledge of all the important events in their lives and almost all the unimportant ones. And by rights of this possession, it tolerated no secrets. (Naylor, 1991)

We feel comfortable in the presence of our close friends. We earn and jointly create the freedom of our friendships. Time together, straightforward talk, shared stories, and mutual respect produce the "co-knowledge" cradling friendship. I believe that friends do retain some secrets because of needs for privacy and respect for each other's vulnerabilities (Rawlins, 1983a, 1983c). Yet friends also co-create deep understandings allowing for shared moral visions and rights unique to their friendship. Ann Patchett keenly captures this special private domain with her friend Lucy Grealy:

> Our friendship was like our writing in some ways. It was the only thing that was interesting about our otherwise very dull lives. We were better off when we were together. Together we were a small society of ambition and high ideals. We were tender and patient and kind. We were not like the world at all. (Patchett, 2004, p. 73)

This book examines the unique spaces, the singular worlds that friends accomplish. I will probe the contingencies of friendships: their vulnerabilities and contributions to the larger social contexts in which they occur, the similarities and differences they recognize and suppress, their storytelling and dialogues, their shared and risked identities. Though offering peace, friendships are seldom completely placid. There is always more to friendship than two persons' lives.

Around 10 years ago I read a newspaper story that I haven't been able to forget. It seems a man living in a small town in the midwestern United States, who I'll call Hank, was about to go bankrupt. However, Hank had come up with a solution to his financial problems that he confided to his best friend, who I'll call Barry. Hank informed Barry that he had decided to set fire to his own business. He figured that the insurance settlement on the total loss would clear up his debts and put him in pretty good shape to start fresh with another venture. Soon after their conversation, Hank torched his store. Unfortunately, the flames destroyed more than he planned. Before the local fire department could extinguish the blaze, it burned down most of the block of buildings making up the economic center of the small town where they both lived. Due to the circumstances of the fire and some incriminating evidence about its cause, Hank was charged with arson.

As you might imagine, the trial created quite a stir in the little town. Despite the worrying revelation of Hank's financial straits during the proceedings, townspeople had trouble believing that an upstanding citizen like Hank would do such a thing. Influenced by an effective case for the defense, public opinion began to question the evidence of arson. This swing was occurring even though legally clarifying the fire's causes would facilitate reparations made to the other destroyed businesses. Monitoring the events closely, Barry was torn. On one hand, he was Hank's longtime friend whom Hank had entrusted with the guilty secret. Most of us would agree that the loyalty and confidence of friendship is a sacred trust. Close friendship is one of the things that make life worth living. What kind of person would betray his best friend's trust? On the other hand, what Hank did was wrong. To make matters worse, Hank's self-serving, premeditated action had caused fellow citizens considerable trauma and economic damage. What kind of citizen would protect such information and turn his back on his home community when it deserves justice? Where did Barry's true loyalties lie in this situation? Well into the trial, Barry decided to come forward and reveal that Hank had confided his intentions to him. Deeply moved and visibly upset, he told reporters after his testimony that while he cared about his friend like a brother, he felt the results of Hank's actions went beyond the trust of two friends. Barry felt he would never be able to look the people of his hometown in the eye if he did not tell the truth about the fire's cause.

What would you have done? For some time I have discussed this story with students and friends and not everyone's answers are the same. This story raises some of the questions about friendship that I address in this book. For one thing, people want to know more about the friends' conversation. Did Hank approach Barry for his opinions on the plan, or did he simply declare it as a foregone conclusion? Hank clearly trusted his friend's confidence, but did he seek Barry's judgment before making the decision? Did Hank consider the burden he imposed on Barry by confiding this criminal intention? How much thought did Hank give to the position in which he was placing Barry? What about Barry? Did he just passively listen to Hank's plan? Or did he question his friend, engage him in dialogue, and urge him to consider other scenarios? Did he play out other stories that might influence Hank to think differently about his current situation, his financial options, or the consequences of this drastic action? How these friends went about *making choices* is an important consideration.

This story also poses larger questions about the relative duties of personal friendships pursued in private versus broader civic friendships conducted in public. Under what conditions does one of these relationships exert the greater claim on us when pitched against each other? Do our duties to our community surpass our duties to our close friends as in the case of Barry and Hank? Or should our loyalties to our close friends trump our duties to our community?

Cross-cutting tensions between duty to the collective and loyalty to specific friends arise in particular circumstances. One famous example involves Brutus and Cassius, supposedly trusted friends of Julius Caesar, assassinating Caesar because they believed their action was for the greater good of Rome. "Et tu, Brute?" bespeaks Caesar's sorrowful awareness of his personal friend's betrayal. As a result, in *The Inferno*, Dante placed Brutus and Cassius in the innermost rings of Hell for their violation of personal friendship. Dante believed they belong in the hottest part of Hell because they betrayed their loyalty to their particular friend out of perceived duty to the impersonal state. In dramatic contrast, Cicero saluted friends who upheld their duties to the Roman state over personal loyalties. He believed there cannot be a viable state if people do not place duty to it above their personal attachments. Indeed, the private moral visions of friends can promote factions and divisiveness within the collective order. In this book I consider further the cross-cutting pressures that can arise between impersonal duties to broader collectives versus caring for the needs of personal friends. Sometimes our friends may act selfishly as in Hank's case. In other cases, our friends who challenge the impersonal political order may be courageous forerunners of necessary social changes.

What considerations would you find important in choosing between your close friend and the demands of your larger social world? Maybe you presumed that Barry and Hank lived in a homogeneous community. In this case if Barry identified closely with everyone else involved because of their similarity to him, perhaps it was easier for him to act for the greater good of his community. After all, a lot of folks just like him had suffered. But what if he and Hank had always been excluded because of their racial, ethnic, or religious differences, or their sexual orientation? What if they had been oppressed as a devalued minority due to their shared differences from the larger community? What if Hank's business endeavors took place in a constant struggle against powerful prejudice? Do any of these factors change how you feel about Barry's choice to testify against him? What if Hank had been systematically denied opportunities by the townspeople because of his differences while Barry was the only person in town who became his friend despite their differences? How do you regard Barry's decision now?

Instead of these two men, what if the story involved a man and a woman? Hank and Mary are the longtime friends. What differences, if any, would this make in your perceptions of Mary's decision to testify against Hank? What if Hank was a woman named Hanna? How would you evaluate Barry's decision to renege on Hanna's trust? What if both friends were women? How do perceived similarities and differences between the friends and vis-à-vis the larger community interact to shape identities, perceptions of relationships, and responses to others? How do the activities of friends relate to matters of social justice? Who (including you, the reader) identifies with whom in these various scenarios, on what bases, and with what consequences?

Why is friendship positioned at these flashpoints? How does friendship simultaneously relate to our identities as individuals and to our participation in larger groups? How is it that we use the same word "friendship" to describe a gamut of relationships from close dyadic bonds to diverse public connections of varying lengths of time and degrees of involvement? The word "friendship" typically implies benign meanings. How does friendship sustain its benevolent, even moral, connotations? Discussions of friendship as a guide to proper conduct appear in numerous contexts. Authors recommend the values of friendship as a moral model for the relationship between family members (Lindsey, 1981), authors and readers (Booth, 1988), co-authors (Lunsford & Ede, 1987), researchers and participants (Newbold Chinas, 1993; Tillmann-Healy, 2003), teachers and students (Jackson & Hagen, 2001; Rawlins, 2000), academic advisors and students (Rawlins & Rawlins, 2005), lawyers and clients (Fried, 1976), and physicians and patients (D. N. James, 1989). What gives friendship this flexibility of application across contexts? What meanings of the term remain consistent and which ones change? What ethical connotations are implied by describing relationships as friendships?

Aristotle (1980) devotes two books of his *Nicomachean Ethics* to friendship. He describes two broad forms reflecting different contexts of friendship—*true friendship* and *civic or political friendship*. Both forms involve distinctive qualities and demands. Even so, in actual practice the two forms overlap in significant ways to compose evolving intersections of social participation. Aristotle extends his notions of true dyadic friendship in describing civic friendship. Civic friendship is equally important because communities where people demonstrate good will, address common concerns, and dwell in peace as political friends enable the continuing possibility of dyadic friendship (Hutter, 1978). The fates of personal and political friendships interweave in actual human circumstances.

*True friendship* (which I also call close or personal friendship) involves distinctive characteristics for Aristotle (1980). Personal friendship occurs between specific individuals and involves *concern for the other person for his or her own sake*. Suttles (1970) terms this the "person-qua-person" orientation of friendship. In close friendship we desire good things to happen to our friend because we care about this particular person. The activities composing personal friendship occur for the most part in private settings out of public eyes and ears. For Aristotle true dyadic friendships also involve *mutual well-wishing*, which includes reciprocated concern and actions to benefit each friend. They jointly experience the gratifications of their friendship. However, Aristotle holds that true dyadic friendships only occur between persons (he said men) who are alike in virtue. In their purest form such friends duplicate each other's essential qualities; a friend constitutes "another self." I consider problems associated with his presumptions of similarity and privilege throughout this book. I give them particular attention in Chapter 7 when considering limitations of Aristotle's notions of political friendship.

Aristotle (1980) contrasts true dyadic friendships with those of utility and of pleasure. The latter are inferior kinds of friendship in which individuals primarily use each other for personal gain or gratification. Consequently, such friendships end when they expend the bases for utility or pleasure. While true friends also share pleasure and can assist each other, Aristotle notes a different primary motive. It is their pursuit of the good life together in light of their mutual well-wishing as intrinsically worthy persons. Close dyadic friendships are the primary focus of Chapters 3 through 6 of this book and are perhaps what contemporary people typically think of when friendship is mentioned.

By comparison, *civic or political friendship* describes a stance toward a number of other persons who occupy shared places and times. The practices of civic friendship connect citizens as friends in public settings and discourses. Such friendships are characterized by *good will*. Political friends wish each other well in their activities as persons occupying commonly held spaces. They actively support each other's performances as citizens through behaving in ways that sustain a hospitable environment for interaction. Of matching importance, political friends devote themselves to pursuing a *common good*. They do things together primarily to serve purposes that transcend the specific desires of the individuals or subgroups performing the actions. Acting as political friends, they orient toward something more encompassing than their individual selves—a commonly recognized good. While they do not necessarily share the same interpretations of the common good, they realize that a larger cause and a broader constituency of similarly concerned citizens benefit from their efforts. Although civic friends may personally enjoy the positive results of their cooperative actions, they do so primarily as members of a political community, not as detached individuals.

Neither communicating good will nor pursuing a common good is first and foremost a personal disposition or merely an emotional tendency (Hansot, 2000). Rather, each is a practice that we choose to perform as a consequence of choosing to live in civic or political friendship with others. Importantly, these practices are not devoted restrictively to others as specific individuals who display idiosyncratic attributes or desires. They are activities performed in concert with other community members with an eye toward sustaining a commonly occupied space in ways that recognize and benefit all participating citizens. Living in political friendship with others involves our ongoing efforts to display good will toward our civic friends and to pursue actively common concerns. When conducted properly, civic friendship provides a basis for belonging as citizens but also a basis for responsible freedom.

Despite their obvious differences, both personal and political friendships suggest benevolent, hopeful orientations toward social life. The concern for a specific other person practiced in personal friendship broadens into the generalized sense of good will practiced in civic friendship. Likewise, the mutual well-wishing performed in personal friendship expands to focus on a common good in civic friendship. We purposefully remove ourselves from responses to specific individuals and concentrate on a broader, shared enterprise. Meanwhile, a social context of civic friendship can facilitate the possibility of personal friendships, even though dyadic friendships are not a necessary or desirable consequence across all public circumstances.

The virtues and vexations of friends' communication have captivated me for 30 years (Rawlins, 2007). In trying to understand the contradictory, situated practices of friends' interaction, I turned early on to a dialectical perspective. From my first presentation of dialectically informed insights (Rawlins, 1979) through early research reports (Rawlins, 1983b, 1983c) to delineating a theoretical account of the perspective (Rawlins, 1989a) to applying dialectical thinking to friendships across the life course (Rawlins, 1992), I have found it to be an enriching, evolving orientation for inquiry. I briefly review this dialectical perspective below. While I have found these dialectical principles helpful in understanding the predicaments and possibilities of friendships, I consider it unproductive to conceive of any fixed, primary set of dialectical tensions. Indeed, it is quite incompatible with the volatile energies and the changing, contextual understandings of dialectics to do so (Henry, 1965; Rawlins, 1998b). Lured by questions of friendship, I devote much of this book to probing *the dialectic of individuation and participation* for the first time. Chapter 2 describes *individuation* as identifying an individually embodied self or a social group as a distinct entity separate from others. Communicating individuation occurs concurrently with *participation,* identifying self or groups as relational entities necessarily connected with others. In conversation with insights provided by dialectical thinking, I detail in Chapter 3 and exemplify in Chapter 4 the interconnections of storytelling and dialogue characterizing friends' discourse.

The dialectical perspective employed here involves four basic elements: totality, contradiction, motion, and praxis (Rawlins, 1989a). *Totality* highlights the vast interrelations constituting social life. All friendships are affected by social and political forces. In turn, friendships influence all areas of society. *Contradictions* are incompatible yet mutually conditioning aspects producing the dynamic pulse of human relationships. For example, as we noticed in the story of Barry and Hank, the contradictory demands on friends can arise from simultaneous, opposing private and public responsibilities. *Motion* describes relationships as always changing from barely noticeable to dramatic ways. Stasis is an illusion; communicative life inherently responds to discourses already in play. People grow closer and farther apart, affecting and affected by big and small personal and external events. *Praxis* describes the private and public world-shaping reflexivity of social action. Constrained by and responding to our circumstances, we make active choices as subjective agents. Our choices create objective conditions that we must then address. We are simultaneously subjects and objects of our own communicative actions. What objective conditions requiring response did Hank and Barry create for themselves as a result of their actions? How did Barry's testimony shape his and Hank's choices for the rest of their lives? All of our choices both open up possibilities and constrain further choices between our friends and in society.

I have previously described six dialectical tensions in the ongoing communicative achievement of friendships (Rawlins, 1989a, 1992). The *dialectic of the private and the public* articulates the tensions of friendships occurring across a considerable range of social relationships. Friendship can arise voluntarily as a freestanding bond, or as a dimension of other relationships like marriage, family, neighborhood, work, and politics. We choose our friends within the constraints of our situations. Dyadic friendships are subject to review by other more normatively located relationships. Friendship occupies an uncertain position in the hierarchy of relationships because it *complements, fuses with, competes with, or substitutes for* these other personal and social relationships (Hess, 1972). For example, between people who are musical composers, sports teammates, scholars, or politicians, friendship can *complement* the otherwise professional or instrumental relationship. In contrast, becoming friends might *compete* with the organizational requirements and expectations of a superior/subordinate arrangement. Further, friendship can *fuse* so completely with spousal or sibling bonds that it becomes difficult to decide which type of relationship is being enacted. Finally, when we are without kin, friends may *substitute* for our family (M. Friedman, 1992; Lindsey, 1981). The peculiar *double agency of friendships* allows them to course in and out of private and public life, simultaneously serving (and risking) personal and social integration (Rawlins, 1989b, 1992).

The *dialectic of the ideal and the real* expresses the interplay between the cultural ideals of friendships and their problematic achievement in concrete circumstances. Important ideals of human relationships are associated with friendship across times and cultures (Aristotle, 1980; Brain, 1976; Paine, 1969). Across cultures friendships embody esteemed qualities of human relationships, including trust, loyalty, generosity, and concern for the other's welfare for his or her sake (Aristotle, 1980; Brain, 1976; Krappmann, 1996). A humanizing blend of personal autonomy and social participation lives at the heart of friendship. Friendship can foster responsive and responsible freedom. Our choice to befriend others enhances the relationship's ethical significance (M. Friedman, 1992). In contrast to categorically enforced, compulsory duties, we voluntarily negotiate the covenants of friendship. Fulfilling our freely chosen obligations to one another as friends attests to our very characters as social beings and our capacities to make promises to others (Grunebaum, 2003).

Aspiring to equality also characterizes friendship. Friends seek ways to treat each other as equals despite differences in personal characteristics or social circumstances. The practices of equality constitute one of friendship's staunchest ethical potentials. Finally, the mutuality of friendship simultaneously benefits the other as well as the self. Paine (1969) asserts that the notion of a bargain takes on a different meaning between friends. He states, "Expressed as a bargain, A, in his concern with *his own side* of a bargain with B, is, in friendship, *also concerned with* B's, and vice versa" (p. 512, original emphasis). We acknowledge self-regarding concerns but view them as fundamentally altered by the mutuality of our friendship (Mills & Clark, 1982; P. H. Wright, 1984). However, friendships are mostly unprotected by legal, kinship, or religious sanctions. They are actively negotiated in personal and political contexts and highly susceptible to their social circumstances. Accomplishing the ideals of friendship requires facing the realities of cultural life.

I refer to *the dialectic of the freedom to be independent and the freedom to be dependent* as "the dialectic of conjunctive freedoms." This dialectic is a vital focus of this book. Acting upon these contradictory freedoms uniquely positions friends' activities of individuation and participation in accomplishing their identities together (Rawlins, 1983b; Wiseman, 1986). Friendship is founded upon connected, responsible, positive freedoms. It requires unforced yet mutually contingent choices to respond to each other as friends. Friendship cannot be demanded. Between friends, exercising the freedom to be independent creates distance from the requirements of the friendship; it asserts individuation.

We pursue distinct projects and utilize our singular potentials. Yet our friend simultaneously grants this freedom with confidence in our participation in shared friendship. Our freedom to be independent is experienced in conjunction with our freedom to depend on our friend. We understand our separation as a moment within an ongoing relationship that includes the open invitation to call upon our friend.

The *dialectic of affection and instrumentality* formulates the tensions between caring for and using friends. As Aristotle (1980) notes, friendship's affections ideally involve caring for others as an end-in-itself. Regarding our friend merely as a means to self-serving ends, rather than serving the friend's well-being, sullies the ideals of disinterested affection for our singular friend. Meanwhile, participation in friendship includes relying on others for assistance and to complete ourselves even as others rely on us to fulfill themselves (Bakhtin, 1990). Friendship arises from affection for one another for our own sake (individuation) *and* as a way to belong and prosper with others (participation).

The *dialectic of judgment and acceptance* formulates important challenges within friendships to appraise who we are and who we should become. Because our friends know us well, they perceive us in ways that confirm our own self-perceptions, including our faults and virtues. Our friends accept us for who we are. However, this acceptance arises in light of evaluative standards that we have negotiated. As Rothleder states, "Both creation and judgment are integral parts of friendship" (1999, p. 117). We judge *with* our friends, and we judge each other (Beiner, 1983). In their best moments, friends perform the intertwined motivations of judgment and acceptance as *compassionate objectivity* (Rawlins, 1992). Friends deliberate with us and help us to know where we stand. They compassionately discern differences that matter in our lives even as they affirm meaningful similarities.

The *dialectic of expressiveness and protectiveness* describes the contradictory impulses to be open and candid and to be responsibly discreet in communicating with friends. With friends we speak our thoughts and feelings directly. Even so, across situations we recognize matters about ourselves that should remain private as well as issues that our friends consider too sensitive or volatile to discuss (Rawlins, 1983a, 1983c). Forming friendships involves engaging these dialectical challenges in a benevolent spirit. We experience these dialectical tensions of friendship as creative but often demanding opportunities to respond to valued persons.

Living in a world increasingly divided by differences, we are bombarded with examples of corporate greed and daily violence. We live in times of harried personal lives, diminishing existential connection, and increasing alienation. In these disheartening circumstances, I believe that communicating as friends offers hopeful alternatives. In this spirit, I examine *the compass of friendship* in this book. I intend two meanings of the word "compass." First, I mean the extent to which we can realistically apply friendship's ethical ideals across private and public contexts. What is the practical reach of friendship? What is offered by extending the hand of friendship across the spaces between self and other? How far can we project the humane spirit of friendship in proposing commonalities, recognizing and spanning significant differences? Second, I mean the capacities of friendship for offering moral guidance in our personal and public lives. How can friendship's ethical practices contribute to making choices as individuals and political communities that constructively shape the courses of human events?

Calling others friends involves adopting a benevolent stance toward them. It also means negotiating mutually recognized standards for action. Friends communicate in ways that serve individual needs in some situations and combined interests in others. The combination of ideal expectations and situated achievement of enriching communicative practices leads me to characterize the finer moments of communication between friends in terms of narrative and dialogue. Friendships occur along continua. There is considerable range in the ways that the attributes of friendship discussed in this book are actually realized in specific relationships. While based on friends' choices and practices, all friendships remain highly susceptible to the enabling and constraining features of their circumstances.

Soberly acknowledging limitations, I view friendship as offering compelling ideals and concrete practices for grappling ethically with the challenges of contemporary life. This book explores potential contributions of communicating as friends for constructing identities, dealing with differences, and pursuing well-lived lives. I consider the rewards and challenges of friendship as an interpersonal relationship. I also examine the ethical potentials and limits of political friendships for building meaningfully inclusive communities. Throughout the book I emphasize the capacities of communicating in a spirit of friendship for co-creating and making choices with others.

In developing the positions offered here, I address narratives of friendship from my own life and the lives of persons who generously have shared their lived experiences with me. Informed by Bateson's (1972) notion that all communication contexts are contexts of learning about our diverse premises for communication, I have placed few boundaries on my learning activities in writing this book (Rawlins, 2007). I have drawn upon scholarly essays and research reports across humanistic and social scientific disciplines. I have also studied short stories, novels, and plays shedding light on the joys and predicaments of friends. Newspaper and magazine articles, screenings and transcripts of television programs and movies, everyday conversations recalled or recorded with others, spontaneous and planned interviews, Internet sites, reflections on my own life and the lives of students I am fortunate to co-learn with—all of these discourses inform and enliven this book.

The next two chapters after this introduction outline conceptual foundations. Chapter 2 states my assumptions about human communication underpinning this book. I describe how perceptions of similarities and differences shape communication about selves and others. I introduce the notions of *individuation* and *participation* and examine their dispiriting and edifying modes for co-constructing identities. Chapter 3 relates storytelling and dialogue as vitally interwoven communicative activities within friendships. I envision the ongoing communicative achievement of friendship as involving *a dialogue of narratives and a narrative of dialogues* shaping the identities of friends. Chapter 4 exemplifies these practices of storytelling and dialogue using the afternoon conversation between two lifelong, women friends. Chapter 5 cross-examines undergraduate students' arguments concerning the possibility versus impossibility of enduring, close, cross-sex friendships. Invoking artifacts from North American popular culture and lived experiences, their discussions display gendered identities, sexual orientations and identities, and narratives of romance and the well-lived life. Chapter 6 investigates cross-race friendship between blacks and whites. I exemplify the predicaments and possibilities of bridging racial boundaries through interracial friendships using a literary depiction, published autobiography, and interviews with a male and a female pair of interracial friends. Chapter 7 inspects the ethical profile of friendship. I then consider the potentials and limitations of political friendships for pursuing social change. Chapter 8 surveys the compass of friendship in light of the previous chapters. It reminds readers how friendship embodies an invitation to dialogue, co-create stories, learn together, and make choices across contexts. It assesses the potentials of personal and political friendships for promoting individual and collective identities and well-being.

Thus, this book begins with two chapters of conceptual discussion, and moves through three chapters focusing on dyadic friendships. Yet in discussing dyadic cross-sex and cross-race friendships, I increasingly must address the enveloping discourses and sociocultural contexts that enable and constrain their existence. Acknowledging personal friendships' susceptibility to contextual factors, Chapter 7 necessarily examines ethical and political potentials of friendship for accomplishing social change. Across the book we are drawn from personal and private to political and public contexts of friendship.

Friendships are questions of degree. They exist on a panoramic continuum of everyday contingencies conditioning the participating friends' well-being. Static definitions of friendship fail to capture the lived actualities of friendships—their finitude, flexibility, and fragility. Friendships can present elusive dreams and evaporating hopes hampered by concrete conditions and divisive cultural prejudices. However, they also involve the reassuring presence, the helpful hands, or the tough truths gifted to *this* person when she or he most needs it by someone who cares about that person. They involve as well the groups of concerned citizens who voluntarily share the work of defying the unjust development in a neighborhood, the threats to the safety of children, the needless violence of a polity, and the destruction of our ecosystem.

Let us now explore the situated capacities of friendship to address significant similarities and differences in edifying ways, to help people integrate and distinguish public and private identities and responsibilities, and to make thoughtful, constructive choices. Living friendship requires and facilitates learning, humility, relational integrity, thoughtfulness, and always becoming with others.

# 2

# Making Choices as Communicators

*Similarity, Difference,
Individuation, and Participation*

*"We need each other to become ourselves." We need talk, not
merely to fill a sensory vacuum, but to fill what would otherwise be a far more intolerable void within ourselves, where
we seek an identity. (Kaplan, 1969, p. 99)*

B eing alive is never a static condition. From the moment we draw
our first breaths outside our mothers' bodies, we enter a world of
human activity. Our initial surrounding environment may range from
bustling to tranquil, nurturing to threatening, dry to humid, cold to
warm. Whatever the circumstances, as newborns requiring attention
from others, we immediately begin our incorporation into relationships and our emergence as meaning-making beings. Throughout our
lives, we perform and become aware of our limits and potentials as
persons. Our sense of self arises and is sustained through our interaction with others (Mead, 1934). As human beings, we are always

involved in the process of becoming who we are. This lifelong process of becoming ourselves with others is communication.

In speaking about communication in this book, we encounter numerous contradictions and paradoxes.

(1) Communication always occurs during moments when multiple possibilities are constantly intersecting. Far surpassing our awareness and capacities to respond, a vast world of contingencies and choices *simultaneously* addresses each one of us every second of our lives (Bakhtin, 1993; Holquist, 1990). Meanwhile, these same moments transpire incessantly in a *sequential* passage of time. Our ongoing activities in the face of each moment's unique configuration of historical, natural, and social conditions continually define who we are and who we may become. Reacting without thinking, doing nothing, or acting in consciously determined ways in facing these moments' potentials play roles in forming our possibilities (W. James, 1991). Paradoxically, *simultaneous configurations* and *sequential events* compose the lived temporality of human communication.

(2) The communicative activities of humanity are always already in progress. As a result, *our individual initiations of communication are inherently responses*. As Gregory Bateson (1958, p. 175) observed, we all perform "the reactions of individuals to the reactions of other individuals" in communicating with others. In responding to our social circumstances as we understand them, we simultaneously initiate possibilities for ourselves and others to address. Meanwhile, our beginnings always involve our responses to already emerging conditions.

(3) Our choices are enabled and constrained by historical, natural, and social factors beyond our control. At the same time, we co-construct, select, and negotiate our possibilities to varying degrees through our actions with others in emerging contexts. *As social beings we continually make and are made by the possibilities composing our life circumstances.* This is the *praxis* of everyday life. How much we actively are able to "do" and how much we are passively "done to" varies significantly for individuals across contexts.

(4) Becoming who we are as persons involves perhaps the most fundamental paradox: We are both parts of and apart from social groups. Kenneth Burke described it as "co-existent unity and diversity—'something' in relation to 'something else'—which is probably the basic distinction of our earliest perceptions" (1931/1968, p. 142). On one hand, *we learn who we are and accomplish*

*our identities through our **participation** in enveloping social forma-tions.* We come to know ourselves as members of specific fami-lies, groups, and cultures—as users of particular languages and discursive practices that emerge across historical circumstances. We recognize ourselves and are recognized by others *as parts of* these social formations that transcend us as individuals. For example, I am a member of the Rawlins family, as well as the School of Communication Studies at Ohio University; I am a white, male professor, and a speaker of English as my first lan-guage. The list of possible social groupings used to identify me through association could go on indefinitely depending upon which aspects of my being-in-the-world I or others find relevant to employ in describing me. That is, I am also middle-class, het-erosexual, middle-aged, near-sighted, right-handed, and a fan of Joan Armatrading. Commonalities are sought here to connect me with others in identifying myself.

On the other hand, *we simultaneously learn our distinctive capacities and accomplish our identities as singular, embodied beings through our **individua-tion** from enveloping social formations.* We come to know ourselves as unique persons who manifest variations from definitive characteristics, discourses, or practices of inclusive social groupings of all sizes. We recognize ourselves and are recognized by others as *apart from* some of the same social categories with which we can be identified. For example, I may see myself and/or be seen by others as a liberal versus conserva-tive member of the Rawlins family, a qualitative versus a quantitative scholar, a "sensitive" versus a "macho" male, an English speaker with a faintly hick versus highbrow accent. The categories used to divide self and others are potentially endless. I am also a qualitative scholar who prefers ethnography and narrative inquiry to conversation analysis, as well as a musician who prefers to play acoustic guitar. In these instances differences are highlighted to distinguish me from others.

## ❖ PERCEIVING SIMILARITIES AND DIFFERENCES

This book will examine implications of this paradoxical process of simul-taneously invoking similarities and differences in making sense of who we are with and in contrast to others. Our perceptual process of noting similarities and differences goes on constantly, even as we act and com-municate in ways that change their significance or create new align-ments among them. Reflecting the inherently paradoxical nature of identification, John Dewey stated, "One always identifies by discovering differences that are characteristic" (1931/1988, p. 208). Kenneth Burke echoed, "One talks about a thing by talking about something else" (1931/1968, p. 141).

But what *are* differences? Gregory Bateson gives us an instructive answer that reads like a riddle:

> A difference is a very peculiar and obscure concept. It is certainly not a thing or an event. This piece of paper is different from the wood of the lectern. There are many differences between them—of color, texture, shape, etc. But if I start to ask about the localization of these differences, we get into trouble. Obviously the difference between the paper and the wood is not in the paper; it is obviously not in the wood; it is obviously not in the space between them; and it is obviously not in the time between them. (Difference which occurs across time is what we call "change.") (1972, p. 452)

From Bateson's words, we learn that *difference and similarity exist only in relationships,* only in the between. Something can be different only in relation to something else. Indeed, it is only different from itself across a span of time, however brief, and we call that "change."

The same goes for similarity. Something can only be perceived as similar in relation to something else that is not identical to it. Of course, a relationship of pure identity is an abstract concept, not a concrete occurrence in the world. Nothing in this world is identical to anything else (otherwise "they" would literally be the same thing). Things can be *perceived* as similar, even to themselves over time. Noticeable differences between them when they are juxtaposed and/or perceived over time make their similarity meaningful. Differences can be concrete (like vision, hearing, taste, smell, or touch) or abstract (like intelligence, friendliness, normality, or democracy). A *threshold* must be reached in social situations for differences to be noticed. Bateson calls these "differences that make a difference" (1972, p. 456). This last point is crucial, and we will examine ways in which both differences and similarities that make a difference are socially constructed, noticed, and named in facilitating and undermining friendships.

What do you notice about persons that distinguish them from others in a social situation and makes you want to approach them for conversation? Or avoid them? Is it their physical appearance? How they carry themselves? Is it opinions you have heard them express or the way they laugh? Some look in their eye, straightforwardness, or ironic manner of speaking? Do the attributes that distinguish them in the situation also make them appear similar to you—in their perceived age, gender, ethnicity, race, social class, religion, intellectual, physical or communicative ability? Or do their perceived differences from you draw you to them? Is it some conscious or unconscious composite of qualities? What do you pay attention to that finds you noticing them? Have you always noticed these same attributes in deciding whether or not you should approach or avoid others? Or have the coordinates on your radar screen changed?

Discerning difference and similarity is highly contextual. The selection and perception of any difference or similarity between people, events, ideas or things is always performed by a subjective observer in a specific time and place in relation to what is being perceived, even when observing oneself (Bateson, 1979; Dewey, 1931/1988). Bakhtin terms the unique spatiotemporal coordinates we occupy each second of our lives "the law of placement" (Holquist, 1990). But how are our experiences of any given time and place constructed? What traditions articulate to a great extent our possibilities and impossibilities, our interests, our projects for this very moment? What is necessary versus optional to occupy our attention? What do we attribute to others and to ourselves, or perceive without thinking? There are certainly many ways to answer these questions about any person. We could focus on physical exigencies. Individuals will understand their immediate physical conditions in varying degrees of conscious reflection depending upon their embodied abilities. A starving person will be especially vigilant about the prospect of food and those who have it. A good swimmer may assume unreflectively that others possess the same capabilities until a situation requiring swimming highlights important differences.

Enveloping cultural discourses and narratives comprehensively pattern the subject positions of everyone involved in the situations just described. Their very bodies are sites of cultural determinations. What categories of nationality, race, class, and ethnicity would make it nearly inevitable in *this* culture at *this* point in history that *this* person would be starving and not well fed? Why do empowered people like the swimmer often take for granted their capacities and privileges and assume that others share them? How are these assumptions culturally constructed, insisted upon, or obscured in any context? Are there discourses that categorically mark others as significantly different in their capacities? More destructively, do some discourses tangibly constrain their opportunities, thus ensuring a significant difference in capacities? What discourses construct the baselines for recognizing what these enabled and constrained persons may take for granted, or for comparing their particular conditions with those assumed to prevail?

We can focus on any number of attributes as we interact with others. The similarities and differences that we select are inherently relational propositions. What *difference thresholds* do we employ in given cases, the "differences that make a difference," and how are they constructed? Meanwhile, what *similarity thresholds*, the similarities that make a difference, do we employ in our treatment of others? The distinctions and similarities we invoke range from the very subtle, like the comparisons drawn between the "big-endians" and the "little-endians" in Swift's *Gulliver's Travels* to the most obvious, such as vivid contrasts or resemblances in skin pigment or hair color, religious or political beliefs, or ideological outlooks. Nonetheless, whether a person splits the egg at the big or the little end is not a subtle distinction for the people who self-identify with these practices. Motivations for selection are always based on our particular interests (Burke, 1966; Dewey, 1931/1988). Identified similarities and differences may be deeply etched in historical animosities or concocted in a given context for specific, opportunistic reasons. *In a given situation, who or what people are identified as, with, or in contrast to, may not involve the same attributes or categories that they deem most pertinent.*

Consequently, it is always possible for selected characteristics to be experienced as arbitrary. Perceiving, selecting, and remarking upon similarities and differences inescapably are activities of social construction. Resemblances and distinctions do not exist in some pristine objective form apart from our taking account of them; their existence is inherently relational. While similarity and difference presuppose existing in relationship, we need to beware of the tendency to map them onto hierarchies or to assume parity among people's situations. We need to be mindful of the implicit topography of our discourses and actions.

Bateson argued that individuals' activities and interpretations are never random configurations in human interaction. Cultural learning and available discourses significantly determine our conscious and unconscious perceptions, movements, language use, and vocalization, as well as the nature of our typical social contexts. For better and worse, traditions inform human interaction. In Dewey's words, "Traditions are ways of interpretation and of observation, of valuation, of everything explicitly thought of. They are the circumambient atmosphere which thought must breathe; no one ever had an idea except as he inhaled some of this atmosphere" (1931/1988, p. 211). Because traditions can be toxic for some even as they enliven others, the close interrelationship of meanings and values will be a watchword of this book. Discriminating among meanings is de facto choosing among values. Who decides and communicates the meanings of the events of our individual and collective lives? Maxine Greene warns that "meaning, and controlling meaning, is the key to oppression" (1988, p. x).

Deciding our own meanings is vital for freedom, and freedom lives at the heart of friendship.

All meanings depend upon the contexts of their construction (Bateson, 1972). Accordingly, our desire (at least provisionally) to respect everyone's meaning-making efforts will find us paying close attention to how contexts of communication activities are accomplished. We will examine how they are negotiated, constrained and enforced, or challenged and changed. I am especially concerned with the ways friendships are defined, discursive activities are labeled, and opportunities for communication are framed and performed.

## ❖ NEGOTIATING CONTEXTS, MAKING CHOICES, AND CREATING MEANINGS

All communicative contexts are reflexive achievements. When we share emerging moments of real time, we co-construct the "now" in which we are living. Under these conditions, when we perceive another person perceiving us, a communicative context develops (Ruesch & Bateson, 1951). Mutual awareness is required for us to engage in communication as opposed to merely assign meaning unilaterally to someone else's behaviors. We can have only limited awareness of the numerous events and discourses invoked in our negotiation of meaningful actions. Moreover, due to our cultural and subcultural backgrounds, we may employ very different premises for interpreting any aspect of what is going on. Even so, *all* behaviors are considered important in shaping a communicative encounter. All communicative behavior proposes corresponding behavior by another person to accomplish its context. Our behaviors may even be coordinated without shared meanings for the situation—which is important to recognize in attempting dialogue.

A young American salesman, new to Japan, may attempt to create a favorable first impression on a noticeably older male Japanese executive. He enters the latter's office with crisp assurance, upright posture, a forthright and (in his mind) friendly voice and an extended hand. The executive may view these as the brash actions of a presumptuous American who is ignorant of the propriety of conveying respect to all elders and superiors through pausing silently and bowing slightly at the threshold of the ranking person's space, awaiting the invitation to enter and speak. The executive's uptake may convey disdain for this aggressive young pup and their meeting commences on rocky footing. Or he may respond mildly, allowing the younger man the opportunity to redeem himself through more appropriate behaviors as their interaction proceeds. Depending on the executive's responses, the salesman faces a differently unfolding context. Yet with minimally shared meanings, they coordinate their actions.

This co-construction of meaningful actions and contexts is not as linear as might be implied here. Like the young salesman in the example above, we enter into communication with others in response to relevant discourses and in light of cultural resources already in play. Available subject positions are already constructed with varying degrees of freedom and constraint. Moreover, the issues at stake may surpass our attempts to control their significance. We are not entirely certain of the precise meaning of our emitted messages until we perceive their reception through the responses of others. Only then do we discover what we actually have been communicating from the outset. These discovered meanings might wisely be regarded as only for the time being and open to revision by the communicators' further actions.

If we think of communicative contexts in reflexive terms, we are less likely to regard persons, actions, or contexts as having some essential, unchanging significance. Negotiating contexts, creating meaning, becoming persons, and performing actions all involve *making choices*. These activities assume significance in reflexive and mutually contingent relationships with each other across time. In defining context, Bateson said, "We may regard 'context' as a collective term for all those events which tell the organism among what set of alternatives he [or she] must make his [or her] next choice" (1972, p. 289). "Context" here refers to a configuration of multiple events posing simultaneous alternatives for constructing further action. Previous and emerging interaction will facilitate and constrain the options experienced as available at this moment for constructing the next. A disdainful versus encouraging response by the executive above is crucial for the young salesman.

Although choices are co-constructed in human interaction, I believe Bateson literally meant that a person "makes his [or her] next choice." All interpersonal events composing a "set of alternatives" simultaneously are partially performed and partially perceived. We construct choices as we select them and select among them as they are constructed. Bateson also stated that *"choices are not all at the same level"* (1972, p. 405, italics added) because of material, cultural, or learned constraints associated with our actions and words. For example, selecting certain words in a given language typically precludes choosing the letters that spell them, and deciding to hold a door open for a person typically precludes billing them for our services afterwards. Similarly, when we choose certain discourses or actions, we preclude or encourage potential expectations in our relationships with others.

In characterizing our lifelong process of becoming who we are with others as one of meaning making, I embrace the fundamental significance of the hermeneutic circle throughout this book. Basically, the concept of the hermeneutic circle depicts our interpretations of cultural activities and texts as arising from recursive interaction among parts and wholes (Bruner, 2002; Gadamer, 1989; Taylor, 1977). These activities and texts can include anything—stories and movies, episodes and conversations from our own lives, and our own and others' life stories. As we read a story, for example, we begin to project some possible overall stories implied by the initial events in the story that in turn render those events provisionally sensible. These early events take their meaning from the role they presumably are playing in the unfolding of these projected possible stories. As further events occur (which in our daily lives often are negotiated with others), they contribute more definition to the "actual" unfolding story. These details divert our attention from some of the alternative possible stories that might have developed (if other events had occurred and the ones that did occur had not). Meanwhile, we attribute certain meanings to the occurring events because the whole story makes our interpretation of these particular actions more plausible. And so on. Interpretation is thus an ongoing circular process.

And it might very well *seem* that when the story is completed, we will be able to settle once and for all what each of the actions in the story meant, as well as a meaning of the story as a whole—perhaps even a moral of the story. However, we realize that this story is itself a moment of discourse and only a part of a larger story (as well as a collection of other stories), which could include, for example, the developing relationship between the author/storyteller and the readers/audience. In this case we are now faced with the interpretive challenge of deciding the meaning of this story as only a part of the larger collection of stories composing our emerging relationships. Multiple morals of our story may arise at different points in time depending on its contingent relationships with emerging and enveloping stories.

For example, at one point in life, being fired from a job could darkly signify failure. Ensuing events over time may reveal that termination to mark the beginning of a wonderful string of successes and blessings in a person's life. The hermeneutic circles involved in our efforts to make sense of our lives' stories constitute a tantalizing conception. The hermeneutic circle embodies the reflexive and paradoxical qualities of human communication as ongoing meaning making that I will explore further in the discursive activity of friends throughout this book.

## ❖ CONSTRUCTING SIMILARITIES AND DIFFERENCES OF SELF AND OTHERS

While discussing how humans use language, Kenneth Burke (1966) said, "Even if any terminology is a *reflection* of reality, by its very nature as a terminology it must be a *selection* of reality; and to this extent it must function also as a *deflection* of reality" (p. 45, original emphasis). I have been discussing the necessity of making selections in communicating the worlds in which we live. Our communicative activities involve simultaneously drawing distinctions and noticing resemblances in our current situation among moments, movements, moods, tones, pulses, breaths, words, foreground, background, physical contact, threatening gestures or starts of surprise, the narrowing glint or inviting twinkle of an eye, smiles and pouts.

While we unreflectively take in most of the features of our surroundings, we also consciously respond to multiple cues transpiring around us. Our meaning-making efforts involve selection—that is, *making choices*—in the dynamic, relational, and reflexive senses of the phrase. The words we use to perform our selections to ourselves, even as we language and body forth our choices to others, communicate our images of the world we inhabit together at this moment (Buber, 1937; Rommetveit, 1980). In doing so, we also propose our images of self and others through the similarities and differences we invoke.

Meanwhile, another's responses to us are always already occurring even as we have been responding through our communication with that person. Both of our ongoing responses affirm, negate, ignore, or render ambiguous the similarities and differences that we have emphasized in proposing our version of the situation. Our respective versions of the situation reflect, select, declare (and thereby deflect) certain identities for self and other.

In John Casey's short story, "Mandarins in a Farther Field," the narrator, McEvoy, works for a Washington bureau during the Cold War. The times have trained him to be suspicious of Russians. He meets Pavel, a Russian cultural attaché, who tries to identify their similarities, even smugly describing a common out-group, as a prelude to possible friendship:

> "This is a very strange city," he said. "I have a very strange feeling that everyone will leave tomorrow. That everyone is here only for a moment. I can't believe that people are born here."

I felt I had a choice between two answers. One was that seventy-five percent of the population hadn't been born here. And other statistics. The other was that I had.

"It seems like Potemkin villages," he said. "Like Hollywood made it for making films. I can't find its core. However," he added, "I am not completely lost. There are details that are familiar, that are similar."

"Like what?"

"Those statues where we saw each other. They could be in a metro station in Russia. Except perhaps we would have machines in place of horses. But still—something crude and powerful. And the Indians in their—" He made a circle around his head with his finger.

"Turbans."

"—turbans, coming to get degrees in engineering, or asking for money, food, dams. I don't mean to condescend," he said. His English had got even better. "But they are similar, here and there," he went on. "And you and I are similar details."

"I don't know about that," I said, and told him about the report on me—"bright but not too bright."

"Oh, yes, yes," he said. "You can't imagine how similar." (Casey, 1979, pp. 32–33)

No language can escape categorization, and the hazards of using any language include being used by that language (Burke, 1966). We may unreflectively allow the discourses intersecting at our subject positions and social locations to shape our selections in characterizing self and others. We need to be wary of this categorical tendency in making sense of ourselves, others, and our worlds. Because we are hermeneutically recursive beings, we continually constitute categories through our selections, and we make selections on the basis of the attributes defining categories that we have found useful.

For example, we produce the category of "friend" in our daily lives through the people we choose to describe by that term (and negatively through the people to whom we refuse to apply it). We also use the characteristics we associate with friends to recognize this possibility in our encounters. This simultaneous categorizing of self and others involves us in the social reproduction of significant differences and similarities.

Such discriminations occur through discursive practices deployed moment-to-moment in interaction. In considering the communicative practices of friendships, I am concerned with inclusion, exclusion, recognition, and indifference as everyday social accomplishments.

Our capacities for perceiving self and others are dynamically interrelated. Working with Bakhtin's ideas, Michael Holquist (1990) stipulates important contrasts in self's and other's perceptions of their shared time and differentiated spaces at given moments. As Self we experience the space we occupy as "the center of perception" (p. 22). The events of the world, including others' activities, transpire around us and are witnessed from this vantage point. The other's space is perceived as a "neutral environment" or not as significant as our space. Meanwhile, our time as the perceiver is open-ended and "unfinished," brimming with the potential for further deeds. In contrast, we perceive the time of others as "closed and finished." In our eyes, the other's actions are discrete occurrences; (we might say, "signed, sealed, and delivered"). The other's actions are there for us to decipher and evaluate. Moreover, we are able to see more of the other than he or she can, which Bakhtin (1990) calls "the excess of seeing" (p. 12). We can see the other person's face that the other person can see only in a mirror. And we can witness others' reactions to that person in ways he or she cannot. Unfortunately, certain conceits potentially derive from this self-centered sense that we can correctly read the other.

As soon as the story is told from the vantage point of an other, all our orientations immediately apply to her or him as well (that is, to *each other*). This is the existential privilege of perceiving our world and speaking in the first person—we are all potentially selves and others. As we witnessed in the interchange above between McEvoy and Pavel, there are shifting centers for perceiving the world, different points of view, according to who is uttering the pronoun "I" (Holquist, 1990). Whether or how this voice is heard will concern us in this book.

There is ironic value in this asymmetry of perceptual fields. Holquist states, "It is only from a position outside something that it can be perceived in categories that complete it in time and fix it in space" (p. 31). He further explains, "It is only the other's categories that will let me be an object for my own perception. I see myself as I conceive others might see it. In order to forge a self, I must do so from the *outside*" (p. 28, original emphasis). In short, we need each other to learn who we are in a world of others. As McEvoy reflects in describing the further development of his friendship with Pavel:

> It was always a daydream of mine to take an intelligent, appreciative foreigner on a tour of Washington. Pavel even wanted to see where I

went to high school. In fact, he even wanted to hear detailed accounts of the football games I'd played in. It was nice. My ordinary childhood had never seemed so exotic to me. (Casey, 1979, p. 33)

From the dawn of consciousness, we fundamentally depend upon others' reactions in constructing our identities (Mead, 1934).

"Self" and "other" identify dialectically entwined vectors of human experience. The very idea of a self requires the idea of an other even as it contrasts with it. Notions of "self" describe events in our world discerned inside and outside our bodies that are taken as continuous with who we believe we are. In contrast, notions of "other" describe events in our world observed both inside and outside our bodies that are taken as different from who we believe we are. Ironically, we are fated to conceive of ourselves based largely on our perceptions of others' responses to us, and their discourses in pursuing activities of mutual interest (Mead, 1934). We can only describe ourselves from outside of ourselves. In these interchanges others' discourses and perceptions become part of our experiences of self, even if they may also be perceived by us as alien. As a result, McEvoy becomes a more exotic version of himself in light of Pavel's stated perceptions of McEvoy's childhood. Meanwhile, we recognize others in part through projections of ourselves and our discourses in pursuing activities of shared interest. Our discourses and perceptions become part of the other's experience, even if the other may perceive them as strange. Experiencing personhood involves experiencing "oneself *as* another" to use Ricoeur's (1992) phrase.

❖ ACHIEVING AND (MIS)PERCEIVING IDENTITIES THROUGH THE DIALECTIC OF INDIVIDUATION AND PARTICIPATION

Throughout life, the ongoing accomplishment of oneself *as* another and one's self *with* others involves contingent communication. Our identities and senses of self derive from two dialectically interconnected sets of activities. Because these two facets of achieving identity cannot exist independently, the order in which I discuss them is arbitrary. *Individuation* involves activities that recognize the boundaries identifying us as a distinct entity separate from others. *Participation* involves activities incorporating us with others and identifying us as a relational entity connected with others. Individuation and participation exist on a continuum. Sometimes they complement each other in achieving self's identity; at other times they anchor radically contrasting bases for action.

Both of these ways of cultivating identity involve continual communicative activity and sense making of prior and emerging understandings of our self, others, social collectives, environments and even the human condition. Individuation and participation shape and reflect our perceptions, internally directed discourse (thought), externally directed discourse (communication), and observable cultural conduct (actions). *Individuation and participation implicate each other in their meanings and consequences. They are always already present simultaneously for human action and identity.*

Observing Lucy Grealy confidently performing her own poetry in college before they later became lifelong friends, a shier Ann Patchett recalls, "I believed we had something in common even though I wrote short stories." She continues:

> People liked my work but had trouble remembering me. . . . Unlike Lucy, I had a tendency to blur with other people. I had come to Sarah Lawrence from twelve years of Catholic school where we were not in the business of discovering our individuality. We dressed in identical plaid skirts, white blouses, saddle oxfords, and when we prayed, it was together and aloud. It was impossible to distinguish your voice from the crowd. There is an art to giving yourself over to someone else and as a group we mastered it. While Lucy had discovered that she was different from all the other children in her grade school because she was sick and was different from all the other children on the hospital's cancer ward because she continued to survive, I had discovered I was so much like every other little girl in the world that it always took me a minute to identify my own face in our class photo. Still, I thought, in my shyness, my blurriness, it would not be so unreasonable to think that the famous Lucy Grealy and I could be friends. (2004, p. 4)

Early in their acquaintance, Ann's identity primarily derived from blending in (participation) while Lucy's identity came from standing out (individuation). Even so, Ann senses commonalities that might support a friendship between them.

There are various ways in which ascriptions of similarity and difference affect our ongoing projects of individuation and participation. Accordingly, I propose below what I consider to be edifying compositions of similarities and differences in performing identity through individuation and participation. I also will register what I consider troubling discursive trajectories. In all instances, meanings of discursive activities are contextually based. Writing about them here renders them static. Doing so risks distorting their susceptibility to alternative meanings in emergent cultural contexts.

Abraham Kaplan asserted:

There is, I think, a basic dilemma of identity: I need the other for my identity, but the other is at the same time a threat to my identity. The dilemma might be put in this way: How can I be what I am without fear of being different from you, and how can I be with you without fear of losing my identity? (1969, p. 103)

*the departed example*

The interconnected activities of individuation and participation perpetuate this dilemma. On one hand, *individuation* is premised upon noticing differences and drawing distinctions. As Burke (1969) teaches us, an unavoidable counterpart of asserting what or who I am as a distinctive identity, is asserting what or who I am not. As such, individuation can lend itself to pronounced separation from others, concerns with one's rights as an individual, to individualism and visions of integrity based on self-sufficiency. The potential for misperception is inherent in this identity project. *The Primary Misperception of Individuation is to emphasize self's differences to the neglect of significant similarities with others.*

On the other hand, *participation* is premised upon noticing similarities and pursuing commonalities. Participation seeks connection with others, assumes responsibilities of becoming part of something larger than ourselves, embraces identity as part of a collective and notions of integrity based on interdependence. This identity project also includes its own potential for misperception. *The Primary Misperception of Participation is to emphasize self's similarities with others to the neglect of significant differences.* The risks of these misperceptions, which we will examine in greater detail, expand the questions composing Kaplan's dilemma of identity. The first question becomes, how can I be what I am without fear of or exaggerating my differences from you and your differences from me? And how can I allow you to be who you are without fear of or compelling your being too different from me? The second question becomes, how can I be with you without fear of or exaggerating my similarities with you and losing my identity? And how can I allow you to be with me without fear of or compelling the loss of your identity? We will explore capacities of friendships for addressing this dilemma throughout this book.

Achieving identity is so complex because our identities are ongoing, situated, relational accomplishments. As Laing (1969) observed, "All 'identities' require an other: some other in and through a relationship with whom self-identity is actualized" (p. 82). Our communication with every person we encounter says in effect, "This is how I experience myself in relation to you. How do you experience me and yourself in relation to me?" Our responses to each other may affirm, negate, or ignore our proposed self-images, what Laing (1969) respectively terms confirmation, rejection, and disconfirmation. There is breathtaking potential for impacting our own and others' experiences of selfhood and social identity in our responses to each other. In fact, Buber (1957, p. 99) once held that "a society may be termed human in the measure to which its members confirm one another." However, it is possible that neither of us will perceive the other nor be perceived in the ways that we would like.

Let us consider a few interactional possibilities for problems arising from this inevitable trafficking in images. I will use two persons, Sandy and Olivia, to dramatize a potentially troubling situation involving significant differences between us. Their situation—unfortunately common today—is one in which each person's strangeness to the other constitutes a potential basis for considerable distrust, even hostility. What is associated with Self on each side is imbued with goodness and safety and what is associated with Other is imbued with evil and threat. In this encounter the two Selves, Sandy and Olivia, are simultaneously each woman's Other. Sandy potentially exists as an Other for Olivia, and Olivia potentially exists as an Other for Sandy. I ask: What images of Olivia's self does Sandy presuppose to communicate in ways consistent with who Sandy perceives her own self to be? And vice versa for Olivia. How closely or remotely do these images of the other woman accord with how that other woman actually perceives her own self? How much "room to move" does each allow herself and the other in their interaction (Laing, 1968, 1969)? We will consider some of the images potentially affecting their interaction developed from the vantage point of Sandy for purposes of clarity. Everything described here would also simultaneously apply from Olivia's perspective.

> There are Sandy's own images of herself, and there are Sandy's images of Olivia.
>
> There are Olivia's own images of herself, and there are Olivia's images of Sandy.
>
> As their interaction unfolds, we may justifiably ask:
>
> To what extent do Sandy's own images of herself correspond with Olivia's images of Sandy?
>
> To what extent do Sandy's images of Olivia correspond with Olivia's own images of herself?
>
> To what extent is either party able to perceive her own self accurately over time or across situations?

Does she behave differently toward the other woman, perhaps with increasing distrust or hostility, while believing that she has remained the same (that is, true to herself)? Are Olivia's actions actually coming to resemble Sandy's image of Olivia, and if so, why? Does Sandy refuse to relinquish divergent images of Olivia, despite changes in Olivia's actions, and if so, why?

To what extent is either party able to perceive *self* in the *other?* I use italics here because there are two generic ways we can hear this question—the first refers to *perceiving oneself in the other,* the second refers to *perceiving the other's own selfhood.* If Sandy does not see the significant ways in which Olivia is similar to Sandy's own self, Sandy commits the Primary Misperception of Individuation. There are always ways in which we share the human condition, even if they comprise a "trivial minimum" (Rommetveit, 1980). If Sandy does not see the ways Olivia's own self exists on terms significantly different from Sandy's own self, Sandy commits the Primary Misperception of Participation. Assuming that others actually resemble us deep down despite apparent differences denies the integrity of their identities as self-recognizing others.

To what extent is either party able to perceive *other* in the *self?* Once more, I use italics to stress two ways of noticing this predicament—the first refers to *perceiving the other's qualities in oneself,* the second refers to *perceiving the self's own otherness when viewed by others.* If Sandy cannot perceive the meaningful ways in which she resembles Olivia, she again commits the Primary Misperception of Individuation by insisting upon irretrievable differences in the face of important commonalities. If Sandy cannot perceive the consequential ways that her own self is significantly different from Olivia's own self, that is, the otherness of Sandy's self to Olivia, then Sandy commits the Primary Misperception of Participation. Sandy falsely assumes the primacy of her own experiences as the epicenter of the knowing world from which all comparisons are made. *For every way that the other is (perceived as) different from or similar to self, there are ways that self is (perceived as) different from or similar to the other.* There are comprehensive challenges in trying to overcome our self-centered windows on human events, people, and possibilities.

Sustaining our lived sense of identity continually requires reconciling our *self-identity* (our perceptions of our own identity) with our *meta-identity* (our perceptions of how others perceive our identity; Laing, 1969). There may be circumstances when we experience close agreement in these aspects of our social identity. In such instances we are responded to in ways that confirm our sense of self. For example, we believe we are competent and others treat us in ways that affirm our self-image. But multiple situations occur when we are treated in ways that clash with our self-perceptions. We may encounter others who constantly question or undermine our self-perceptions as competent.

Depending upon the significance of our self-perceptions and the condescending others in our lives, our self-identity potentially becomes destabilized by such disconfirming reactions. In situations of unbalanced power, we may be forced to distrust our own experiences of ourselves and feel compelled to fulfill more powerful persons' specifications for our own identities (Laing, 1972). These can be soul-sapping instances of becoming-Other-to-oneself, leading us to search for individuals who will confirm our valued identities.

## ❖ CATEGORIES AND IDENTITY CONSTRUCTION

The activities of individuation and participation involve several modalities for achieving identities that exist on a continuum. On one end of the continuum, we can self-identify primarily using terms, attributes, and activities that distance us from social collectivities. We are our own persons who resist being placed in general categories, and we want to be taken on our own terms as individuals. Whether and to what degree we are identified by others in ways that confirm this robustly individuated self-identity is another matter. On the other end, we can describe ourselves with extensive references to encompassing social groups. We recognize ourselves as belonging to enveloping cultural memberships that are significant in saying who we are and what we stand for. We do not know ourselves meaningfully apart from these categories of belonging. Once again, whether and how others identify us in similarly socially determined ways is important.

These modalities of self- and other-identification combine, complement, and contrast with each other in given cases. Our individualistic discourse or singular actions may simultaneously invoke identification with a specific social group by us and others. For example, a person may speak with a hick accent associated with less prosperous or educated residents of a given area. If this "identification with" is asserted by others as his primary identity, he may resent it, especially when he would not describe himself in this way. He may insist that such classification of self is demeaning when done by others and only dignifying when performed by himself. Indeed, we may recognize our own uniqueness as well as our affiliation with others through using a broader identification in specific situations all the while insisting that we are *not merely a member of a category*. Hearing another describe us in categorical terms may insult our dignity.

Images of self communicated intentionally and unintentionally by others always compose potential instances of confirmation, disconfirmation, and rejection of valued identities (Laing, 1969). The line separating valued acknowledgment from disturbing assimilation of our identity is permeable and circumstantially negotiated. Achieving our social identities involves the ongoing reflexive negotiation of self- and other-recognition, self-descriptions and descriptions by and of others. Moreover, all of these identity-making activities transpire in conjunction with the discursive activities of individuation and participation.

As previously mentioned, every act of describing persons (including ourselves) invokes categories that risk crimping humanity. We have already considered the necessity of stepping outside of ourselves in order to reflect upon ourselves. We accomplish this feat using discursive categories to understand our identities at this time and place. But the social categories we use simultaneously shape and reflect pervasive social practices. As Hastrup (1990) argues, "Although the language at one level 'expresses' the social, it is no mirror image of reality. It introduces its own arabesques into the perception of the world" (p. 53). Using the term *semantic density* to characterize the interconnection of "category systems and reality," she explains:

> It refers to the statistical feature of categories, of which certain meanings are socially more significant than others and are invoked more frequently. . . . For instance, when we talk of the Scottish culture the meaning of tartan-clad Highlanders more often springs to mind than the industrial laborers of the Lowlands. . . .

> All categories may potentially yield similar density patterns, because categories always coexist with a statistical feature that is part of their materiality. It entails a pattern of frequency and relative importance that distorts the neat order of classification in which all categories are equalized. This implies that no reality can be exhaustively described in its own categories. Even local language does not re-present reality. (p. 53)

Since categories are caught up in gross material disparities, they perform elevating or denigrating images of human beings, reproducing historical animosities as well as petty prejudices. Words expressing cultural categories often have sharp edges carving stark borders into the fluid possibilities of interaction among peoples with whom we may or may not want to identify.

We choose words to describe ourselves and others in actual communicative situations with other persons. Yet these concrete interactions occur within discursive formations established on societal and cultural levels where individual agency in constituting these discourses is drastically reduced (Foucault, 1970, 1972). Sandy and Olivia don't communicate in a vacuum. They live in a world of languages that existed before they arrived. Consequently, their actual possibilities for making choices are enabled and constrained by the inclusions and exclusions embodied in available discourses. Such exclusions operate with widely discrepant effects. The racist production of whiteness embodying superiority in contrast to nonwhiteness and the heterosexist production of heterosexuality as the basis for contrasting homo- or bisexuality as different and inferior are taken-for-granted norms. Martinez (2000) observes that these exclusions typically have more oppressive consequences than the gradations of exclusion transpiring *within* the preferred categories.

Clearly, all discursive choices in communicating and constructing identity do not exist on the same level. The range of choices open to individuals differs tremendously. In view of the material, existential, and political disparities shaped and reflected by language, how we experience the discursive categories used to describe us depends on a number of considerations. Do they describe core or peripheral aspects of our self-perceived identity? Are they empowering or weakening designations in the specific circumstances in which they are used? Are the descriptions rendered in terms that we would use to portray ourselves? Are they terms we would readily permit anyone else to use to describe us? Do the terms presume specific eligibilities such as personal or political friendship or shared membership in a relevant reference group? Would we recognize ourselves in the others' descriptions of us? In a related vein, to what extents are edifying or demeaning depictions of others entailed by our own descriptions of ourselves? What images of *them* are invoked in our own accounts of us as *us*? In short, what is the nature of the identity work and social placement accomplished through our discourses characterizing self and other?

Buber (1937, p. 16) once stated, "But this is the exalted melancholy of our fate, that every *Thou* in our world must become an *It*." Any characteristic we *respectfully* select out through our discourse to indicate similarity or difference of self and others is also inherently an act of distancing and potential use. We must "other" ourselves to some extent, that is, discriminate ourselves, to recognize ourselves. We perform the same discursive actions justifiably or not in addressing others. In naming our own behaviors, however, we typically do so working within the ongoing narrative of our own lives. How can we aspire to the same practices in perceiving, describing, and communicating with other people(s)? In this book, I will argue that some ways of doing so involve adopting the stances and practices of various degrees of personal and civic friendship.

## ❖ MODES OF THE DIALECTIC OF
INDIVIDUATION AND PARTICIPATION

As I have emphasized, our selfhood arises and is sustained through communication with others (Mead, 1934). Mead argues that during our earliest experiences we are unable to distinguish ourselves from the voices and touches that envelope us. As we learn language from the others in our world, we become able to "self-indicate," that is, to make an object of ourselves to ourselves (Mead, 1934). Social discourse ironically enables this emergence of individual human personification. Thus arise the primordial moments of *the lifelong dialectic of individuation and participation*—speaking language, self emerges as a figure on the ground of others. How do I recognize myself under these circumstances? Buber's (1937) remarkable discussion of the paired words *I–Thou* and *I–It* poetically offers insight:

> The *I* of the primary word *I–It* makes its appearance as individuality and becomes conscious of itself as subject (of experiencing and using).

> The *I* of the primary word *I–Thou* makes its appearance as person and becomes conscious of itself as subjectivity (without a dependent genitive).

> Individuality makes its appearance by being differentiated from other individualities.

> A person makes his appearance by entering into relation with other persons.

> The one is the spiritual form of natural detachment, the other is the spiritual form of natural solidarity of connexion. (p. 62)

Reinforcing the continuous interplay between actions of participation and individuation, Buber further asserts, "No man [woman] is pure person and no man [woman] is pure individuality" (p. 62). Two modes of identification occur in the ongoing construction of detached, differentiated individuality and relationally connected personhood. *Individuation* primarily involves *identification as*, that is, the discrete recognition of self as this or that entity, bounded in space and time, which may be placed in a clearly defined category with other similarly circumscribed members. Based on a specified set of attributes, I demarcate myself (and other individuals) as a particular being, a self-determining origin of human activity. I locate myself (and others) in separate juxtaposition to anyone else. I recognize self and other through identifying each as a certain type of individual.

By comparison (and concurrently), *participation* primarily involves *identification with;* self is recognized as inherently connected with other selves. I know myself in relation to my activities and discourse with associates. As such, it is not clear to me where my concerns and possibilities end and those of my family and friends begin. I understand myself as a relational being and experience myself and others as dwelling within discursive webs of varying degrees of immediacy and shared consequences. My self-understandings arise in light of my involvements with those persons who make me who I am. Alter the persons I identify with and you alter how I recognize myself.

Individuation and participation compose an interwoven continuum of discursive activities transpiring across diverse contexts. Our ongoing identifications of self and others continually evolve communicatively as combinations of individuation and participation. I will describe how similarities and differences are constructed in both edifying and dispiriting ways in performing identities through individuation and participation.

## Individuation

As we have observed, *individuation involves activities defining attributes and recognizing the boundaries identifying an embodied self as a distinct entity separated from others.* Individuation can occur in both edifying and dispiriting ways. On the constructive side, *edifying individuation* is a necessary aspect of self-reference and other recognition. I distinguish myself and am distinguished by others through recognizing those aspects of my being that meaningfully set me apart from other selves. The individual embodied person thus comprises a locus for agency and personal convictions. In this mode of being, I acknowledge these particular words as statements I have uttered, these particular behaviors as actions I have taken, and these particular beliefs as commitments that I have made in circumstances responding to identifiable others and/or exigencies. I identify these actions, utterances, and commitments as mine and in doing so, I may assume personal responsibility for them and for myself. Viewed in this way as *edifying individuation,* individuated self-assertion can perform positive freedom—the freedom to embrace our responsibilities to self and others and to have a say in the events of our own lives (Berlin, 1969).

Equally important, in owning the singular potentials of our time and place, *edifying individuation* recognizes comparable potentials in the embodied existence of other selves. For Bakhtin ethical action and authentic respect are rooted in responsiveness to "the radical singularity of each person at every moment" (Morson & Emerson, 1989, p. 16)—that is, to *each* other. These are not categorical actions; Bakhtin's (1993) concept of once-occurrence insists that every single moment of the responsibly lived life has ethical import. We are addressed continuously by the events of our world in our radical singularity and in once-occurrent moments. Individuated consciousness of our situation allows us to make choices and to create possibilities for self and other. Ignoring our uniquely embodied opportunities to respond to the once-occurring moments of our own lives is to abdicate our personal responsibilities as human beings.

Meanwhile, the ongoing project of individuation is fraught with troublesome potentials. As noted, the Primary Misperception of Individuation is to overemphasize our differences and our uniqueness to the neglect of significant similarities shared with others. The result of this misperception may be some form of self-serving individualism, a *dispiriting individuation*, where an individual disavows interdependency with others (Butler, 1995). Turning inward, we look to a self-sealing rationality for direction in navigating the events of the world. Autonomy is realized as negative freedom—we do whatever we deem correct in the absence of perceived restraints from others (Berlin, 1969). Bateson (1972) saw overweening pride as one worrisome result of such totalizing individuation. He termed "alcoholic pride" the mistaken belief that we can exert unilateral control over systems and circumstances larger than us. He considered such hubris a form of pathology engendering exaggerated (mis)perceptions of control over self, others, and the natural environment. Such inability to acknowledge our interdependence with other beings sharing the planet is toxic for living systems in Bateson's view.

*Dispiriting individuation* invokes rigid demarcations of self and other versus acknowledging a dynamic continuum of self/other formation. It is an invitation to alienation. The ultimate closure is to treat self and/or others as objects or instances of abstract categories, instead of as open, meaningful, meaning-creating beings (though, of course, not so open as to have no integrity or self-determination). A worthwhile credo is, when we make objects of others, we make objects of ourselves. By comparison, when we regard others and our relationships with them as ongoing narrative achievements, we do the same for ourselves.

Whether we practice edifying or dispiriting individuation, change in the self is always occurring. Narrative reminds us that all selves are accomplished continually through time. There is nothing static about lived identities, which recalls the notion that all being is becoming. Our ongoing performances with others of who we are and who we are becoming include questions about whether we accurately or inaccurately "distinguish those performative acts which function as repetitions from those which function as transformations" as well as "the conditions which support one as opposed to the other" (Nicholson, 1995, p. 11). There can be virtue in transforming ourselves and our circumstances, that is, in becoming something completely different from what we were before. In striving for such fundamental change, the idea of the "wholly other" serves as "a regulative principle of hope" (Benhabib, 1995, p. 30). The pinches, of course, involve achieving undistorted perceptions of the degree to which we have in fact changed, and whether the other we are seeking to become is an enriching or degenerate aspiration. How and with whom can we accomplish sufficient distance from our activities of becoming to produce an accurate evaluation of our progress? People similar to me are probably too close to what I have been to appreciate my attempts to transform myself. Persons from the other realm of being I seek to join are likely to be too far from my origins and too close to my aspirations to evaluate either with useful neutrality.

Various identity mistakes are possible. One problem of individuation over time is to perceive ourselves as significantly different from who we were at an earlier point, when actually we are not. This is the illusion that we have become a totally different person who responds in a comprehensively improved way to situations and people. Meanwhile, potentially anyone observing us from some remove would say that we are kidding ourselves and make the same mistakes under new guises that we do not recognize. Whether others will inform us of these illusions is another matter.

The opposite mistake is to see ourselves as being the same person over time when we are not. Believing that we have remained firm in our convictions, for example, enables us to exaggerate our identity as a person of integrity. We may find it difficult to deal with others who respond to us differently since "I am the same person I have always been." Some of the most important challenges in becoming-with-others involve distinguishing illusory from real continuities and changes in our personhood. As well, we hope to realize the worthwhile versus problematic ways we've stayed the same or changed. Simultaneously, it is vital to recognize the social circumstances and relationships that facilitate meaningful changes or continuities in our valued identities. I will discuss ways that friends help to accomplish significant continuities and changes in personal and social worlds, as well as the potentials of friends for muddling matters.

Despite the risks, part of the well-lived life depends upon our willingness as self-determining beings to take responsibility for making choices with others and our willingness to change in response to emerging situations in our world. In this spirit Maxine Greene (1988, p. 3) quotes John Dewey as saying we are free "not because of what we statically are, but in so far as we are becoming different from what we have been." Positive freedom is performed with others in social conditions that enable change to occur. However, as Greene continues, "If freedom comes to mind, it is ordinarily associated with an individualist stance: It signifies a self-dependence rather than relationship; self-regarding and self-regulated behavior rather than involvement with others" (1988, p. 7). This stance toward freedom tends to perpetuate excessive individuation. Participation must coexist with meaningful individuation.

### Participation

As we have observed, *participation* involves activities incorporating self with others and identifying self as a relational being connected with others. Participation emphasizes significant similarities of a self/other among selves/others. *Instead of relying primarily upon our differences to figure ourselves out in contrast to others, participation emphasizes our commonalities in configuring ourselves with others.* Even as he champions the ethical importance of acknowledging self's and other's singularity, Bakhtin observes, "As soon as I think my singularity as an aspect of existence, shared by all existence, I have already exited from my singular singularity" (quoted in Morson & Emerson, 1989, p. 17). Consequently, there are edifying and dispiriting modes of participation. *Edifying participation* requires enacting similarities that make a worthwhile difference in connecting with others. These identifications with others are often negotiated incrementally, exist on continua, and are seldom once and for all. Connections with others may begin with identifying only the "trivial minimum" of ways self and other could possibly construe being-in-the-world even remotely similarly. Such precious sources for mutuality may serve in turn as a basis for "trading on each other's truths" to use Rommetveit's (1980, p. 145) constructive formulation. These attempts to co-orient from our respective vantage points to jointly acknowledged features of the world may hopefully allow the co-construction of places or moments of common ground.

*Edifying participation* expectantly transcends particularities in the human condition, especially given the seemingly endless stream of times and places when human differences are emphasized with lethal consequences. Responding to one such circumstance, Sartre was eloquent in his call to the French people for identification with the Jews in the wake of the vile insanity of Nazism:

> What must be done is to point out to each one that the fate of the Jews is *his* fate. Not one Frenchman will be free so long as the Jews do not enjoy the fullness of their rights. Not one Frenchman can be secure so long as a single Jew—in France or in the world at large—can fear for his life. (1948, p. 153)

More broadly, across diverse cultural circumstances we must deeply acknowledge self's and other's singularity *and* shared vulnerability. This stand is essential even as the other's particular vulnerability derives from categorical prejudices that in *this instance* do not apply to us. We must palpably grasp living in fear of arbitrary threats to anyone's being that stem from the overdrawn identification of us or them *as others.* Exercising positive freedom, participating with conviction— putting oneself on the line—in activities that redress another's distinctive individuated sufferings simultaneously actualizes the humane humanity of self, other, and a community of belonging.

Consider a Palestinian nurse who works side by side with an Israeli counterpart in the pediatric intensive care unit at Hadassah Hospital in Jerusalem. Barbra Victor (2003) portrays their unlikely friendship and edifying participation in working to rescue persons under the most harrowing conditions of divided identities:

> These two close friends, one Palestinian, one Israeli, are good examples of another type of victimization in this ongoing war. Each suffers under the extremist views that have taken over her respective society and which determine, on each side, the political and military actions and the emotional reactions throughout the region. And yet, almost unbelievably, when they are at Hadassah Hospital, a sense of peace and cohabitation prevails, at least in the emergency room and the intensive care unit, where both women, along with other Palestinians and Israelis, work together as they all fight to save lives imperiled by this conflict. (p. 161)

Clearly, these women confront ongoing challenges and gripping necessities in transcending the dispiriting individuation of extreme political identities fueling violence in the region. Together as friends they demonstrate edifying participation by recognizing vital similarities between themselves and others in caring for persons tragically affected by the ongoing violence. In the words of the Palestinian nurse, "You just can't involve politics in medicine because if you do, it will influence you in a negative way to care for your patients. I grieve for all the parents who lose children and for all the children who lose parents. There is no easy answer" (p. 159).

This form of participation articulates admirably the other-regarding potentials of people. It is something to be proud of. At its best, it is not an isolating pride reflecting imperial individuation. Rather, it is a connected pride for humane purposes—what humanitarian and performer Bono calls "pride in the name of love" when singing about Dr. Martin Luther King, Jr. Pursuing the common good transcends individual concerns, but individual courage is required to challenge unquestioned bases for our own identity, to stand up and be counted, that is, to be identified *with* others. These actions sustain self and others' capacities for making choices and lifting voices. Greene (1988) celebrates similar sentiments in her salute to committed participants who risked their separate identities in the civil rights movements of the 1960s in the United States when she observes, "They were discovering their voices and at once reaching toward membership in a tradition" (pp. 94–95).

In the passage below Buber (1937) contrasts love as a way of living in relation with others as opposed to merely a personally embodied, episodic feeling for others. Taken to its ideal, and for many persons most sacred extents, he describes a basis for inspiring engagement with others in the name of something more enveloping than the petty business of everyday grasping based on illusory distinctions:

> Love ranges in its effect through the whole world. In the eyes of him who takes his stand in love, and gazes out of it, men are cut free from their entanglement in bustling activity. Good people and evil, wise and foolish, beautiful and ugly, become successively real to him; that is, set free they step forth in their singleness, and confront him as *Thou*. In a wonderful way, from time to time, exclusiveness arises—and so he can be effective, helping, healing, educating, raising up, saving. Love is responsibility of an *I* for a *Thou*. In this lies the likeness—impossible in any feeling whatsoever—of all who love. (p. 15)

First, Buber is stating that we achieve positive freedom through taking a stand because of love and concern for others. Recalling Bakhtin, through such eyes others are regarded in their concrete singularity; they become "successively real" to us. We see them for who they are and acknowledge their differences, even as we face each person as part of something larger, namely *Thou*. Buber means God by *Thou*. For some readers the inescapable power of Buber's insights is only possible through preserving this meaning regardless of their particular God (Pfuetze, 1954). Other readers may interpret *Thou* as the spirit of humanity, or as all that is hopeful and compassionate in the human condition. In either case, individual persons are simultaneously regarded as singular embodied presences and as connected to a common wellspring of their humanity. Moreover, the "exclusiveness" that thereby "arises" is *the fundamentally connected form that each person becomes in an I–Thou relationship with each other.* In these profound moments of relationally achieved individuation, that is, in edifying participation, love is equated with responsibility for recognized others who are essentially similar to us in their capacity to love.

Despite the worthwhile potentials of affirming our commonalities with others, this outlook can be taken too far in concrete circumstances. The Primary Misperception of Participation is to emphasize our similarities with others to the neglect of significant differences. What I call *dispiriting participation* is premised upon similarity that effaces meaningful variation in human beings. An example is requiring people to speak an alien language in the same manner as a dominant group in order to participate fully in some collective enterprise, like taking part in a class discussion or town meeting, or working for a corporation. The shadowy risk of dispiriting participation is that practices, values, or sufferings crucial to others make no difference to the dominant group. Such *indifference* to others' unique identities and circumstances also may derive from plain neglect. We are simply too preoccupied with ourselves to notice how our descriptions of and actions toward others compromise them. More actively, our indifference to others may take the form of lumping others together indiscriminately by acting as if what happens to them makes no difference to us. Worse still, we may believe we need to assimilate others' identities in order to confirm our own. Colonized others may be or feel compelled to mute their own distinctive voices to accommodate the dulling demands of the colonizer. In such circumstances, some persons perform negative identification. In aping the practices of a despised, dominant other who has determined legitimate selfhood, these persons emulate the dominators' worst characteristics and become caricatures of those in power.

Navigating our lives in a sea of humanity, we may commit misperceptions of participation and lose touch with the unique significance of our own personal existence. Laing (1969) reminds us that a fundamental desire of all persons is to make a difference to others. In moments of extreme self-doubt we may believe that our actual presence on the earth makes no difference to anyone. These are times when we particularly need confirmation of our singular value from fellow persons. Feeling acknowledged and cared for by people in our world may call us back to ourselves through meaningful connections with others. However, such moments may make us especially vulnerable to recruitment into a total-izing collective that wants to provide us with an unquestioned identifi-cation as one of *Us*, with little room for meaningful differences or human singularity.

Unfortunately, the transition can be very easy from undue self-effacement based on forgetting about the significance of our own life to corporate pride based on over-identification with collective images and purposes. Indeed, there are troubling well-known collective trajectories. On one hand, we can strongly identify ourselves as a certain kind of people, enforcing an exaggerated sense of our differences from all others, whom we regard as homogenous alien groupings. Such a "We/They" outlook is variously described as "group egotism" (A. Kaplan, 1969) and "groupthink" (Janis, 1972). It can be dangerous to be over-unified and afraid to face differences, that is, to encounter and put faces on them (Levinas, 1969). *We need to be continually vigilant about solidarity becoming insularity.*

A problem of participation in such circumstances is mindless con-formism, that is, the failure to register significant differences between our thoughts and feelings and those of others within the group when it would serve our and other affected parties' best interests to do so. People participate in and identify with social groups composing a for-midable spectrum from those with world-enhancing and humanizing purposes to those with vile, genocidal agendas. The true characters of many enterprises are difficult to decipher during early activities when they are cloaked in seemingly high-minded discourse. They may be inherently at cross-purposes or imperceptibly take pernicious turns in the course of sustaining themselves in what their members and leaders perceive as hostile environments.

Achieving sufficient distance to understand the possible errors of our ways may be difficult to accomplish. As Laing (1968) pointed out, two key questions persist in appraising our involvements with others. First, am I in or out of formation? That is, am I sufficiently similar to and in step with the individuals composing the social collective I am hoping to belong to? This is an important question involving inter-linked concerns of individuation and participation and their possible errors. In some situations it is admirable to join others with whom we identify and share important convictions despite other apparent but less crucial differences. In doing so we can perform our integrity and moral courage and constitute *edifying participation*. In other situations, blending unreflectively with a collective due to arbitrarily celebrated similarities may derive from ignorance and/or moral frailty. Some circumstances involving such *dispiriting participation* and failure to assert significant differences from others occur out of fear or naked coercion. Associates monitoring us typically will answer the question of whether we are in or out of formation regardless of our feelings.

The second question Laing raises is, Am I on or off course? That is, am I and are we heading in the right direction with our individual, relational and collective actions, or are we misguided? Sometimes individuals or groups are simply being bull-headed, reactive, or narrowly self-serving to insist upon a contrasting point of view, embodying *dispiriting individuation*. In contrast, sometimes our assertions of difference from others with whom we typically identify constitute *edifying individuation*. Our separate activities engage admirable purposes that we have the moral courage to pursue despite encompassing social pressures. Even so, we may choose thoughtfully to acknowledge common ground, participate, and identify with persons and groups with worthwhile aims. However, the redeeming value of these affiliations may not always be determined conclusively.

Though closely related to the first question of whether we can recognize shared bases for identification with others, this second question about the merit of individual and social goals can be considerably more difficult to answer. Clarifying the worth of our purposes may require appraisal by persons sufficiently distanced from our activities to provide "the excess of seeing" (Bakhtin, 1990, p. 22). Only they have the requisite difference in perspective necessary to offer disinterested opinions. Such perspective may be especially helpful if these evaluating persons also have good will or friendship for us and care about what happens to us (Beiner, 1983). In the next chapter we will examine the potentials of narrative and dialogue for communicating friendship and for addressing concerns of identity and belonging.

# 3

# Communicating Friendship

## A Dialogue of Narratives and a Narrative of Dialogues

*Someone asked me why I wanted to know Bernie's story at all. For one thing, because the German crime of the Holocaust never lets me go. But wanting to know about Bernie's "first life" was only part of what motivated me. I also wanted to link it to my own story. To do both, to tell his story and mine—the Hungarian Jewish boy and the young German villager trapped on opposite sides of a mortal divide, who come to America where their paths cross and they can work and play together—this new undertaking came to form the crux of what was important to me: bridge building. (Rosner & Tubach, 2001, p. 22)*

When he was only 12 years old, Bernie Rosner and his family were transported to Auschwitz, where the rest of his family died during the war. That same year Fritz Tubach was 13 and "slated to become a Hitler Youth" (p. 7). His father served in the German army and survived with most of Fritz's family. Meeting and becoming friends in the United States after the war, Bernie and Fritz felt compelled to try to understand each other's tragically divided lives and how they were able to be friends. They decided that telling their life stories together was the best way to recognize their individuated burdens and their shared participation in friendship. *An Uncommon Friendship* (2001) presents the co-told, "bridge building" narrative of their contrasting lives before and during the dreadful events of the Holocaust, and their friendship following the war. In co-narrating their friendship, the men continually address their similarities and their differences in building links. Motivated by shared regard, friends like Bernie and Fritz tell stories to traverse the concrete circumstances of lived, remembered, and anticipated moments.

Communicating as friends responds to the questions composing the principal dilemma of identity (A. Kaplan, 1969) noted in the last chapter. Recall the first pair of questions: How can I be what I am without fear of or exaggerating my differences from you and your differences from me? How can I allow you to be who you are without fear of or compelling your being too different from me? The spirit of friendship understands these questions as shared invitations to *edifying individuation*. Living in friendship involves acknowledging our own time, place, and possibilities while also respecting the comparable potentials of our friend's unique existence. Acknowledging our respective differences does not require hierarchically contrasting them. The second pair of questions is: How can I be with you without fear of or exaggerating my similarities with you and losing my identity? How can I allow you to be with me without fear of or compelling the loss of your identity? The spirit of friendship comprehends these questions at the same time as shared invitations to *edifying participation*. Living in friendship celebrates our significant similarities that connect us and enliven our differences.

In this chapter I maintain that the communicative activities of telling stories and pursuing dialogue are important for situating participants' concerns within friendships. I describe storytelling as fundamental for performing identities as friends and community members. Then I celebrate dialogue between friends as involving an enriching array of communicative practices. Finally, I examine how narrative and dialogue interweave to accomplish humanizing friendship as *a dialogue of narratives and a narrative of dialogues*. Telling stories and engaging in dialogue within friendships achieves, cross-examines, and performs identities as friends.

## ❖ STORYTELLING BETWEEN FRIENDS

Jerome Bruner (1996) observed, "We live in a sea of stories, and like the fish who (according to the proverb) will be the last to discover water, we have our own difficulties grasping what it is like to swim in stories" (p. 147). In understanding our lives as navigating a sea of stories, we also realize the vital roles our friends play in composing our narratively constructed worlds. Friendships emerge among the personal, relational, and cultural narratives of our lives. Negotiated within a host of stories already in progress, *friendships are ongoing narrative achievements reflexively shaping our identities, convictions, participation, and possibilities.* When we choose our friends, we not only are selecting co-actors in the stories of our lives, we are selecting co-authors and co-tellers. Poignantly over the course of shared lives, we also come to serve as trusted curators of the stories of our friends' lives, even as they preserve our co-told and witnessed narratives (Rawlins, 1992). Viewed in these ways, the narrative activities of friendship include significant privileges and responsibilities.

First, *narrative activity between friends is fundamentally concerned with the meanings that we assign to our experiences and lives.* Meaning making is fundamental to human existence. What interpretations do we construct with our friends for our lived experiences? What significance do we attach to the occurrences of our lives? How, for example, should we understand events in our careers, in our local community and world events, in personal projects, and in the lives of loved ones? Carr observes that "meaning is thus central for the understanding of the course of life because it encompasses and orders the things we value and the purposes we pursue" (1986, p. 77). In telling each other our stories, friends co-construct the ongoing personal and social significance of our endeavors, setbacks, accomplishments, and hopes.

Second, *telling stories together explores the points of view and particularities of each friend's individuated life.* A friend's story is not an abstract treatise. It is not told, at least initially, to formulate some broadly applicable insight. The narrative activity of friends is especially interested in understanding the details of how *this* friend experienced *these* moments of living her life in concrete conditions with palpable consequences for her and the persons she cares about. The friend's distinct point of view fuels the uptake of *this particular* story. Arthur Bochner remarks, "Every narrator has a stake in her story; she is never indifferent" (1994, p. 31). The storyteller, our friend, embodies a unique locus for evaluating occurrences and possibilities in her world. As Carr (1986, p. 59) argues, the narrator's point of view "transforms events into a story by *telling* them," elaborating further, "what is essential to narration is not that it is a verbal act of telling, as such, but that it embodies a certain point (or points) of view on a sequence of events" (p. 62). Stories are formed when we organize events, choosing what aspects to include and emphasize. Narrating our point of view highlights which parts make a difference to us. We encourage our friends to tell the stories that they want or need to relate. We want to know what matters to our friends in the events they are recounting. We try to see the occurrences of their lives through their eyes.

Third, *telling stories is an embodied effort that involves the simultaneous and consequential activities of speaking and listening.* We share the moments of storytelling with friends who through their hearing and co-telling help us learn about life. In Frank's words, "Stories are the ongoing work of turning mere existence into a life that is social, and moral, and affirms the existence of the teller as a human being" (1997, p. 43). Through articulating one's point of view on lived experiences, self achieves discursive distance from personal events by making them objects of mutual experience as accomplished in a story (Berger & Luckman, 1966). Suppose Brian tells Alicia a story depicting his emotional strains during a troubled evening with a romantic partner that led to their breaking up. Alicia now understands specific exchanges between Brian and his partner that caused him both anguish and pride. If either of these friends faces a similar situation in the future, they can refer to this previous incident, identifying particular actions or statements as worthwhile or regrettable when they narrated it together. Ironically, stories at once compose distanced renderings of personal experience as well as the opportunity for another person's empathy and enhanced immediacy to self. In this way, stories connect persons with their friends.

That both self and other hear the story self tells has important implications described eloquently by Arthur Frank:

> Storytelling is *for* an other just as much as it is for oneself. In the reciprocity that is storytelling, the teller offers herself as guide to the other's self-formation. The other's receipt of that guidance not only recognizes but *values* the teller. The moral genius of storytelling is that each, teller and listener, enters the space of the story *for* the other. (1995, pp. 17–18, original emphasis)

As much as we offer or request guidance through telling a story, our friend is summoned as a witness to the story. Through narrating ourselves to a friend, we become accountable to our self and to our friend. Stories are driven by their central characters. As in the example involving a romantic relationship breakup above, telling personal stories offers opportunities to review and rehearse our actions as narrated characters. These actions performed in the stories of our lives and our narrated responses to their impact on others display versions of our own moral characters.

In witnessing a friend's story, we necessarily engage in the dialectic of judgment and acceptance (Rawlins, 1992). How do I evaluate my friend's actions in this narrative? Do I withhold judgment based on my perception that my friend just wants to be heard and accepted for whom he is or is trying to become? Or because of my overall acceptance of him as my friend, do I respond as an evaluative witness to his story, voicing my judgment of actions? In what spirit was his story shared with me? Given our friendship, what is my most edifying response to the testimony to his character portrayed in his story?

What testimonies do we choose to relate and witness in friendship? Although the actions involved in telling and listening to stories are individual, each one suggests a reflexively negotiated social ethic (Frank, 1995). Frank (1995) observes, "The self-story is told both to others and to one's self; each telling is enfolded within the other. The act of telling is a dual reaffirmation. Relationships with others are reaffirmed, and the self is reaffirmed" (p. 56). In affirming the person's actions within the narrative of his life, which is simultaneously a life shared with friends, the listener acknowledges that person's moral claims at that moment. In doing so, both narrator and witness should heed MacIntyre's (1984, p. 217) warning concerning the narrative formation of selves: "I am forever whatever I have been at any time for others—and I may at any time be called upon to answer for it—no matter how changed I may be now." This is why there is both delight and embarrassment in reuniting with old friends. They know us as we once were.

For example, responsibilities that Brian has embraced or shirked in his stories to Alicia about his romantic involvements will always say something about him. Arras (1997) remarks how listening to narratives affects listeners as well: "But once one actually sits down to listen to the other's story, one opens oneself not simply to the possibilities for acquiring sympathy and tolerance, but also to the possibility of radical self-transformation" (p. 75). He adds later, "In this way, an awareness of other stories leads to an awareness of the limits of our own" (p. 76). Our friends' stories change us. Hearing Brian's stories about episodes with romantic partners prompts Alicia to reflect on her own experiences with romantic partners.

Fourth, *in sharing narratives friends are concerned with the existential and cultural contexts in which the narrated events transpire.* We want to probe the enveloping circumstances that frame and give meaning to the events depicted in our friend's stories about his life. What is selected for inclusion and exclusion is important. The setting for the story matters. What conditions sustain the possibilities and impossibilities of our friend's and others' actions in this story? In Brian's story of a romance gone awry, what kinds of pressures was he under to treat someone he loved in this way? Why wasn't he able to take more time and try to understand her side of the situation? Why did walking away from this person he once loved make sense to him? What will he do now? Friends want to understand the enabling factors and constraints of each other's circumstances. Our narratives reflect our experiences of strategic and unavoidable distributions of resources and power in shaping our choices (Peterson & Langellier, 2006). Given the material, social, and existential conditions of our lives, how much agency do we portray in shaping the events in our stories?

Through the eyes of the storyteller, what does this story reveal about the assumptions, everyday activities, practices, and values of the local culture in which it occurs—be it a family, workplace, political association, or romantic relationship? What practical and moral issues are at stake in the community presupposed by the story? In listening to friends' stories, we recognize the wisdom in MacIntyre's assertion, "For the story of my life is always embedded in the story of those communities from which I derive my identity" (1984, p. 221).

Indeed, fifth, *as friends we compose and enact versions of our own identity as individuals and community members through storytelling*. Frank (1997) asserts in detail the importance of stories for affirming that we belong to a community. Narratives also serve reflexively to constitute communities:

> Stories are told as claims to membership in communities, but the community is not already there, waiting for the story. Communities are formed out of stories; the story is a reflexive affirmation that a gathering of people *is* a community, or even that two people can become a community. The communal act of telling, hearing, and recognizing a story is how a group becomes a community. (p. 36, original emphasis)

Through relating our experiences in a story told to others, "individuality folds into community" (p. 37). Undertaking this narrative activity together constitutes a basis for understanding a connected basis for our identities. Frank concludes, "The call to stories is a call to the common work of *finding out what the experience we share might mean as an identity*" (1997, p. 37, original emphasis).

The characters that we present as ourselves in a story imply personal attributes, as well as the social groups and types of people we identify with and those we reject. Our actions in a story dramatize making choices, thereby invoking moral values. The positive values may involve enacting various degrees of personal and social responsibility, cooperation, courage, loyalty, and concern for others' welfare. Negative values may include insensitive actions, shameless self-promotion, crass opportunism, bigotry, deception, and exploitation. However, the values that appear to be negative and positive may take on different valence due to the moral visions forged narratively among friends within encompassing cultural orders. Opportunism may be celebrated as a positive value in certain circles, and certainly not "crass." Reflecting our disadvantaged circumstances, we may tell stories celebrating our resourcefulness in earning money or landing on our feet when the chips are down. Further, what one community regards as bigotry another community may narrate as upholding the necessary boundaries between the community and those who should be excluded. Unfortunately, through such community stories, ranging from dyads to larger social groups, the other becomes marked as the *other* that is devalued and dehumanized.

But we also tell stories to humanize ourselves and others and to celebrate values that connect us. Our discourses do more than instruct us about what is good and what is bad. We are also instructed about whom and what is *worthy* of being valued and disvalued (Laing, 1972). When we narrate and identify with stories upholding values in our community (of 2 or of 2000), we become part of those narratives, and their values become part of our characters. Our narrative identities therefore involve a life-long process of construction and reconstruction with other persons. Hearing and telling stories together displays the subject positions we believe are available to us and the possibilities and limits of identifying with others. Burrell and Hauerwas concluded, "The test of each story is the sort of person it shapes" (1977, p. 136).

Finally, *friends seek to understand how events unfold in time through telling narratives.* What do our friends select as the significant events that occurred earlier, setting the stage for this story? What events do they identify as pivotal in composing the story? What have been the consequences of the story's events from the vantage point of the present moment of telling? Moreover, how are these events arranged in the plot of the story as it is told by our friends? In Bruner's words a friend's narratives enact and reveal "a structure of committed time" (1996, p. 133). What do our friends' stories reveal about how they understand the temporal organization of their lives? Perhaps indicative of a frantic culture or a beleaguered life, some friends never seem to have enough time for anything. Their stories bespeak endless demands and time pressures and embody this frustration. Other friends' stories suggest such emptiness, material deprivations, and constrained opportunities that time seems to burn upon them without meaningful purpose. The minutes of their days seem to stretch bleakly into only more of the same. Other friends seem to relish the moments of their lives. They tell stories of moments savored, choices deliberately measured, people cared for, even as they take the time to share their tales of those moments with us.

The narrative activities of friends pore over descriptions of each person's time and place in their moments spent together telling and listening. Co-narrating friends want to emphasize their capacity for choice or scrutinize its limits. They take seriously each other's say in co-telling the stories of their individual lives and the narrative of their life together. As Bruner (1996, p. 136) states, "Some element of freedom is always implied in narrative. . . . Agency presupposes choice." Encouraging our friends to tell stories simultaneously inspires them to understand themselves as possessing agency and to envision alternative possibilities. Gergen and Gergen (2006, p. 113) hold that such support to craft narratives presupposes the significant question: "Is the narrative we are fashioning together 'actionable'?" That is, is it "capable of being put into daily practice"? This involved stance enjoins friends to share responsibility for our envisioned choices and actions. Can we really do this, and what might happen if we do?

Friends support our active, mindful presence in our everyday moments, our refusal to play a cameo appearance in our own lives. Positioning ourselves strongly as choice makers in the narratives of our own lives derives from a rich sense of the unfolding temporality of our identity. We make choices through dedicated activity in the always contingent present, "the point of tension between self-identity and self-transcendence" (Crites, 1986, p. 171). In the "double concentration" of the present moment, persons engage in the "self-recollection" necessary to sustain a viable "self-identity" consolidated from the past. Meanwhile, persons muster the hope and effort for "self-transcendence" to pave the way for positive future changes (Crites, 1986, p. 171).

At numerous points in our lives it can benefit us to seize the moment, to pause and reflect upon the person we have been and might continue to become. Doing so involves examining how our past actions and decisions have shaped how we see ourselves now. What have I done that makes me proud and contributes to the person I believe I am today? What significant things have I done that I regret and still shape how I see myself? Honestly assessing my "self-identity" at this point in time allows me to envision and perhaps do things differently in the future. I may take action to transcend this current identity. The present moment is when I may begin optimistically to rise above my past identities. In their roles as benevolent co-authors, friends help create our engaged presence in co-authoring our moments together as self-recognizing persons. In doing so, they help us to sustain and direct the productive tension of self-identity emerging from our past and self-transcendence leaning into our future.

I recall talking with a close friend of mine when I was leaving a university where I had worked several years. In presenting the fit I perceived between myself and my two work choices, I told my friend (and myself) a story of my life that recollected my youth playing rock and roll. My unfolding story recalling this past would have me choose the job near the coast with no doctoral program. After minimally fulfilling my responsibilities, I envisioned spending my days strumming a guitar by the ocean. My friend listened carefully to me but did not accept this version. He told me that he understood I loved playing music. But he also said that during the years he had known me, he had observed my passion for working with graduate students. He said, "I know you would like to see yourself as some Jimmy Buffet whiling away your days by the ocean side. But that is not your story. Your story involves you going to a place where you can continue to educate grad students. You have a lot more to contribute to your field before you answer this beatnik call." His narrative highlighted contrasting past actions and lifelong convictions. His version convinced me to rethink my story and to select the position that challenged me to continue to work with new scholars.

Telling stories together thus highlights our conceptions of turning points in our lives, including the ambiguities, contingencies, and passions that provoked our actions (Bruner, 1996). Some of these turning points develop incrementally, almost imperceptibly, across everyday activities. We may not even notice certain daily occurrences as important until our friends point out their potentials to us from hearing our stories. Meanwhile, we may realize the significance of seemingly mundane events in the very process of narrating our activities to our friends. More dramatic turning points—a proud accomplishment, a new relationship or opportunity, a disappointment or betrayal—may compose the occasions for telling stories to our friends in the first place.

Together friends negotiate the *narrative punctuation* of the events in their lives. As MacIntyre (1984, p. 212) observes, "there are many events which are both endings and beginnings." Friends may decide together when a particular story actually began. Does this recent occurrence really constitute a new turn or is it merely another instance of a larger pattern? Has this co-worker or romantic partner turned over a new leaf, or is this simply a momentary blip on the screen? Should this remark be interpreted in an offhand or deeply foreboding manner? Further, as trusted curators of each other's stories, sometimes friends offer us a summary appraisal. Having heard our tale of recent developments, our friend may say, "This is not your story. You need to be careful. You are changing in ways that will be difficult to reverse. This needs to be put to rest; you need to walk away from this situation." At another juncture our friend may say, "Whether you want to acknowledge it or not, this is your story and always has been. Stop kidding yourself. Whatever it takes, you need to see this through."

Friends help us claim our being-in-time forged across noticed and overlooked moments. They help us to identify who we are through helping us locate where, with whom, and how we belong. As our stories unfold with our characters etched in *time,* do we consider our beliefs and actions to be in accord or in conflict with *the times* (Barros, 1998)? What communities subsume ours in the telling of these times? Under the care of our friends we continually monitor the potential "was and is self" (p. 13) that dynamically marks the transition from past complacencies and oversights to present discontents and motivations. With whom do we share our stories? Perhaps the troubles in society we perceive as dyadic friends might benefit from a hearing by a greater number of potentially like-minded souls. Perhaps there will be a broadening of our concerns as a result of shared tellings. A larger community of civic friends may allow us to transform into our envisioned identities through crafting new narratives together. Performing these more inclusive civic stories with others constitutes "a horizon shift from the personal me to a political me" (Barros, 1998, p. 7).

For example, I know two persons in my town whose personal stories, one as a compassionate individual and one as a horse lover, were told initially only to their close friends. Now their stories are co-told with fellow community members as narratives of social change. Their narratives have come to include more characters, personal and civic friends who have worked with them to found a flourishing shelter for homeless persons and to establish a center for rehabilitating cast-off or condemned horses. In both cases the visions and identities originally expressed in their personal narratives have transmuted into political identities serving larger interests. They have involved community members in stories enlarged by broader caring and commitment.

To summarize, stories *demonstrate friends' meanings and points of view* to one another. We co-tell our stories with friends through *engaged speaking and listening.* In sharing narratives we reveal the *existential and cultural contexts* of our actions. As friends we also *identify ourselves as connected to specific communities* through our narratives. Finally, telling stories reveals the *temporal organization* of friends' lives. Friends help us preserve the integrity of our narrative identities through how we relate the choices we make in life. In telling stories with friends we seek to understand ourselves in time and receive support for our struggle with personal, cultural, and political situations. Our ability to narrate self-assertion, belonging with others, and valued existential continuities in the face of changes composes our narrative integrity pursued with friends.

## ❖ PRACTICING DIALOGUE BETWEEN FRIENDS

Conversing with friends is one of life's pleasures. Friends' talk together runs the gamut from brief exchanges to long phone conversations, from chatting during meals, projects, or recreational activities, to pointed discussions of serious concerns (Rawlins, 1992). During times with our friends we exchange stories and cross-examine viewpoints, transitioning in and out of light-hearted and deeply significant discourse. Feeling free to do so is one of the gifts of friendship. My examination of friendships across the life course identified "somebody to talk to" as one of the three most important benefits of close friendship named by persons from late adolescence to old age (Rawlins, 1992).

While talking together with friends includes a range of discourses, it also emphasizes existentially significant conversations. On occasion friends actively seek to sort out a personal concern or a larger question. They want to talk through problems and possibilities in the presence of someone they trust. I hold that interwoven with their storytelling is the pursuit of dialogue. I want to present seven aspirations of dialogue that I believe epitomize constructive communication between friends. Following this discussion, I will describe how dialogue intertwines with narration to individuate and connect friends throughout their moments of friendship.

First, *dialogue involves exchanging, questioning, and responding to individual points of view on relevant matters while sustaining our communicative relationship.* Posing, taking seriously, and responding to each person's viewpoints regarding issues of mutual concern motivate dialogue. Accordingly, we may engage together in dialogue to learn about and refine our questions and points of view. But we also actively practice dialogue as an energizing end-in-itself. Friends talk. In order to exchange viewpoints and foster ongoing connections with others, there are intrinsic as well as extrinsic values in communicating according to the dialogical stance.

Second, *in dialogical activity, the personhood of others is considered sacred.* Consistent with the ideals of friendship, embodying a dialogical outlook embraces Martin Buber's (1937) I–Thou regard for persons as ends-in-themselves—as the very persons they are. This treatment of others contrasts with the I–It orientation, which objectifies other persons, seeing them primarily as tools to carry out our plans and projects. However, Buber (1937) wisely recognized the impossibility of sustaining an I–Thou stance indefinitely; it is only achieved in sterling moments. In actuality, both I–Thou and I–It orientations toward other human beings are lived in tension with each other as the concrete exigencies of material life fate us to I–It activities. Even so, recognizing the emptiness of treating others as objects, Buber (1970, p. 85) pronounced, "without It a human being cannot live. But whoever lives only with that is not human." This tension resembles the dialectic of affection and instrumentality, which friends must manage continuously in their interactions (Rawlins, 1989a, 1992). Our interactions involve caring for friends for their own sakes, but also calling on them for help. Our deep regard for our friends' irreplaceable presence in our lives shines through in our moments of dialogue.

Third, *a dialogical outlook understands human identities as accomplished in historically situated relationships and as simultaneously involving similarities and differences between people.* The singularity of each of us derives from our placement during each moment of social life at a complex intersection of discourses, cultural traditions, and emerging potentialities (Bakhtin, 1981; Gadamer, 1989). Facilitating the pertinent identities of each participant during our moments of interaction thereby becomes a primary requirement of dialogical interaction. Negotiating identities occurs reflexively as part of the ongoing activities of defining relationships between people. As we identify ourselves and others through how we communicate with them, we define our relationship. Meanwhile, as we mutually define our relationship, we enable and constrain our relevant identities. Defining our relationships involves recognizing the similarities and the differences that matter to us in constituting our respective identities at this specific time and place. As noted above, between friends our meaningfully shared similarities can constitute bases for *edifying participation* and our significant differences can facilitate *edifying individuation* in social interaction.

For example, Alicia is Brian's supervisor at work. Their company has clear policies concerning hierarchical relationships that require them to address each other as Dr. Johnson and Mr. Evans. This sanctioned definition of their superior–subordinate relationship specifies manners of speaking and comportment between them that function to confirm the primary definition of their work relationship for them-selves, their colleagues, and clients. These practices perform their work identities in ways that highlight differences in their job experiences, qualifications and status while ignoring their respective genders and races.

Meanwhile, Alicia and Brian have become friends because of common interests in bicycling, music, and physical fitness. When they dialogue about matters outside of work, they try not to invoke their work-related identities that position them hierarchically and under-mine their abilities to talk as equals. Instead, they draw upon the per-sonal attributes that connect them as friends. In their dialogue addressing the local politics surrounding a new bicycle path, Alicia's identity as an African American becomes relevant because she notes that part of the proposed route uproots numerous African American families who have lived in the area for generations. Brian is European American and cannot share with Alicia in significant existential depth that specific racial and ethnic identity. Even so, as a friend and person concerned with social justice, he embraces her point of view despite his excitement about expanded biking opportunities at the outset of their dialogue. On another occasion the friends may primarily recognize the salience of their different identities as a heterosexual male and a heterosexual female in dialoguing about Brian's problems with the woman he is dating. But when they discuss proper diet and fitness regimes in preparing for a long bike tour together, their contrasting identities as an African American female and a European American male have minimal if any bearing on their discourses. They speak in this situation primarily as dedicated friends and disciplined cyclists.

Fourth, *an indispensable watchword of a dialogical stance is respect for self and other(s).* Participating in a genuine spirit of dialogue mandates simul-taneous self-respect and respect for others. Entering into dialogue means that we must represent our own convictions. In dialogue we always have a say in shaping the events of our lives. Speaking our mind and hearing our voice addressing others constitutes the communicative integrity of our point of view. Simultaneously, entering into dialogue means respect-ing other persons' differences, thoughts, and feelings. In opening dia-logue with them, we allow other persons to be who they are. Within the limits of constructive conversation and our own self-respect, the stance of dialogue requires us to hear and respect the other's point of view, regardless of our agreement or disagreement with it.

Similar demands are posed by the dialectic of expressiveness and protectiveness (Rawlins, 1983c, 1992). In expressing thoughts and feel-ings to friends, we embrace the responsibility to protect our friends' and our own privacy, areas of vulnerability, and threats to dignity. Speaking in these ways promotes trust *both* in the honesty of our expressions *and* respect for the friend's and our feelings. Fulfilling the simultaneous expectations of expressiveness and protectiveness renders us trustworthy as communicators within ongoing friendships.

Fifth, *dialogue requires active, mutual involvement by all parties in the emerging process of conversation.* Entering into dialogue with another person means being fully present, psychologically and emotionally, to the other (Buber, 1956). Such committed participation in conversation with the other creates the mutuality of dialogue celebrated by Buber (1937). Dialogue demands paradoxical work to sustain itself. On one hand, it involves surrendering oneself to a process of interaction that transcends the self. On the other hand, it involves active *thoughtful* participation (Koehn, 1998). Thoughtful participation means devoting careful attention to the substantive matters at stake *and* concern about the friend's well-being. In Bateson's (1972) terms, both reasons of the heart and reasons of the mind have their place in the robust dialogue between friends.

In perceiving our needs to talk, friends dedicate the effort to cultivate our contingent opportunities to be fully available in each other's presence. We limit distractions and are mindful of the time and place of the dialogue in each other's immediate lives. We understand that it is important to optimize the circumstances for dialogue to occur. Our friend may be too emotionally involved in events to be able to talk about them constructively at this moment. Likely interruptions or insufficient time may also threaten the natural unfolding of our dialogue. When, where, and how can we have this conversation in the best possible circumstances?

To engage in dialogue, active, careful, and responsive listening is crucial. Motivated communicators understand the creative and confirming powers of listening in nourishing each other's willingness to speak. In listening, as in all facets of dialogic activity, we must realize the significance of nonverbal communication. All behaviors occurring between friends—bodily movements, gestures, and tones of voice—qualify and are qualified by the context in which they occur (Haley, 1963). Bakhtin insisted that the intonation of voices paints audible pictures of the persons being addressed and therefore constitutes the expression through sound of social evaluations (Holquist, 1990). We are wise to remember that the overall composition of these embodied activities continuously defines identities and relationships during all face-to-face social interactions, including dialogue (Haley, 1963; Rawlins, 1987).

Moreover, dialogical partners embrace the potentials of silence in each other's presence. Silent moments provide opportunities to pause and reflect on what has and has not been said. Participants should not feel pressed to speak when they would rather hold their peace. Such co-achieved silence emerging through the very moments of engaged discourse ironically provides necessary distance from the interaction. Being able to be silent together is part of being able to talk together.

Sixth, *conversing in a dialogical spirit involves standing our ground and allowing others to happen to our self* (Stewart & Zediker, 2000). We enter into dialogue holding the convictions that make us the very persons we are (Buber, 1956). Even so, we approach dialogue with a willingness to risk change. A dialogical ethic regards self and others as unfinished, engaging with others in moments brimming with potentialities for becoming other than who we were at the outset of our dialogue (Buber, 1956; Frank, 2002; Todorov, 1984). In practical terms this means that we may have provisional goals for speaking with others but no fixed conclusion envisioned for our conversation. We may know what we are going to say at the outset of our dialogue but not know precisely how we are going to respond to the other as our dialogue unfolds. In this regard, the spirit of dialogue avoids fixed or predetermined goals and especially self-regarding agendas in speaking with others.

Finally, *dialogue may demonstrate the intractable constraints of relationships.* At the same time that dialogue may affirm our humanity, open up possibilities, and generate new understandings, the converse is also true. In-depth, committed discussion may reveal the undeniable constraints of our abilities to converse and positions we cannot or refuse to modify (Burbules, 1992). We are finite, culturally situated beings overdetermined in many ways by our histories and the discourses at our disposal. Speaking together magnifies the concrete differences in power, resources, and backgrounds that may dictate our experiences of each other. Through dialogue, we may primarily discover the boundaries of our respective languages for creating comprehension of each other and our respective worlds.

Despite such frustrations, accomplishing these mutually recognized limits to our understandings of each other through dialogue is valuable (Gurevitch, 1989). In the spirit of dialogue and friendship we address the practices and conditions under which we speak together in the interests of improving one another's possibilities for freedom, self-determination, and voice. Communicating in such inherently respectful ways, hopefully we set the stage for "trading on each other's truths" (Rommetveit, 1980) in other occasions where our differences are not so daunting.

❖  NARRATIVES, DIALOGUES, AND FRIENDSHIPS

Storytelling and practicing dialogue are not distinct activities. Narratives allow us to dramatize the situated actions of specific characters occurring across time; they perform temporally mediated activities and experiences. By comparison, through dialogue we can embody ideal practices in conversationally addressing our concerns; we converse respectfully about meaningful matters. However, in the actual discourse of friends, the communicative activities of narrative and dialogue interweave considerably—so much so that they seldom occur separately. Many of our co-told stories emerge through dialogue, and our conversations with friends often consist of co-told stories.

First, *both narratives and dialogues are vivid ways of sharing and shaping a specific person's point of view.* When someone tells a story or articulates a position in a dialogue—we become privy to that individual's window on the world. Telling our stories and stating our views means discursively accomplishing and owning our distinctive worldviews with others. It is a crucial lynchpin connecting dialogue and personal narration (Black, 2008). Whose perspective do we choose to embody as a storyteller and character in our discourse with friends? To what extent do we actively individuate ourselves in our stories, taking responsibility for our actions and viewpoints? To what extent do we perform ourselves as belonging to or identifying with groups or collectivities that make us who we are? What or whose languages do we speak as we express ourselves in dialogue? The language we utter constitutes a point of view (Bakhtin, 1981; Burke, 1966; Holquist, 1990). Both telling our stories and participating in the back and forth of dialogue with friends allow us to utter and to hear our personal understandings of how we see ourselves at the time and place of these activities.

Second, *storytelling and pursuing dialogue are invitational discursive activities* (Foss & Griffin, 1995). Both are welcoming endeavors that actively seek other communicators with whom to co-create understandings and special moments of possibility. Narrators must have audiences who function to varying degrees as co-tellers and addressees in constituting meaningful narration. Storytellers want to share their tales with responsive others. Likewise, embodied dialogue requires at least two participants to deal earnestly with each other's views. The ideal stance of dialogue involves a receptive, inclusive, respectful turning to the other (Buber, 1937). In short, narrative and dialogue create openly shared frameworks for edifying discursive participation. Both are inclusive ways of simultaneously connecting with others and performing individual points of view.

As such, third, *meaningful dialogue and storytelling both emphasize the creative, ethical, and mutually affirming significance of engaged listening.* Narrating experiences and pursuing dialogue together are active communicative achievements that emphasize embodied speaking and listening. Effective storytelling and dialogue require all participants to give themselves to these discursive moments, to be fully present for the other communicators.

Fourth, *among friends participating in dialogue and storytelling may constitute ends in themselves.* Each activity involves potentially enriching activities for taking pleasure in each other's company. Telling stories together enjoyably transports friends to other times, places, and possible versions of selves. Narrative provides ways to reminisce about personal, romantic, recreational, family, work, and political activities that we have accomplished in the past. Favorite stories are retold in dramatizing us as characters involved in the events of our friendship. Similarly, dialogues involve us meaningfully in the mutual cross-examination of issues we consider important. We enjoy hashing out things through dialogue with our friends. Both storytelling and robust dialogue enliven our time spent with friends.

Fifth, *the discourses composing their dialogues and narratives generate moral visions for friends.* These communicative activities demonstrate moral convictions relevant for friends either as common principles or as matters disputed in a spirit of good will and respect. Thinking out loud, respectfully challenging each other's positions and likewise being held accountable, and talking through matters of contention constitute the moral contours of dialogue. The circumstances and actions depicted in stories and the narrators' responses to their consequences also embody moral choices for friends. Co-told narratives and engaged dialogues give voice and intonation to the friends' values. Both conversational activities vibrantly perform persons' convictions, doubts, and decisions.

Sixth, taken together, *narrating stories and engaging in dialogues constitute significant discursive activities for making choices as friends.* Choices are not uniform in significance or implication (Bateson, 1972). I intend "making choices" here in two senses. On one hand, friends work together to envision *new* sets of alternatives composing their lives. In our best capacities as co-narrators and dialogical partners, we do not confine ourselves merely to given options. On the other hand, having identified the range of choices we perceive as available, we jointly select with our friends from that array the most favorable alternative. As my friend and colleague Raymie MacKerrow has put it during our conversations, *there is a vital difference between choosing the choices* (co-constructed as available to self) and merely *choosing* (from a finite set of already stipulated options). Friends make choices together in both senses.

Conjunctive freedoms live at the heart of friendship. In connecting with each other, friends help friends formulate our capacities for individual agency. Through our narrative and dialogical activities together, we make choices by discursively constructing the constraints and potentials of our subject positions. We enhance our perceived options for experiencing, communicating, and acting. We facilitate each other's "room to move" (Laing, 1969). In addressing together questions such as who am I, where do I stand, what can and should I do, self-told narratives position us meaningfully in depicted time(s) and places(s). These stories allow us and our friend to experience our circumstances and the identities we consider relevant to perform. Meanwhile, through dialogue we directly articulate positions and feelings about the issues raised by our friend. These activities feed off of each other in discursively constituting our identities and possibilities.

Both narrative and dialogue conceive and communicate our being-in-the-world as unfinished and unfinalized by others (Frank, 2002). In contrast, a principal danger of categorical thinking is to perceive people and their possibilities in ways overdetermined by their identification with restrictive categories. Such discursive closure is imposed by registering abstract attributes largely considered to exist outside of time. Narratives can make use of the "sense of an ending" (Kermode, 1966) to achieve provisional closure derived from their present vantage point of telling. Even so, narrative perception resists discursive closure in its openness to the interpretive complexities of concrete circumstances and to future events. Dialogue also resists discursive closure in its openness to other voices, languages, and points of view, and its recognition of multiple versions of the world existing in simultaneous juxtaposition at any moment in time (Bakhtin, 1981; Bateson, 1979). The closures accomplished in a story and through dialogue are provisional, continually revised by discursive activities and actions performed over time with others. Moreover, both activities consciously dwell within the ever-freshening potentials of meaning making in hermeneutic circles. There is always the necessity of (re)positioning friends' dialogic and narrative activities within the unfolding horizons considered relevant to their collaborative meaning making (Gadamer, 1989; Kepnes, 1992).

❖  INTERWEAVING NARRATIVE AND
    DIALOGUE IN DISCOURSES OF FRIENDSHIP

Co-telling narratives embodies and can create dialogue between friends. The dialogues of friends turn into various degrees of shared narration. Each discursive activity can be used to constitute the other activity. Narratives may be told to support or illustrate one's position in a dialogue, and replaying a dialogue may be employed as the format for telling a story. Co-telling stories and engaging in dialogue may literally constitute ways friends structure their clock time together. Meanwhile, temporality may be performed in important ways "within" their stories and dialogues—for example, when a friend relates in three brief sentences the condensed story of her job interview or trip back home. Or the way a complicated history of a situation may be summarized thematically as one statement in a dialogical exchange: "You basically have wasted your semester partying and working at that stupid job."

Bakhtin characterizes all language use as inherently dialogized. He discusses dialogue more as a condition of discourse than as an ideal practice. In his view all words are always already crisscrossed with myriad meanings stemming from the words' numerous uses throughout history and in the present. In "Discourse in the Novel" (1981) Bakhtin distinguishes between internal and external dialogue. *Internal dialogue* describes the dialogical interplay of multiple languages and voices taking place wherever discourse occurs. It is an inherent property of all language use. His term *heteroglossia* describes tensions occurring at every site of language between *centripetal* forces endeavoring to centralize and restrict the possible meanings of words and *centrifugal* forces seeking to expand their diversity of meanings. This contest among numerous possible languages and meanings is simultaneously a contest among numerous worldviews. As we have noted, for Bakhtin language is a worldview; controlling meanings is controlling possible worlds.

When we listen to our friend's story about the events surrounding her recent decision to forego a vacation, we might say, "When you say you have been reviewing your 'productivity,' all I hear is your company speaking. What is it that *you* want to do?" The language of "productivity" bespeaks a different worldview—that of a demanding corporation—from the one we believe she should use to envision her options. We call attention to the internal dialogue percolating in the very language of her story. One question for friends is, to what extent do we constrain and to what extent allow the multiple languages simultaneously constituting the internal dialogue of our stories to be heard and considered?

In contrast, for Bakhtin (1981) *external dialogue* refers to observable ways of organizing the discourses and voices occurring in a narrative. Presenting the conversations or dialogue of characters in a sequential turn-taking mode is a common example. The unfolding exchange of turns at talk by characters constitutes a significant feature of many stories. Key events in stories often take the form of pivotal conversations presented as external dialogues. Note that this alternating of speaking turns actually is a mundane meaning of conversation or dialogue, which does not necessarily involve the ideal practices discussed above. Even so, the routine alternating of turns at talk constitutes the majority of "external dialogue" in our everyday lives.

How our lives are lived through time and how they are enacted in discourse involve crucial dynamics interanimating narratives and dialogues. For one thing, both types of discursive activity try to comprehend the first paradox of human communication discussed in Chapter 2. Communication always occurs in moments where multiple possibilities *simultaneously* address us, yet these same moments transpire incessantly in a *sequential* passage of time. Characteristic performances of this challenging paradox of temporality initially distinguish narration and dialogue. Narratives typically stretch across time with an identifiable beginning, middle, and end (regardless of how these occurrences may be rearranged in actually telling the story. For example, some stories start in the middle and then flash back to the beginning). In grappling with the sequential unfolding of complex configurations of human possibilities, actions, and events, narration accents linear time.

In contrast, dialogical temporality accents the multiplicity of possibilities simultaneously available (yet unfolding) during every moment of human discourse (Kepnes, 1992; Ricoeur, 1981). The discourse of dialogical temporality strives to embrace the simultaneity of multiple potentialities juxtaposed at given moments in time (Bakhtin, 1981; Buber, 1937). Actively engaging together with this rich configuration of possibilities is an aspiration of dialogue (Buber, 1956). Even so, Buber (1937) cautions us about the limits and evanescence of these authentic encounters. These "moments of meeting" cannot be sustained (Cissna & Anderson, 2002).

Despite their contrasting temporal accents, both narration and dialogue struggle with the paradox of sequence and configuration in communicating possibilities and consequences. For example, there are meaningful though reflexively blurred differences among: (1) living our unfolding story of a trip to visit our friends; (2) co-telling the events of the story of our trip as they are emerging as parts of "the" story; and (3) co-telling a story of the trip after it ends. Mink (1970) stipulates that "following a story" occurs while events are happening and contrasts with "having followed a story," which transpires after the fact. The first he likens to traveling on the currents of a river in anticipation of what will occur next. The latter he likens to viewing the river from above and being able to see simultaneously what takes place in the river both downstream and upstream, which he terms "configurational" understanding. In his view, human events are *first* lived and *then* narrated.

Carr (1986) disagrees, stressing that we live the unfolding temporality of our lives as already narrative in composition. We understand our experiences as meaningfully storied, just as we can anticipate the resolution of a suspended chord in music or the return of an echo in a canyon. We have the possibility of (co)constructing emerging pivotal events in shaping the narrative composition of our lives without the necessity of "having followed" them. His point is that we do not live our lives merely as a series of minimally connected "nows" only deriving their significance as parts of a story told after the fact. We have provisional, narratable understandings of our unfolding moments as they occur. Sometimes we even have an anticipated story in mind. Based on such recognitions, we have a say (with others) in shaping the stories composing our lives.

Likewise, there are significant differences between: (1) a dialogue about important issues pursued in the fullness of undetermined moments of engagement; and (2) representing that dialogue as a completed story after the fact. The simultaneous play of potentialities opened up by devoted conversation is significantly diminished when described merely as sequentially unfolding occurrences (Gadamer, 1989). Dialogue does not achieve its lived traction by its partners reaching for another moment in time or communicating primarily as if they knew how things could or should turn out. All our questions in dialogue may only produce better questions or tacitly acquired knowledge of each other that serves further dialogue. Describing the fits and starts and the creative risks of dialogue after the fact as a completed story often misses the dedication of dialogue partners to living and understanding to their fullest the possibilities offered by the co-achieved moment at hand. It is difficult to capture this present. Consequently, while narratives composed across time through dialogues can be instructive, the truly transformative moments of dialogue transpire during our shared presence and engaged participation.

Kermode's (1966, 1979) work demonstrates two positions concerning the tensions between the sequences and configurations of lived time (Kepnes, 1992). One position, "the sense of an ending" (Kermode, 1966) argues that the ending of a story provides the closure necessary to view the narrative as a determinate whole. We can then employ the hermeneutic circle to understand the meaning of the story's events in their interrelations as parts of a meaningful whole. We may also further probe their meaning through assessing the events' linearly conceived role in leading up to the story's end. This position relies on the endings of stories to tie things together, providing the necessary resolution of ambiguities. In doing so, it presents life in light of its overall sequence, tilting toward the future with a "when it's all said and done" basis for assigning significance to actions. In contrast, the later Kermode (1979) ironically comes to view narratives as performing "the genesis of secrecy." Various moments in stories are viewed as "impression points," continuously posing multiple opportunities for interpretation and not foreclosed by the story's ending (Kepnes, 1992).

Kepnes (1992) uses Buber's work to suggest a dialogically informed image of narrative temporality. Rather than viewing events in stories—and by proxy the moments of our lives—as deriving their primary significance from what they contribute to completed stories, Buber's narratives propose a strongly dialogical "sense of the middle" (Kepnes, 1992, p. 96). They embody the understanding that most of the events constituting the narratives of our lives transpire during an extended middle where life is actually lived. The actions we perform do not necessarily derive their principal justification from how things began or how they end. Much of the excitement of life derives from experiencing the events of our lives from the vantage point of an indefinitely unfolding present. In other words, it arises through grasping how the potentialities of dialogue interanimate the co- and multi-authored moments of our storied lives. A variety of "befores" and "afters," and "was and is" selves (Barros, 1998) make up our ongoing sense of the middle. This sense of every moment's rich offerings sustains continuities and emerging versions of selves versus merely a quest for resolutions. Meanwhile, through dialogues and stories we identify and co-construct with friends *our shared sense of the turning points that matter* in our lives (Bruner, 1996). One of the key synapses connecting the narrative and dialogical activities of friendship is living together what is tried and true in our worlds and the "pivotal points in time when the 'new' replaces the 'old'" (Bruner, 1996, p. 144). A mutually renewed sense of the middle through retelling our shared stories continually offers a narratively performed invitation to ongoing dialogue between friends.

Thus, narrative, dialogue, and the stances and spirit of friendship interweave and enfold into each other. I envision the ongoing communicative achievement of friendship as involving *a dialogue of narratives and a narrative of dialogues.* In personal friendships *both* the experiencers *and* what has been, is, could be, should be, and will be experienced are reflexively eligible for (co)narration, questioning, and dialogue. The discursive actions of friends are both *about* our lives and *make up* much of the substance of our shared lives. Our discourse addresses and constitutes our lived experiences. Our spoken and written utterances in this dialogical activity also compose performances of our characters in the story of our friendship.

We continuously are addressed by the events of the world and other persons, including our friends (Bakhtin, 1990). How we respond shapes our character. In the presence of others we make choices and memories to which we in turn are answerable. *Friendship involves the co-authored story of ongoing questions and answers raised by lives that take others into account.* Narratives of friendships encompass selves, others, selves-in-relation-to-others, and the events and times of friends' lives.

Are narratives heard in a dialogical spirit? Do we as listeners hold on to our convictions while allowing the other to happen to us through their stories? Do we cross-examine stories and exercise our judgments? "He did what? Tell me this again." "Are you going to stand for this?" "Do you think this is fair to her?" "What are you going to do now?" "How much time do you think you have?" "What can I do to help you?" Friends negotiate together the meanings and punctuation of stories. What parts do we consider important to attend to? What is the relevant encompassing frame of reference from which we position ourselves hermeneutically and determine the meaning of these events? The (co)telling of stories transmutes into dialogue as the positions embodied in related events are explored and questioned.

Pursuing dialogue together transmutes into a co-telling of narratives as particular events and characters are emphasized in depicting their contingent and reciprocal effects over time in concrete circumstances. Telling each other stories may constitute the back and forth of friends' dialogue. Swapping yarns and fish stories; relating incidents of heroism, missed chances, triumphs and regrets all vividly embody positions on issues at the heart of the matter. Bruner celebrates the dialogic capacity of storytelling for calling attention to what people are taking for granted, shaking up their "unconsciousness of the automatic" (Bruner, 1996, p. 147). The stories we exchange may challenge how we've been living. Bruner elaborates, "Confrontation is strong but risky medicine for unawareness. Its active ingredient is thwarted expectation, finding that your narrative version of reality clashes with what subsequently transpires or with the reality claims of others" (p. 148). Despite the risks he considers storytelling within close friendship to be one of the precious few "privileged forms of confrontation . . . where *prise de conscience* is the objective of the whole exercise." Indeed, stories often perform valuable service dramatizing and clarifying contrasting positions in dialogue between friends.

## ❖ CONCLUSION

Friends strive to communicate in ways that respect each other's similarities and differences, distinctive points of view, choices, and strengths. The conjunctive freedoms and other dialectical tensions of friendship shape and reflect the individuation of friends through participation in shared moments of their lives. Friends become themselves partly through the belonging they negotiate with each other. In this ongoing process, practices of narrative and dialogue interweave in performing the identities, actions, and values that are important to friends. Friends co-construct the grounds for appraising each other as persons and as participants in a shared moral vision. Our dialogues cross-examine our narratives, demarcate our individuated positions, and dramatize premises for celebrating differences that matter between us. Pursuing dialogue and telling stories also dignify our significant similarities that enable us as friends to identify with each other.

These discursive activities position us to varying degrees as absorbed participants and distanced spectators in our own and each other's lives. Combining a stance of involvement, participation, and identification with friends—with one of disinterested appraisal by an individuated other—facilitates judgment with friends (Beiner, 1983). Such meaning making is accomplished through an ongoing process of oscillating moments (Kepnes, 1992). At one juncture, we try passively to understand another's narrated experiences and dialogical positions on that other person's own terms by being receptive to the new perspectives their words disclose. At another point, we actively sift these provisional understandings through our own life events, terms, and worldview. As friends we evaluate the applicability of what we are learning in our individual and shared lives. How are the insights of these dialogues enacted in the unfolding narratives of friends' lives? To what extent will such understandings change how we perceive things and react? What are and will be the consequences of our discourses? Friendship is an interested relationship. Engaging in these processes with the good will of friendship hopefully co-constructs thresholds of similarity and of difference that allow for more edifying participation and individuation.

The dialogue of our co-told and co-witnessed stories may compose significantly the enveloping narrative of our friendship. Meanwhile the developing story of our relationship is in dialogue with other relationships. How are the narratives of our friendships positioned vis-à-vis other cultural narratives of the well-lived life? How does the narrative of our friendship embody and question prevailing cultural narratives about matters such as gender, sexuality, work, race, ethnicity, embodied abilities, romantic love, marriage, family, religion and spirituality, political involvement, and patriotism? How do we position our friendship through narration? What stories do we tell ourselves and others to justify the time spent in our friendships? Because of its often contingent status in the hierarchy of social relationships, time spent with friends may be viewed as a measure of our freedom of choice in patterning our lives (Naegele, 1958). All of these considerations may be matters for dialogue and narrative reflection among friends.

# 4

# Making Meanings
# With Friends

*Two Women's Storytelling and Dialogue*

Fifteen years ago, Cindy Marshall, a close friend and a scholar/teacher with whom I worked, talked, sang, and laughed for a number of years before her untimely death, returned home to Maine for the summer. We had discussed several times my interest in studying recordings of friends talking together. Cindy was kind enough to speak with several people in Maine who she thought might be interested in tape recording some of their time spent talking as close friends. She informed these persons that their spoken words would be closely scrutinized and written about by me, a professor and a scholar of friendship with whom Cindy worked. Many of them were surprised to learn that scholars actually were studying how friends communicate and were eager to participate in the project. The freely offered and

*Source:* An earlier version of parts of this chapter appeared in "Making Meanings With Friends" by W. K. Rawlins, in *The Meaning of "Relationship" in Interpersonal Communication*, 1998, edited by R. L. Conville and L. Edna Rogers, Westport, CT: Greenwood Publishing. Copyright 1998 by Greenwood Publishing. Reprinted with permission.

naturally occurring discourse of one pair of these participants provides the primary basis for this chapter's discussion.

There was no interview protocol or schedule of questions guiding these two friends' interaction other than the fact that they knew I was interested in their friendship. Their talk went where they took it during their shared "vivid present" (Schutz, 1970). Nearly everything I say about these friends I have gleaned from listening repeatedly to them talk with each other across 90 minutes of audiotaped interaction, transcribing their conversation, and studying their transcribed words. Some years after publishing an earlier discussion of their conversation (Rawlins, 1998a), I met the two women whom I refer to below using the pseudonyms Karen and Chris. Having read my published account, each informed me how impressed she was by the accuracy of my insights about their friendship, saying independently that I was "dead-on" and "had nailed it." At that time I thanked them for their encouraging feedback and again for sharing with me the opportunity to learn from their lively, revealing conversation and to write about their discourse as friends. Profoundly for me, I was able to express my gratitude to them in the very room where they recorded the interaction I engage with again in this chapter.

By their own reckoning early in the conversation, Karen and Chris have been friends for some "thirty years and counting." One late summer day it rained in Maine, and Karen took the afternoon off from her job at a local swimming pool. She and Chris met at her home; Karen put a microphone in a coffee cup on the table between them, turned on and tested the cassette tape recorder, and they began to talk about their lives and friendship. The tape machine clicked off after the first 45 minutes, whereupon they cooked a meal together, sat down to eat, flipped the cassette over, turned the recorder back on again, and talked for another 45 minutes.

Numerous vibrant, touching, funny, quizzical, mundane, and panoramic moments appear throughout their recorded talk. I am fascinated by the depth and variety of meanings their interaction exhibits. I have studied relational communication for 30 years yet am struck continually by just how nested each woman's life is with the other's. Their families, memories, trips, jobs, judgments, disappointments, and possibilities intertwine. At several points I have taken out maps of Maine and the United States, even a globe, trying to visualize their mentioned locations and travels. Among topics specifically involving their friendship, I have also reflected on sailing, parenting, the breaking and mending of bones, hearts and homes. I have heard laughter, strained and absent voices, individual and shared worlds being constructed or rebuilt.

I believe their conversation exemplifies the attributes of story-telling and dialogue between friends discussed in Chapter 3. The narrative qualities of their interaction are apparent in their practices of expressing and trying to comprehend each other's meanings for the events of their lives and friendship, and exploring their respective points of view. They make the effort to speak their outlooks and listen carefully to each other, performing the connected basis of their identities through their discourse. They also seek to understand how events unfold in time through each other's stories. I notice moments of dialogue interwoven with their storytelling through their questioning and responding to each other's points of view on matters of shared concern. These women communicate respect for each other's personhood while openly acknowledging the similarities and differences in their identities. Sustaining mutual involvement throughout their unfolding conversation, they preserve their own convictions while remaining open to each other's influence. They also demonstrate the limits of their dialogues.

I am convinced that it is impossible for me to say anything that remotely approaches the richness and vitality of their interaction as it actually occurred, much less objectively account for its "variance." Neither am I interested in identifying through formal conversational analysis the "routine methods" these women ostensibly utilize to accomplish the sequences of talk I present here. Instead, I want to narrate my perceptions of the overall contours of their talk together. I will re-present selected portions of their discourse, and offer interpretations of the communicative practices and features of narrative and dialogue I perceive these women accomplishing in their talk as friends. In short, I want to share with you my experience of these moments of their friendship as composing both *a dialogue of narratives* and *a narrative of dialogues*.

## ❖ BEGINNING THE CONVERSATION AND THE STORY OF KAREN AND CHRIS'S FRIENDSHIP

*Karen:*   That says "Record Battery," and I don't know why that's on; I don't know if this is recording. My name is Karen Wilson.

*Chris:*   My name is Chris Keyser.

*Karen:*   And we have been friends [laughing] for thirty years.

[Tape recorder turns off.]

*Chris:*    Isn't that in the middle? [referring to the microphone]

*Karen:*    Okay.

*Chris:*    The microphone is in the coffee cup between us. Now let's see what happens [laughing].

*Karen:*    [Laughs] Okay.

*Chris:*    Thirty years and counting . . .

*Karen:*    Thirty years and counting, yes, okay, we, we got to be friends first in Burlington, Vermont, which is not where we are now . . .

*Chris:*    No, our husbands were acquainted.

*Karen:*    Our husbands taught at the same school.

The conversation begins with attention to the task of managing the tape recorder. In their opening discourses they individually state their names (using identical sentence forms). Following Karen's lead, they laughingly recognize themselves as friends for "thirty years." Chris modifies the description into "Thirty years and counting . . . ," registering the ongoing nature of their relationship, which Karen repeats. They self-identify as persons who met through their husbands in a different city from where they now live. The women commence this co-told story of their friendship utilizing the narrative convention of starting at its chronological beginning. From the beginning of this tape they connect their individual identities with their friendship over considerable and still unfolding time, and with respect to their husbands.

It soon becomes apparent in co-telling the narrative of their first meeting at a cocktail party and talking there about enjoying summers in Maine that the women have different stories about who first came to live in Maine permanently and when and how it was accomplished. Establishing their individual and shared positions on this question of "Who stayed first?" becomes a matter of weaving together personal stories that differ in nuanced yet seemingly significant ways concerning time lines. Each narrates linear sequences of events contingent upon co-occurring configurations of relationships with her respective parents and increasingly problematic husband. The shared story of their friendship is simultaneously a negotiated story of their individuated lives. For example:

*Chris:*    The only reason I went back to Burlington later that fall was to have a legal confrontation . . .

*Karen:*    Um hm [sort of laughing in a knowing way]

*Chris:*    Uh huh [mildly laughing] with my husband

*Karen:*    Uh . . .

*Chris:*    and the lawyers, etc., etc. because I had absolutely no money, and so they were trying to rectify that. And then I came back on the Greyhound Bus. And stayed.

*Karen:*    Well, here we are on this tape and I've gotta say that's news to me.

*Chris:*    [Laughs turning into a brief dry cough] Unless I'm really . . .

*Karen:*    Really! No I had it in my mind that *we* had come here first. I mean to stay.

Performing this initial dialogue of their personal narratives during the tape recording produces explicitly acknowledged "news" to Karen about this question of "Who stayed first?" The answer nevertheless seems to have only provisional status for the two friends. After the passage quoted above, Chris tries another approach to establish a shared chronology (that the friends employed at other junctures during their conversation). She uses the birth year and resulting age of one of her children to locate relevant events of the friends' lives in time. Even this seemingly objective method is not satisfactory although it doesn't seem to matter to the friends:

*Karen:*    I think maybe there were some years in there that we've both lost. [laughing] We've shuffled . . .

*Chris:*    We've shuffled. [laughing] Well, never mind, let's go on.

I find this echoed notion of shuffling suggestive. On one hand, it harks to the sequential jumbling of playing cards in a deck as analogous to rearranging events of linear time. Meanwhile, what these women actually have "shuffled" are configurations of interrelated, meaningful events and people—like configurations of suits depicted on playing cards. This locution also trades on the figurative notion of the "hands" persons are dealt and draw at different moments in their lives.

Then the women narrate their divorces from their first husbands. Their co-telling of each story involves one friend encouraging the other to clarify her points of view on the related events. As well, they support the other's pluck, decisions, and positive self-image in the face of transgressions by these men. Yet each person's story also embodies one more self-promoting take on the "chronology" of their permanent relocations in Maine; it suggests how she was the first to come "to stay." Differing subject positions continue to swim in the waters of their shared narratives. Even so, Karen provides a coda for this opening section of their conversation that returns them to a narrative present emphasizing similarity: "So now Chris is divorced and Karen is divorced."

In their talk the women sort through sequences and configurations of involvements and choices that transpired in the past. In Mink's (1970) terms, they are co-telling the story of their lives as friends "having followed" it up to now. There are, however, any number of "impression points" (Kepnes, 1992) from their lives that they could select to focus on together. Part of the dialogue—that is, the back and forth exchange of viewpoints, questions, and responses—of their co-narration concerns deciding precisely which events, characters, and versions of selves they will relate together. They also decide together the significance these happenings held then and now for them as the key protagonists. Among other issues, they are establishing together the meanings for each woman of her "was and is self" (Barros, 1998), that is, her self in the past and her self now.

❖  NARRATING DIVERGING LIFE PATHS

Urged on by Karen, Chris then narrates an extended period of her life that discloses important facets of her existence and identity that differ from her friend. Her story begins with her dating a lobster fisherman, deeply enjoying his island house with their combined four children, marrying him, and moving into his large home in a harbor town. She continues:

Chris:    And we commenced to have stepchildren and children and all
          manner of things. Dogs and many cats and all this menagerie.
          And I became a stern person in the summer weather. (heh
          heh)

Karen:    (hm hm hm)

Chris:    What luck. And after a couple years we bought, our mutual
          interest in a boat, we bought a large sailing vessel, a schooner,
          in preparation for charting the seas of the world. [laughs] And
          uh at some point we, after two or three years of false starts
          and things, we did actually sail the schooner to Florida
          and the Bahamas and back again. And uh, although I didn't

realize it at the time, that put paid to that marriage. [laughs] So that was that.

*Karen:*   [laughs]

*Chris:*   After some time had gone by, we separated . . . And Karen was always there and always supportive to me through all these vicissitudes, the good and the bad, the ups and the downs, and we could really lay it on each other.

Asked by Karen about the origins of her persistent interest in travel, Chris continues her story. Separated now from her second husband, convinced he was seeing other women and weary of the cold Maine winters, she "flew the coop" and began traveling repeatedly to warmer climes—Florida, the Virgin Islands, and Puerto Rico. She describes an epiphany that occurred on one of her trips: "This is what I want! Hot sand, ocean!" Drawing on her experiences sailing with her second husband and working as a breakfast cook during the winter in Maine, she landed a job with a yacht charter venture in the Virgin Islands. In narrative terms she exclaims, "That was the second big chapter in eye opening and feeling like this is where I belong." Even so, she eventually returned to Maine due to "the pull of my kids" and the fact she "still wasn't divorced!" The latter condition she recalls and exclaims in a whisper during her telling. Chris's tale portrays a free spirit, someone who likes warm weather and all things nautical, with the moxie and resourcefulness to pursue and support her excursions.

At this point Karen notes how Chris's traveling marked a significant change in their life patterns as friends, "Well, that was, you know that's interesting when you're, at least when you're talking about friendship because, up until then, basically you and I had been running along, ahem, [clears throat] in similar sort of, yeah

*Chris:*   parallel at least

*Karen:*   grooves. And at that point, we stopped running in similar grooves

*Chris:*   Right.

*Karen:*   because I in the meantime had hooked myself up into the Prospect Harbor School. And was beginning to count the number of years of service that

*Chris:*   Right.

*Karen:*   I had

*Chris:*    Ah yes

*Karen:*    And was, you know, plodding faithfully forward towards retirement. And, not always liking it. And then I got this summer job

*Chris:*    Right.

*Karen:*    down at the pool which I've done for eighteen years now. Which was

*Chris:*    Um hm.

*Karen:*    more plodding and more being in a rut and . . .

*Chris:*    and more being in Prospect Harbor.

*Karen:*    More being in Prospect Harbor. And my mother had come to live with me, which, eh ahem, [clears throat rhetorically] you know, added another dimension to responsibilities that I had here. And so the way we ended up was I was plugged in, and you were basically plugged out. [chuckles]

*Chris:*    [chuckling too] I was plugged in, seasonally.

*Karen:*    Yeah, Chris was running; she was running back and forth between summer

*Chris:*    Back . . .

*Karen:*    [phone rings] and winter . . .

*Chris:*    and Florida and . . . [Taping is interrupted.]

Qualified by chuckling, Karen characterizes herself as "plugged in" and Chris as "plugged out" of life in Maine. Chris, also chuckling, modifies this depiction of herself in Karen's story, stating she was "plugged in, seasonally," which Karen then describes as "running back and forth." Granting the good humor of this friendship, contrasting moral visions inform the divergent patterns of these friends' lives at this point in their story. Chris pursues pleasure freely; Karen embraces responsibilities faithfully. After answering the phone, Karen summarizes her perceptions of how removed the friends became from each other's worldview due to their contrasting lifestyles—to the point of having no "real empathy." At the same time Karen suggests that the spaces and differences separating them did not prevent them from talking with each other. She recalls, "And I, I didn't understand that, and Chris didn't understand what I was doing, and neither of us had any real empathy for the other one's point of view. But it didn't make any difference, in terms of friendship, because we kept on talking about the things that troubled us."

At this point in the dialogue about lifestyles embodied in their co-told narrative of friendship, Karen tells a story about an incident involving one of Chris's children. The event occurred while Chris "went someplace in the winter" and her daughter stayed with Karen. It is the first time she has ever told Chris the story. Although I will not divulge any details here, this vignette could be heard as a dialogical gambit by Karen and a possible indictment of Chris's lifestyle and parenting choices in the past. Chris gracefully sidesteps the tacit invitation to justify herself or respond with stories about past parenting in their talk, remarking, "Why that was another story." She brings matters crisply to the present observing, "My kids are wonderful." Then she explicitly, if somewhat haltingly, acknowledges where Karen seemed to be taking their own story before this digression:

*Chris:*    Right, anyway, um, but I remember uh going, let's see now, oh yea, then uh, that's true what Karen said, we still had, we had lots to talk about even though we were on different tracks, and we always could, regale each other with both the good and the funny things and the bad things, and the things that blew us away, and made us depressed, and all that, and uh, and

*Karen:*    um hmm [slightly laughing]

*Chris:*    so that was a big help always, still is.

## ❖ SHARING STORIES OF DIVORCES AND TRAVELING TOGETHER

A paired exchange of divorce stories follows. On Chris's part, she had to have a hip replaced several years after her separation from her second husband. In a bittersweet sequence of actions she learned that he had generously kept her on his medical insurance all this time because she "had never dreamed of having insurance." But he also never visited her in the hospital. While she recuperated at her daughter's home and made plans to work in Florida the next winter, she received a "little missive" that he had initiated divorce proceedings. She concludes, "Well anyway. This was another chapter. And it was horrendous [laughs] terrible. Anyway, we won't go into that. But um, I seemed to have a very hard time with this divorce, whereas I hadn't with my first divorce. Um but emotionally, and it took me very many years to really be through with it, I mean really a lot of years [laughing]. And then Karen stood by me."

Karen responds, "Well of course at the same, not at the same time, but in similar vein, my missive was, my missive appeared upon my pillow on July 8th of whatever year that was, saying you know I can no longer [laughs], "I can no longer

Chris:    [laughs]

Karen:    live without Leanne. Do not try to find me."

Chris:    I, I remember that day!

Karen:    Remember that? Yeah.

Chris:    My God, between the shower and the . . .

Karen:    Holy smokes. So of course I immediately popped onto the telephone and spent hundreds of dollars trying to find him, which I did in fact do. But, uh, [slight laugh] hmph Chris was there, listening to me on my diatribes. I was, I knew, oh, years before that that we should be divorced, and

Chris:    Right.

Karen:    I didn't want to do it myself, because, you know, I had done it once.

Chris:    That's right. It's painful.

Karen:    and I figured you know I'm not going to try to hold marriages together for the sake of the kids.

Chris:    That's right.

Karen:    So what was hurt, my pride was hurt.

Chris:    Yeah.

Karen:    But that didn't mean I talked any the less now did it? [laughs]

Chris:    Well no, but you had a, a lot of anger too, which was the thing

Karen:    Oh yeah, I still have a lot of that.

Chris:    I know you do. I know you do.

Karen:    I . . . The man is an asshole.

Chris:    [laughs]

*Karen:*   Forgive my language.

*Chris:*   [laughing] That's alright. It's free Karen; the air is free. [laughs]

*Karen:*   The air? Oh whatever. Um, bump up the volume.

*Chris:*   Yeah, well right, well it was a whole bunch, about different circumstances, but anyway it was the same kind of a big jolt.

*Karen:*   Big jolts, right?

*Chris:*   Big jolts.

*Karen:*   And then the big jolts stopped.

*Chris:*   Uh huh. Well?

*Karen:*   Don't you think? I'm not talking about kid jolts.

*Chris:*   No.

*Karen:*   No kid jolts is a whole other story.

*Chris:*   Right, can't get into that.

The women are negotiating the meaning of their divorces. In doing so, they also review, justify, vent, and support each other's past decisions. One witnesses that they still speak together about emerging concerns in the ways they narrate themselves as having spoken together in the past. They also agree that they won't discuss "kid jolts." As proposed earlier by Chris, Karen agrees they are "a whole other story."

At this point the women address how Karen became interested in Chris's "track"—"because I got pretty damn bored with my own track." Karen states laughingly, "All I wanted by this time was to get out!" To which Chris replies, "So then I jumped in cause I said, 'I know how you can get out. I know, I know, I know!'" The friends begin making choices together that find them traveling extensively. Karen goes on an exchange teaching program to California, where Chris visits her twice. The women then relate a sequence of travels and temporary jobs throughout the western United States. With obvious delight they recall visits to the Grand Canyon, Arizona, Navajo country, the Painted Desert, the Petrified Forest, Oak Creek Canyon, Utah, and Zion that demonstrate their enjoyment of traveling together. Several minutes are devoted to the mutual pleasure of reminiscing about this period in their friendship. Yet in narrating their travels, they also describe incidents revealing starkly different preferences: Chris loves heat, Karen cold; Karen smokes, Chris despises smoking; Karen loves and Chris hates shopping.

For the most part, these differences are narrated as handled well throughout their travels. Even so, two incidents stand out. The first is a minor altercation that occurred in Las Vegas. They describe together their contrasting reactions to being assigned a hotel room that had a broken air conditioner. It seems a minor tiff that they laugh about later. However, the second incident is one Karen wants to discuss "before this thing ends" [meaning the recording session]. She puts her cards on the table:

*Karen:*   But I'll tell you what I haven't forgotten; I have not forgotten Harlingen, Texas.

*Chris:*   Alright we had another disagreement.

*Karen:*   We have never talked about Harlingen, Texas.

*Chris:*   No we should talk about that, right.

*Karen:*   This is brand new tape. (Heh heh heh)

*Chris:*   This is real; this is uncharted territory.

*Karen:*   Chris, this is the year when I'm doing the Southwest, right. I'd retired.

*Chris:*   Right.

*Karen:*   and Chris is still pursuing "back to the sun in the wintertime," and she had never been to south Texas,

*Chris:*   Right.

*Karen:*   the Rio Grande Valley, so she went there.

*Chris:*   Right.

*Karen:*   And I had gone to Alamogordo, New Mexico, and had spent the month of November quite happily in Alamogordo, which was too cold for Chris. We had talked about, you know, getting together here, getting together there. And I think that we were planning to do Christmas together anyway.

*Chris:*   Yeah, but we should say that our thermostats are diametrically opposed.

*Karen:*   They are; they are; they are . . .

*Chris:*   Karen likes coolish, sunny but coolish; I like tropical, and sunny.

Karen:    Yeah and I get very uncomfortable in tropical.

Chris:    Right, so we knew that, but . . .

Karen:    We knew that but . . .

Chris:    But.

Karen:    So then, Chris had an accident in her truck, and she totaled the truck . . .

Chris:    [gaspy laugh]

Karen:    and she [laughing a little], there she was in Harlingen, Texas

Chris:    Harlingen, right

Karen:    with no wheels, no insurance, and no money

Chris:    Heh, huh. Right.

Karen:    And she called me, or I called her, some, somehow

Chris:    I did have insurance for the other car, but not for mine . . .

Karen:    not for your own

Chris:    Right.

Karen:    The fat point is you were stuck . . .

Chris:    I was there.

Karen:    And I, like this conquering hero . . .

Chris:    [laughs] while curious

Karen:    decided that I would ride to her rescue.

Chris:    Right.

Karen:    So I suggested that she find us an apartment . . . then she

Chris:    Well, one little thing was that before uh the accident, we had talked about we were gonna rendezvous someplace . . .

Karen:    Um hm

Chris:    in a warmer climate

Karen:    Yeah.

Chris:    but we weren't, we hadn't determined where or when at that

Karen:    where or when

*Chris:*   point.

*Karen:*   I think we were thinking about Christmas weren't we?

*Chris:*   Were we? I don't remember now. But it doesn't matter. Whatever, but any way it was the point anyway.

*Karen:*   So, here we are; Chris finds the apartment . . .

*Chris:*   Right.

*Karen:*   which is on the second floor

*Chris:*   Right.

*Karen:*   And a perfectly pleasant apartment

*Chris:*   But it was a good apartment, yes it was.

*Karen:*   It had, you know, two bedrooms . . . and it's a damn good thing it would turn out.

*Chris:*   Bear in mind that I had to find this without a car, and with my landlady telling me I couldn't use her phone. [gasping laugh]

*Karen:*   Yeah, it was a job.

*Chris:*   Heh heh, and walking on one crutch . . .

*Karen:*   It was a job.

*Chris:*   And anyways, anyway we had this apartment.

*Karen:*   We had this apartment, and the, because of the landlady, I guess, Chris after a lifetime of putting up with me, had suddenly become allergic to smoke. And so she laid down the law that I could only smoke in my bedroom, which pissed me off.

*Chris:*   No I didn't lay, we talked about it on the phone, I didn't lay down that law, I, I, about the little porch, the outdoors and the open windows and door [The tape recorder stops.]

These women have beautifully co-authored the exposition, setting the stage to revisit through co-narration their "disagreement" that occurred in Harlingen, Texas. It promises to be a true dialogue of their respective narratives pursued for the first time in these moments of taping. We can witness their thoughtful listening, qualified encouragement of each other, the way they agree about certain matters and "stand their ground" concerning others, all the while allowing the other woman to happen to her in dialogically rendering the frame for this tale (Stewart & Zediker, 2000). Karen informs their electronically mediated and time-delayed audience, namely me, "This is brand new, tape." And Chris certifies, "This is real; this is uncharted territory."

We are offered tacitly opposing sketches of the characters and situation that are consistent with other moments of this conversation. As narrated by Karen, Chris, ever shunning the cold, does not join her in a city in New Mexico "too cold for Chris." According to Karen, Chris is still pursuing "back to the sun in the wintertime," has totaled her truck, and is "stuck" in Harlingen "with no wheels, no insurance, and no money." Ever responsible, Karen "decided I would ride to her rescue," only to discover that Chris had found a "second floor" apartment and had "laid down the law that I could only smoke in my bedroom, which pissed me off."

While agreeing on several points, Chris's co-narration contests or qualifies several points of Karen's scene setting and characterization. Chris finds it important to register that "our thermostats are diametrically opposed," that she did have insurance covering the other car though not her own, that she was simply "there," not "stuck," and that Karen was as "curious" as she was heroic in coming to Harlingen. In Chris's story, she finds "a good apartment" without a car or telephone and "walking on one crutch." She maintains they discussed the smoking policy on the phone and that "she didn't lay down that law."

As fate would have it, the tape recorder stops shortly after this point at the end of the cassette's first side. The friends' exchanges on the second side of the tape lead me to believe they actually discussed this incident further while they prepared dinner and the tape was not running. I am left wondering about what happened between these two friends at Harlingen, Texas. How did their contrasting narratives of that time play out in their dialogue? Did they air and reconcile their differences through the dialogue of their narratives that afternoon? Did they decide to limit their recorded talk about it? If so, how did they make this decision? What would this discourse further reveal about their friendship's communicative practices if I could have heard it? I comfort myself that I am fortunate to have been able to listen to the dialogue and narratives that they performed on tape and shared with me.

❖  SIDE TWO OF THE TAPE—CONVERSING
    ABOUT PETS AND POLICIES

*Karen:*    a proper break. [laughs] We [coughs] we've just managed to amicably cook and share uh rice pilaf, Spanish style, and peas, and what are these Chris? These good things?

*Chris:*    They're garden vegetable patties of some sort, produced by the green, Jolly Green Giant [laughing] people [laugh].

*Karen:*    [laughs too] We didn't fight even once while we . . .

*Chris:*    No, no we didn't.

*Karen:*    while we were cooking these things.

*Chris:*    No we were quite happy. [laughs]

*Karen:*    Um hm. [laughs]

*Chris:*    And sounds of eating now, and chewing

*Karen:*    Um hm.

*Chris:*    Talking with mouth full.

*Karen:*    We're sure you're dying to listen to this part.

*Chris:*    Umm. [agreement]

[sounds of silverware being used and glasses]

The friends' discourse on the second side of the tape differs markedly in one important respect from the first side. On the cassette's first side, they primarily address in the present stories of their past from their mutual if differing standpoints of "having followed" the narratives (Mink, 1970). It seems, however, that the "brand new" and "uncharted" discussion of the events in Harlingen that presumably occurred during the break in taping repositioned their talk to focus on concerns actually arising in the present. Thus, a strong "sense of the middle" (Kepnes, 1992) characterizes the women's dialogue on this side of the tape—simultaneously co-telling and following life as it unfolds in the present as an emerging dialogue and narrative adventure.

Prompted by a phone call by one of Karen's children, at this point in the tape Karen and Chris have been talking about their relationships with their adult children, their children's relationships with each other, and the difficulties of coordinating family get-togethers during the current summer.

*Karen:*    [to her cat] Are you a nice kitty? Are you a nice kitty?

*Chris:*    [almost to herself] Anyway, I decided not, decided not to think about it, 'cause whatever will happen, will happen.

*Karen:*    [to her cat] Okay, check it all out. Put your nose right on it. See, there's nothing there that you want. Nothing.

| | |
|---|---|
| *Chris:* | Tell you what I'm getting into more lately is, [pause] not doing anything . . . |
| *Karen:* | [chuckles in a low-pitched, almost encouraging way] |
| *Chris:* | [laughs briefly] |
| *Karen:* | [chuckles in the same cadence as before, yet higher pitched] |
| *Chris:* | about, not feeling that I have to make things, I have to somehow help things along. |
| *Karen:* | Um hm. |
| *Chris:* | I've just; I've gotten to the point where I'll, you know, I sort of whipped myself into a frenzy when I was there, that bad week that last week that I was there, and I was so depressed, getting the house ready, that somebody might come, that some friend might come, or Loretta might come, or some unknown person might come, and, and I went around sweeping and . . . |
| *Karen:* | My God Chris. |
| *Chris:* | dusting . . . |
| *Karen:* | That *is* depressing. |
| *Chris:* | And, I wanted to have the house look nice and then I, I kinda got a hold of myself and I thought— |
| *Karen:* | Hahahaha [rapid high-pitched laugh] |
| *Chris:* | You know!? |
| *Karen:* | Yeah. |
| *Chris:* | Really here! Um. You know, I don't even *know* if anybody's coming, and, and, and it's beautiful weather, and you know I don't want to be doing this. And I got sort of mad at myself and mad at the house, and, and so since then I've sort of got this idea like, whatever happens, you know, then Julie started in about maybe cousin Alice coming from Georgia, and when could I get her out there, and I said, "Julie, I can't do anything about, given the information that I have, I can't do anything about it, I uh, I'm glad for you to stay there. For Alice to stay there, whoever comes, that's good. But I can't make any more efforts over it; I've just had a summer of planning for things that didn't happen and getting ready for things that didn't happen, and I can't do, and I don't want to do that anymore." |

*Karen:*    Mmm.

*Chris:*    I mean I didn't say it in that way to her; but that's the way I feel, basically. I'm just gonna look after what I have to do for myself and for my cat.

*Karen:*    Yeah.

*Chris:*    And keep myself there. And if they fall into place, good; if they don't, too bad, you know?

*Karen:*    Yeah.

It may seem odd to begin this section of the conversation with Karen speaking to her cat. But talking about pets and talking to Karen's cat are integral moments of the later part of this visit. At various points in the conversation, talking to the cat seems to provide a breather in their conversation, which often allows a new topic to emerge. For example, immediately prior to this passage the women had been discussing some of the problems involved when their families would converge on their homes during the upcoming Labor Day weekend. Karen's talk to the cat transitions into a more general discussion of doing less for company.

.—Listening to this passage, I want to register the significance of laughter apparent throughout the friends' dialogue and my challenges in re-presenting this discourse to readers. Laughter is a vital part of their interaction—there are low, almost mocking chortles; metered laughs, like Karen's in the previous excerpt, that increase in pitch and seemingly urge the other woman to continue and to feel good about what she is saying; wheezy, surprised laughs that turn into coughs and then more laughter; wary, questioning laughs that sound unsure where the talk is turning and at whose expense. Laughter adds gusto and a risky, joyful timbre to their talk. In its ambiguity and teetering emotions, it sounds from the depths of a robust, longstanding connection. As Bakhtin usefully worried, how do we render in words the singularity of such intonation at the heart of communicating in relationships (Todorov, 1984)?

Of course, multiple voices also intersect as an "internal dialogue" as these friends speak (Bakhtin, 1981). Note, for example, how Chris quotes her own utterances to her daughter, Julie, in her talk with Karen. I find intriguing Chris's admission that the version spoken here is an altered one. In this reenactment, Chris seems to dramatize for her friend what she really felt (or is now experiencing that she felt) in addressing Julie. This quotation of herself embedded in her talk with

Karen allows Chris to speak more candidly in relation to her daughter than she did in the actual circumstances. Further, Chris appears to be rehearsing a more assertive identity and position on family visitors through this rendering of herself to Karen. On her part, Karen responds throughout in actively confirming ways. Their dialogue continues.

*Chris:*  I mean it was, I just got burned out when I tried to get Mary out, that was one thing with Mary, you know I felt like I was under the gun the whole time!

*Karen:*  Well . . .

*Chris:*  I had to try to get out and, you know, worked up a gigantic phone bill. Both of us tryin' to make connections and tryin' to go. Finally, I just said, "Well, you know, somebody up there is telling us the word is no—Hmhmhmhm [chuckles quietly, rising slightly in pitch]

*Karen:*  Hm [laughs briefly]

*Chris:*  —and I'm willing to listen to that." Hmha, and Mary really wasn't, 'cause of course she wanted to go so bad. And I didn't blame her, I understood exactly how she felt and said, "There's gotta be a way." Um. I threw in the towel first because over the years I've learned that when it comes up no, seven or eight times that you better listen. Is that what it is, what the answer is is NO? [laughs]

*Karen:*  Yeah.

*Chris:*  No way.

*Karen:*  Yeah.

*Chris:*  And it just kinda, and I just like blew a gasket I guess, and just thought, "I can't go through this anymore; [quietly] I don't do this anymore. I don't."

*Karen:*  [big sigh] I don't know, I can't get ready for things; I, I don't, it's been a long time since I've been willing to get ready for things.

*Chris:*  Really?

*Karen:*  No.

*Chris:*  I've started, this has been quite sudden with me, 'cause usually that's what I spend half my life, getting ready for things, and see—

*Karen:*    I mean for people—

*Chris:*    No, I do too, yeah!

*Karen:*    visitors, you know, coming to this house. [Walks into the kitchen] Hey, they take it as they find it.

*Chris:*    Oh I, well . . .

*Karen:*    And if they don't like it, I can show them where the door is. [She's running water, doing something in the sink.]

*Chris:*    Right. Well, I guess it wasn't so much the house, it was uh I was upset about everything on the island anyway, and then—

*Karen:*    Yeah well you deserved to be.

*Chris:*    And that was another feature of it that [long pause] I just . . .

*Karen:*    Here, look out the door [talking to the cat].

*Chris:*    [laughs] [to the cat] Look at the rain.

*Karen:*    [to the cat] Yeah right, it's like getting your playpen.

*Chris:*    Hahahahun.

*Karen:*    [to the cat] Do something besides whine at me; what's the matter with you? Ho God!

*Chris:*    Ha ha ha, I think he probably resents this other person here.

*Karen:*    No she doesn't, it's just, it's a, it's a need for attention, I don't know, I don't—

*Chris:*    Yeah but if she maybe doesn't have your full attention or something. Are we still on this thing here? [referring to the tape recorder]

*Karen:*    Yeah.

*Chris:*    Oh jeez me, why don't we, we've got to talk about, I've got—

*Karen:*    We're supposed to be talking about friendship, but—

*Chris:*    We got Harlingen right.

*Karen:*    Harlingen, but . . .

I hear a variety of things transpiring during this excerpt. Some of the understated drama of their conversation is nicely displayed. Chris is still talking about the effort involved in receiving visitors at her island summer home. With vigorous phrases she recounts her burnout, feeling "under the gun" and working up a "gigantic phone bill" in trying to arrange Mary's visit. Finally, she quotes herself as citing "somebody up there" as intervening in this mythic quest and the other woman's reluctance to accept a negative answer. Chris characterizes the episode as blowing a gasket for her and meditatively quotes her immediate thoughts to Karen, "I can't go through this anymore." At first, it sounds like a conclusion she reached in her mind at that time. However, when she repeats it quietly, "I don't do this anymore. I don't," it sounds like she is again contemplating a new personal policy aloud to Karen, rather than reporting on her reactions in the past. Chris's present expression of these thoughts is quite pensive yet conclusive in tone.

Beginning with a large sigh, Karen echoes her frustration about the time involved with "getting ready for things" for visitors to her home, and observes spunkily that "Hey, they take it as they find it," or are shown the door. She emphatically endorses Chris's distress about recent events at the island, stating explicitly, "Yeah, well you deserved to be." In short, it appears they have had a fairly thoughtful discussion about their attitudes toward preparing for company. However, when Chris seems to continue this topic, Karen responds to her cat's meowing to go outside. Both friends laughingly tease the cat about the rainy conditions, subtly establish its sex, and critique its apparent need for Karen's "full attention." The cat has occasioned comic relief and perhaps a new topic of conversation.

Interestingly, at this point Chris asks whether they are still being taped. Her surprised, somewhat flustered reaction to Karen's affirmative answer intrigues me as the would-be eavesdropper embodied by the machine. It appears that she had forgotten their conversation is being recorded, which supports my perceptions of the mostly uninhibited, authentic qualities of their interaction. Karen reminds her they are "supposed to be talking about friendship." Chris observes, "We got Harlingen right," referring again to their discussion during the break of their quarrel while traveling revealed toward the end of the tape's first side.

### ❖ PERFORMING A DIALOGUE OF NARRATIVES ABOUT CONJUNCTIVE FREEDOMS

In the next section of their conversation, Chris initiates a poignant dialogue about Karen's unavailability and minimal communication the previous winter. They address a predicament in their friendship that I consider a significant dialectical tension facing close friends—the dialectic of the freedom to be independent and the freedom to be dependent (Rawlins, 1983b, 1992). I have stated, "Time apart can be interpreted either as an assertion of friends' faith in their bond or the possible beginning of a new period of separateness that may jeopardize the friendship. During the period of separation, there is really no way of telling exactly which is the case, except by renewing contact" (1983b, p. 261). Imagine how intrigued I was to stumble on these two friends explicitly considering the lived dynamics of this dialectical principle when Chris pointedly raises them as a concern.

*Chris:*    Well the other thing, I've got to say this before we get back into that [laughs] Harlingen [laughingly said] who-knows-what,

*Karen:*    [laughs with Chris]

*Chris:*    but I have to tell you now. Last winter, after, after last fall [long pause] you were going to Portland for the, for the first time— [serious tone]

*Karen:*    Yeah.

*Chris:*    and . . . getting an apartment, all that stuff. And we, I went down to see you once. [slow, measured pace and tone]

*Karen:*    Right. [quickly inserted]

*Chris:*    And then um, we had a few, I don't know how you pronounce it, desultory?

*Karen:*    Desultory.

*Chris:*    Letters. [brief laugh]

*Karen:*    Um hm.

*Chris:*    [laughs] missives floating back and forth.

*Karen:*    I get the feeling here that there's something between us? [said with a quizzical expectant laugh]

*Chris:*    Then . . . a little longer silences and longer silences.

*Karen:*    Yeah.

*Chris:*    And I got quite upset.

*Karen:*    I know; it was my fault. [quickly interjected]

*Chris:* Well, I'm not saying fault, but the thing is Karen that I decided that the crux of it was that [puts food in her mouth] we're friends of this long and good standing, [pause] and I didn't know what the *hell* was going on. I didn't know if you were dead or alive.

*Karen:* I was pretty near dead.

*Chris:* Or in the hospital, or what. But I had no way of, I mean except to call your son and say, you know, "Is your mother okay?"

*Karen:* Did you?

*Chris:* No. I didn't.

*Karen:* Oh. Yeah well; I don't know whether he could've answered you or not.

The above excerpt opens with a distinctive mix of laughter and deliberately paced interaction, momentarily achieving a questioning, ambivalent atmosphere. After laughing about Harlingen, Chris clearly wants to talk with Karen about their, but mainly Karen's, actions the previous winter. Chris initiates the topic of their gradually losing contact in a markedly measured sequence of turns, even dwelling on the correct pronunciation of "desultory" in recalling their letters. Karen responds to each of these speaking turns promptly and tersely, which functions to magnify their segmented quality. After Chris seems to laugh a little nervously, Karen senses "that there's something between us?" registering this questioning observation with a watchful laugh. Chris then asserts that the "little longer and longer silences" made her "quite upset," and Karen instantly replies, "I know; it was my fault."

In my opinion, less than ideal contact is a condition many adult friends face (Rawlins, 1994). Such separation is primarily a relationally negotiated pattern that friends may handle in multiple ways, ranging from ignoring to explicitly addressing the issue. Evidently, Chris cares enough about the matter to raise it with Karen but is not interested in assigning blame or "fault." It is a rather sophisticated communicative challenge for her to bring up this concern without hurting or angering Karen, which may be the reason for her tentative approach. Once the issue is on the table, Chris immediately clarifies that "the crux of it was we're friends of this long and good standing," that she was uninformed, and that her worries centered on her friend's well-being. In my judgment, a vexing past situation in this friendship has been opened sensitively for their present dialogue as friends.

Yet, as someone who has listened to this conversation many times, I read these and the next few lines as initial expressions of some deep-seated themes in their ensuing dialogue. Specifically, Chris states, "I didn't know if you were dead or alive," to which Karen replies, "I was pretty near dead." Then Chris observes that the only way she felt she could learn if Karen was okay would be to call her son. Karen immediately asks if she did; Chris says no; and Karen states, "Yeah well; I don't know whether he could've answered you or not." Here is my interpretation of these lines: Chris worried about Karen because she cares for her and can be anxious about her health. Even so, Chris respects Karen's privacy and freedom within their friendship. She recognizes that an unobtrusive way to inquire about Karen would be through Karen's son, though Chris chose not to do so. Karen acknowledges the legitimacy of Chris's concerns when she says she was "pretty near dead," however literally the expression is meant. Then, Karen momentarily puts Chris on the spot and seemingly tests her sincerity by verifying whether she did contact Karen's son, then immediately excuses Chris by doubting whether he could have answered Chris. Karen's wry expression of this last statement could imply a variety of meanings: He might not know because he was not in touch with his mother either; he was in touch with his mother, but neither he nor she knew for sure whether she was "okay"; he knew his mother was not okay but would be hesitant to convey that to Chris. Regardless, it seems that Karen confirms the validity of Chris's worries last winter as well as Chris's reluctance to contact Karen directly or indirectly.

*Chris:*    Well the thing was, I thought [long pause] and then finally, I guess it was Julie, my daughter, said, something about that you were hav—, were in one of your stages where you didn't wanta communicate, you were withdrawing and whatever, whatever.

*Karen:*    Yeah, I was.

*Chris:*    And I thought, "Well that's okay; everybody has these times when they feel this way." But I feel like you should *alert* people that *care* about you [laughs] to the fact that this is what is goin' on—

*Karen:*    [laughs] Yeah . . .

*Chris:*    "I'm going into my cave. See ya in the spring," or whatever. Or "I don't wish to have anything, writing or any communications for a while. Not to worry. Adios. Bye to everybody, Hasta la vista or whatever."

*Karen:*   Yeah.

*Chris:*   Or something, because I [pause], I [pause], I . . .

*Karen:*   You were worried.

*Chris:*   It was very hard on me to not know and then to hear third hand, I mean maybe I, I didn't take the responsibility of following it up or making any, after a couple, writing a couple of times; but I felt like it would be a help to me to know that, not to know that you were having a depressed, hard time, but to know that you, you didn't want to be bothered with having to write or correspond, or to talk on the phone or see anyone, or whatever it was. But even a, a postcard to say this, or to say, you know, "Leave me alone" [laughs] or whatever.

*Karen:*   [laughs in a quiet, understanding way]

*Chris:*   And, or whatever you were thinking, [pause] would have been a help to me, because I find, I felt like you know maybe we're never gonna talk again, maybe we'll never see each other. I didn't know what exactly what was going on. And I—

*Karen:*   Well I didn't know what was going on either.

*Chris:*   No, I know you didn't.

At this point Chris recalls thinking, and her daughter confirming, that perhaps Karen merely wanted to withdraw from social contact for awhile. After Karen agrees, Chris quotes her thoughts to herself at the time that such feelings are commonplace and "okay." Even so, she believes that Karen "should *alert* people that *care* about you to the fact that this is going on . . ." They both laugh at this rather paradoxical recommendation to communicate to significant others that she does not intend to communicate with them. Chris rehearses two voices for Karen here: a humorous one that trades on a hibernation metaphor, and then a more serious, explicit statement with Spanish flourishes at the end that seem to add a comical flavor. As Karen affirms this idea, however, Chris surrenders her comic tone and makes the frank request, "Or something," haltingly trying to offer her reasons, "I [pause], I [pause], I . . . ," which Karen completes for her, "You were worried." In short, Karen again recognizes the emotional basis of Chris's concerns and legitimates Chris's suggested policy for communicating social withdrawal.

Chris further elaborates her anxieties about not knowing about Karen and about learning of her through others, acknowledging that she was partly responsible for losing contact by not following up on her early letters. Nonetheless, she repeats her desire to be informed when Karen "didn't want to be bothered with having to write or correspond, or to talk on the phone or see anyone, or whatever it was." The friends laugh together at the suggestion that Chris would prefer "even a, a postcard" or a brusque, "Leave me alone" to ambiguous silence. Chris remarks that last winter she was not sure if they would ever talk or visit again, that she "didn't know exactly what was going on." Once again, Karen responds, "Well I didn't know what was going on either," implying that her being on the "sending" side of her own silence was possibly as frustrating and confusing as being on the "receiving" side. Chris immediately confirms Karen's reflection, saying, "No I know you didn't."

Chris:    But the thing is. [pause] However much you want to struggle through things on your own, and I know that every now and then we have to do this on a lot of things, [pause] but I, I would just hope that you could say, "I need to be by myself, I need to be incommunicado;" or whatever. However you phrased it. And then I'd say, "Oh yeah. Well that's good. I know that. That's what's happening to Karen now; and that whatever it entails I don't know, but I know that that's the way, that's her pleasure right now to do this time, to frame it out this way." Now I can accept that, I have always accepted everything else that—

Karen:    [laughing sardonically] Ha heh "She's thrown my way."

Chris:    No, I mean between us, both of us, back and forth have accepted pretty much, may have been some bumpy spots and all, but we could live with it, and we could go on. And then, and so I felt that, well one of the worst things anybody can do to *me* is from, prior history, is to not let me know what the hell is going on.

Karen:    Yeah, I can understand why you would feel that way.

Chris:    That is the worst thing that could, if, I don't care, I can cope, if I (heh heh) . . .

Karen:    I'll just get this.

Chris:    [chuckles] I'm spitting rice on the floor.

Karen:    (hahahaha) [laughs quietly in a little bit of a high pitched titter]

*Chris:*    Um, and then you know since my father's illness and death
and all when I wasn't told, and I've always had that feeling
that [long pause] if you lay it on me I can somehow get a handle
on it, I can work at least on doing that. If I don't know, and if
it's secret and I'm not supposed to be told anything, that is
devastating . . . to me. So there. [The passage beginning with,
"if you lay it on me" is quite emotional in tone and then gradually tapers back into a more ordinary conversational one.]

Again Chris acknowledges Karen's and most persons' need to
"struggle through things" independently while also repeating her
hope that Karen will inform others when she feels that way. Then Chris
rehearses what she would say to herself upon learning "That's what's
happening to Karen now." These statements clearly endorse Karen's
actions. Chris comments on her ability to accept Karen's needs to be
alone, as well as "everything else that— . . ." As Chris searches for
words, Karen concludes the sentence in a sarcastically laughing
manner, "Ha heh 'She's thrown my way.'"

This can be heard as a rather complex occurrence in their conversation. Basically, Karen ventriloquizes Chris's voice here in nuanced
yet revealing ways. First, by using the third person ("She's" instead of
"You've thrown my way."), Karen grammatically converts the implied
trajectory of the sentence to resemble Chris's previous statements *about*
Karen in the past, rather than something she is *now* saying *to* Karen.
Through this formulation Karen seems to suggest subtly that Chris is
reluctant to address her directly. Second, using the word "thrown"
rather than the diplomatic wording Chris has previously employed
colors Chris's statement as recalling unpleasant surprises. Karen's version changes Chris's statement from one about acceptance into one of
judgment. For Karen to have Chris say, "I have always accepted everything else she's thrown my way," in a sardonic tone significantly
shapes the spirit and implied meaning of Chris's unfinished sentence,
in my opinion. In Karen's version Chris is not accepting Karen; she is
judging her, and speaking in the third person objectifies her further.

Chris seems to pick up on Karen's characterization of her, protesting,
"No," and proceeds to describe "bumpy spots" occurring in their relationship, "between us," that "both of us, back and forth have accepted
pretty much." Yet her initiation of this segment of the conversation does
constitute a judgment of Karen's actions last winter. Despite Chris's
desire to grant Karen the freedom to be independent, Karen's unan-
nounced, extended silences troubled Chris. Accordingly, Chris restates
what earlier in the conversation she, without assigning blame ("saying

fault"), deemed "the crux" of the issue. Using almost identical words as earlier, Chris states, "One of the worst things anybody can do to *me* is from, prior history, is to not let me know what the hell is going on." Interestingly, she does not emphasize the word "hell" this time, and the entire statement is said in a way that suggests she is repeating an important point she has already made. Realizing its significance Karen says empathically, "Yeah, I can understand why you would feel this way."

As Chris begins to discuss this "worst thing," a brief humorous interlude occurs due to her "spitting rice on the floor." Then we learn that because of the secrecy surrounding her father's death, Chris feels strongly about not being told things. One of the most emotional passages in this talk is her statement, "If you lay it on me I can somehow get a handle on it, I can work at least on doing that. If I don't know, and if it's secret and I'm not supposed to be told anything, that is devastating . . . to me." With Chris's personal associations registered, the significance of her feelings about not hearing from Karen is thrust into a new light. The immediate result in the dialogue is that Karen begins to narrate and explain her actions.

*Karen:*  Well, see I wasn't consciously trying to keep secret; I, I, I certainly was not thinking about anything but myself.

*Chris:*  No,

*Karen:*  Right, you know—

*Chris:*  No.

*Karen:*  I wasn't thinking about, you know, my effect on you—

*Chris:*  No, of course not

*Karen:*  and I wasn't thinking about my effect on Sandy either—

*Chris:*  No.

*Karen:*  and I didn't communicate with her any more than I communicated with you—

*Chris:*  No, it was everybody, and I understand that.

*Karen:*  No and now that it's later I am ashamed of that, but, at the time I just didn't want to do anything except, you know, sit in my chair and take my daily Prozac.

*Chris:*  Yeah.

*Karen:*  Which was a disaster. [said with a brief scornful laugh]

| Chris: | Was it? |
|---|---|
| Karen: | Oh yeah, Christ. |
| Chris: | How long did you take it? |
| Karen: | I took it for about four or five months. |
| Chris: | Really, Kar? [asked in a quiet, deeply concerned voice] |
| Karen: | Yeah. And at the end of it, I was beginning to think, you know, "Hey, why bother?" |
| Chris: | Yeah. |
| Karen: | "Why bother at all?" |
| Chris: | Yeah. |
| Karen: | And at that point I thought, "Why don't you just stop this?" |
| Chris: | Yeah. |
| Karen: | You know so, I just call, I just stopped taking it— |
| Chris: | Yeah. |
| Karen: | and uh, I did call the doctor, and say, "You know, it uh," and left a message on her, I don't know, with her nurse or some damn thing, but I was . . . you know not getting the benefit— |
| Chris: | Was this a medical doctor that had given you this? |
| Karen: | Yeah. |
| Karen: | Yeah. *Chris:* Oh. [simultaneously in quiet harmony] |
| Karen: | Yeah. *Chris:* Hmm. [simultaneously in quiet harmony] |
| Karen: | Yeah. |
| Karen: | [brief mocking laugh] Jean thought I was, what a heart attack waiting to happen, you know and all those lovely things. |
| Chris: | Right. |
| Karen: | I don't know; it was just a bad |
| Chris: | a bad time |
| Karen: | a bad time. |
| Chris: | Oh yeah. Must have been awful for you. |

At the beginning of this excerpt, Karen immediately addresses Chris's use of the word "secret," asserting that "trying to keep secret" was never her conscious goal. Secrecy suggests deliberately concealing information or selectively excluding others (Rawlins, 1983a). In contrast, during this period Karen recalls being focused only on herself without considering the "effect" of her seclusion on Chris or Sandy, another close friend of hers. Further, she describes being equally uncommunicative with both women. After responding supportively to virtually every point Karen makes here, Chris acknowledges the blanket nature of Karen's retreat, saying, "No, it was everybody, I understand that." Removed in time, Karen admits being "ashamed" of seemingly abandoning her friends but now adds that her self-absorption included a disastrous drug prescription.

As she listens to her friend, Chris proceeds to ask brief, interested questions and to give positive minimal responses (Maltz & Borker, 1982) that may facilitate Karen recounting this lamentable period lasting "four or five months." Karen reenacts her thoughts "at the end of it" to Chris when she concluded to herself, "Why don't you just stop this?" Karen reports, "I just stopped taking it," and narrates leaving a message for her doctor to that effect. Sounding critically concerned, Chris asks, "Was this a medical doctor that had given you this?"

At this point a brief exchange occurs that I want to describe in detail because it illustrates the rhythm and musicality of these friends' conversation and my extreme limitations in trying to render it for readers. As my transcription above tries to depict, here's what happens: After Chris asks this question, Karen says, "Yeah," then in a gentle manner repeats, "Yeah," this time accompanied by Chris saying "Oh" in soft, higher pitched harmony, followed immediately in the same cadence with Karen saying "Yeah" again, this time with Chris simultaneously voicing "Hmm" in the same dulcet harmony; and then Karen utters one last solo "Yeah." It is a musical coda of sorts for the story just told, followed by Karen's piqued observation that "Jean thought I was a heart attack waiting to happen; you know, and all those lovely things." Then ensues an interaction confirming the negative nature of this period, which both friends concur was "a bad time" for Karen. And Chris observes compassionately, "Must have been awful for you."

*Karen:*    And I didn't, you know, the only people that I knew were like Michael and Tina and the kids.

*Chris:*    Right.

*Karen:*    And that was all I wanted to know.

*Chris:*   That was all you could do—

*Karen:*   If they had anybody over for dinner, you could be damn sure I wasn't there.

*Chris:*   Right. [walks into kitchen] No, I know how you can't deal with anybody, and don't want to. [from another part of the room] I'm gonna have some more rice, now.

*Karen:*   So . . .

*Chris:*   I don't know how I could still be hungry, but I am . . . Well—

*Karen:*   Chris, I apologize. I apologize, and I—

*Chris:*   No, I, it's not a thing for an apology, I'm just saying, in the *future* when the storms come, don't—

*Karen:*   I'll do it, Ha ha.

*Chris:*   Try to raise the pennant and say, "Storm signals are flying here."

*Karen:*   "Storm signals are flying," okay. [said mostly to herself seemingly in rehearsal]

*Chris:*   Or some such ilk, and um, and just so I can say, "Okay." And I, I would do the same, I mean—

*Karen:*   Ah but you, dear heart, are going to be at sea.

*Chris:*   [talking with food in her mouth] Only nineteen days, I mean not for the rest of the winter, [laughing a little] I hope, unless we're blown way off course!

*Karen:*   Noo, I, I, I hope I sincerely hope for my sake that this winter will be purposeful,

*Chris:*   Yeah.

*Karen:*   and maybe even interesting? Nah.

*Chris:*   Well why not?

*Karen:*   [whispers] That's too much.

*Chris:*   You've got all of Portland at your feet! [laughs]

During the above segment, Karen indicates that her sole contacts during this time were her son and his family who live in the immediate vicinity, and only if they did not have dinner guests. Walking into the kitchen Chris voices her understanding of her friend's desire to avoid people. When Chris returns to the table, Karen tentatively begins, "So . . . ," and then calling her friend by name, says quite sincerely, "Chris, I apologize. I apologize, and I—." Karen seems to register her realization that even though Chris now understands and accepts her retreat, she hurt Chris deeply by shutting her out and providing no indication of what she was going through. The friends have returned to "the crux" of their dialogue after considering in depth each woman's story of her experiences of "last winter."

Chris cuts short Karen's statement, once again insisting, "It's not a thing for apology." Instead, Chris wants to establish a forward looking practice in their friendship. Tuning into their shared history living on the coast of Maine, Chris uses nautical terms, "I'm just saying, in the future when the storms come, don't—." Before hearing the rest, Karen laughingly interjects, "I'll do it." Chris continues, "Try to raise the pennant and say, 'Storm signals are flying here,'" which Karen immediately appears to rehearse aloud. Chris states that such a signal will allow her to respond, "Okay," and that she will indicate likewise, should she require solitude.

Having agreed to this procedure, Karen promptly steers their conversation to the fact that soon Chris will literally be "at sea." Chuckling, Chris replies that she will sail for "Only nineteen days" and not the entire winter "unless we're blown way off course!" Karen, in turn, wistfully hopes for a purposeful and interesting winter, to which Chris encouragingly responds. Just beyond this transcript the women begin to analyze together Karen's constraints and opportunities in Portland during the approaching season.

## ❖ INTERWEAVING NARRATIVES AND DIALOGUE IN THE TALK OF TWO FRIENDS

This talk reminds us what it can mean to converse in a close, long-standing friendship. This chapter addresses only a 90-minute conversation, a fleeting episode in this friendship of 30 years. But perusing this slice of life reveals much about the ebbs and flows of communicating with a close friend. This discourse illustrates the enjoyment of conversing with a long-time friend and for these women in particular, a shared appreciation of the drama of everyday life, its continuous production of comic and tragic events, and the need to make sense of them.

In trying to comprehend their lived experiences together and apart and to situate the choices shaping their lives across times and places,

Chris and Karen tell each other stories. The *narrative activities* of friends described in Chapter 3 are richly illustrated in their conversation. First, the women work to establish their meanings for a range of personal and joint episodes through carefully exploring their stories. As enacted by Karen and Chris, these meanings are active, collaborative, ongoing, and cumulative accomplishments. They frequently are created by the participants from highly nuanced behaviors, prosodic cues, or word choices. These meanings symbolically reproduce mutually recognized events that occurred or are unfolding in real time and concrete settings with genuine consequences for the friends and/or persons they care about.

Second, each woman's voice as a narrator embodies her specific point of view on related events. What particulars of divorces, seasonal changes, jobs, decisions, deaths, and travels are selected for telling by each of these women? Which details matter to her in the stories and why? What subjects does she want to downplay or avoid? How does she recall experiencing narrated episodes? What differences do the occurrences and persons selected for narration make in each woman's life and her experience of their friendship? Each woman seems dedicated to performing her own while also honoring her friend's perspective.

Third, the co-telling of these narratives is a dynamic communicative activity with each woman vividly relating her experiences as well as listening carefully and responsively to her friend. These friends seem to feel free to experiment stylistically and with multiple voices in their talk. Throughout their discourse they quote their own and others' thoughts and statements in colorful and sometimes admittedly fictional ways. Each feels encouraged to narrate and dramatize events in ways that allow her to role-play, rehearse new identities, and explore different characters. Meanwhile, they actively listen to each other, providing frequent verbal and nonverbal responses and asking effective questions. Each is a dedicated witness to her friend's testimonies (Frank, 1995).

Fourth, in recounting their stories together, the women are keen to portray the perceived contexts of their actions and decisions. It is important for their actions to be understood in terms of the circumstances they now believe they were facing then. For example, personal financial situations, treatment by others, and existential outlooks are depicted as facilitating and limiting their options in ways the women must address in their stories. I am fascinated by how their conversation builds on itself, with events, people, periods and places crossreferenced and indexed multiple times as they co-tell the stories of each other's opportunities, choices, and relationships.

Fifth, in a related fashion, the women's stories portray the connected basis of their identities throughout their discourse. Karen and

Chris's communicative relationship with each other is mediated by numerous other relationships—with prior spouses, children, in-laws, friends, co-workers, and employers. The co-telling of their friendship for much of the first side of the tape emphasizes their relationships with prior spouses as especially significant in constructing their past identities. However, in the more present-oriented second side of the tape, relationships with their children and their families provide the salient relational contexts for narrating their identities. As a negative example, I find it intriguing that the two friends collaborate in avoiding past parenting episodes in co-narrating their friendship. Relating events specifically focusing on child-rearing or "kid jolts" is termed "another story" in Chris's words and "a whole other story" in Karen's. While somewhat unavoidable in the overall configurations of their lives at given points, the primary identities as friends they co-narrate here do not emphasize their past parenting-related identities with their children or vis-à-vis each other. Focusing on such parenting practices might invoke pronounced differences that occasion too much judgment and strain the fabric of their connection.

Finally, from its inception, this conversation may be viewed as seeking to understand through stories how the events of their intertwined lives occurred across time. Their talk involves the ongoing narrative punctuation of when important moments of their lives began and what marked their ending or transition to "another chapter," to use Chris's words. They use stories to characterize sequentially the beginning of their friendship, their respective arrivals "to stay" in Maine, the slow demises and the abrupt endings of their marriages. Meanwhile, they employ stories to describe the configuration of pressures perceived as operating simultaneously for specific events to be understood after the fact from their present vantage point of telling. Thus, these friends co-narrate both sequences and configurations of events to establish together plausible "was and is" selves (Barros, 1998). What aspects of self's and the other's identity do these women want to preserve across time? What aspects should be relegated to the past and laid to rest as a function of unfavorable circumstances? In what ways has each woman changed and stayed the same that constitute a testament to her unique identity as a worthy person and friend?

The ideal *practices of dialogue* discussed in Chapter 3 are also apparent simultaneously as Karen and Chris co-tell the narratives of their friendship. First, to varying degrees throughout their discourse, the two women actively exchange, question, and respond to each other's points of view on incidents and matters of shared concern. The co-narrated prelude to discussing their disagreement at Harlingen, which closed the tape's first side, is a case in point. Performing the back and forth of dialogue, the women address and revise several details framing the events in question as they begin to tell the tale together. Their co-narration involves contesting and qualifying particulars reflecting their distinctively individuated values and identities. As another example, the question of who came to stay first in Maine is addressed by exchanging contrasting versions of the story in dialogical counterpoint. The precise significance of events and claimed identities is a matter for cross-examination at several points in their conversation, yet often with an eye to preserving each friend's dignity.

Second, these two women communicate obvious respect for each other's personhood throughout their talk. An atmosphere of encouragement shapes much of their dialogue. This ambience is probably due to several communicative practices richly evident in their talk. Many risky disclosures are met with confirming responses. Each woman explicitly recognizes the legitimacy of the other's experience at various points. Concern is expressed when the other's narrative seems to warrant it. Unselfconsciously, they exhibit effort and empathy in trying to recognize and dignify, if not entirely understand, what the other is feeling or saying at that moment.

Third, they devote much of their conversation to acknowledging the historically and relationally accomplished similarities and differences in their identities. A vivid dialogue about their individuated lifestyles and identities is embedded in their co-told narrative about participation in their longstanding friendship. On one hand, they hold in common: similar paths to and a love for Maine, "missives" and divorces from prior spouses, a shared sense of humor, enjoyment of laughter and conversation, and pleasant memories of traveling together. They also share recently admitted stances toward preparing for company. On the other hand, they have different preferences concerning weather and ambient temperature, cigarette smoking, and shopping. Deeper contrasts in moral visions and associated identities seem embodied in their depictions of diverging life "grooves," presenting Chris as a free spirit "plugged out" of life in Maine and Karen as the "plodding" responsible person "plugged in" to life in Maine. The depths of these differences animate more penetrating questioning and more pointed narration between the friends at times. Even so, their apparent agreement not to discuss parenting issues suggests a difference that could make a difference in their relationship. The topic may be too painful and judgmental; discussing it could threaten their friendship.

Fourth, the two women sustain active and mutual involvement over the course of their unfolding conversation, which is a hallmark of committed dialogue. Accordingly, we witness a range of emotions expressed and acknowledged in their dialogue—from worried self-reflection and engaged questioning to tentative indulgence, from outright anger to warm confirmation and exuberant laughter. In fact, the terrain of their talk is sprinkled with many species of laughter. The two friends converse with attention and feeling. We sense that these women are very much "in the moment" when speaking and listening to each other. They hang on to each other's words and sighs, responding to nuances as well as to forthright thoughts and feelings. They give each other opportunities to retreat and reflect.

Fifth, reproducing the edifying individuation and participation of hearty friendship, the two women preserve their own convictions while remaining open to the other's influence. Each represents with integrity her own experiences while opening herself to the other's insights and concerned observations. Historically, this is apparent in Karen's account of times when their lives differed so much that there was "no real empathy" between them. Even so, both women acknowledge that their contrasting lifestyles did not prevent conversation nor preclude their desire to hear and consider the other's point of view. Finally, being the persons they are with the constraints of their circumstances, they acknowledge limits in their abilities to change as a result of their dialogues. Even so, as their closing conversation about communicating desired separation attests, they remain willing to express and consider distinctive positions.

This chapter embodies an overarching *narrative* of this friendship as their dialogical exchanges juxtaposing divergent positions reveal their characters, pivotal events, choices, and consequences as individuals and as friends over the past 30 years. Their apparently negotiated decision to address their quarrel at Harlingen while the tape recorder was turned off contributed to the overall narrative of their friendship embodied in this recorded dialogue. Their coordinated avoidance to address past parenting practices and children ("kid jolts") involves "another story," in their words. Consequently, my narrativization of their dialogue involves three sections. The first part focuses on past events starting conventionally with the beginning of their friendship. The Harlingen incident is brought up as "brand new" (Karen) and "uncharted territory" (Chris) at the end of this part. By all indications, the friends discussed the situation in a second, unrecorded part of their discourse while preparing their dinner. The third part occurs on side two of the tape. Their discussion of the contemporary challenges of coordinating visits is prompted by a phone call from one of Karen's children that interrupts the taping. At this point the friends pursue an extended dialogue embodying their "sense of the middle" (Kepnes, 1992) and their co-narrated possibilities emerging continuously in the present.

This chapter also presents a *dialogue* composed of differing as well as common viewpoints performed and interrogated through narratives exchanged between the two friends. Different positions are manifest in the back and forth of their individual and co-told stories. Their individuated perspectives also arise in the distinctive points of view each woman performs in co-telling the stories animating this dialogue.

Here enters my interpretation of how they enact two dialectical tensions potentially inspiring engaged dialogue between friends (Rawlins, 1989a, 1992). At various points in their talk, contradictions involving the dialectic of judgment and acceptance emerge. Tensions arise between each woman's confidence that the other will accept her and give her the benefit of the doubt in most instances, and her expectation that deserved judgments will be conveyed. They notably enact this dialectical tension in the last section of their discourse as they deal with the issue of Karen cutting off contact with Chris the previous winter. This matter further turns on the dialectical tension between granting the freedom to be independent and the freedom to be dependent in close friendship (Rawlins, 1983b). Weaving in and out of critical and accepting discourse, the two women examine in detail through narrated particulars and dialogical counterpoint Chris's legitimate concerns about Karen's seclusion and Karen's understandable need for privacy. Judging together in this way, they establish sensitively a new policy for dealing with such circumstances in the future. Interestingly, it is a paradoxical policy asking each friend to communicate to the other when she is feeling the need not to communicate. The other, in turn, is expected to hear and respect this desire for what it is.

*The talk of these women displays the edifying potentials shared by narrative and dialogic activity.* Both types of discourse interweave in these two friends' talk to shape each friend's individuated point of view. They do so as invitational discursive activities that welcome, serve, and reflect edifying participation as a primary goal. Both narrative and dialogue, as performed by Karen and Chris, emphasize the creative, ethical, and mutually affirming significance of engaged listening. In facilitating belonging and mutually enriching listening, their dialogue and storytelling seem to constitute ends in themselves, regardless of what they might achieve extrinsically for these friends. These two women enjoy talking together. The robust discourses of dialogues and narratives generate and invoke moral visions for these friends.

Taken together, narrating stories and pursuing dialogues constitute significant discursive activities that involve these women in making choices as friends. They decide together meanings for their actions in the past, which in turn confirm their present identities as friends and as individuals. Addressing events in the distant and recent past from the vantage point of the present, they compose their shared sense of turning points that matter in experiencing their lives. I argue that such turning points include valued conversations like this one pursued with friends—ones that embody narratives of dialogues and dialogues of narratives. To a significant extent, *making meanings is making choices as friends.* Accomplishing this choice-making together composes significant moments of the connected freedoms living at the heart of friendship.

# 5

# Talking With College Students About Frontiers and Frustrations of Cross-Sex Friendships

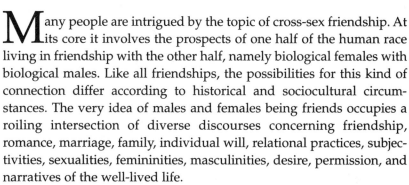

M any people are intrigued by the topic of cross-sex friendship. At its core it involves the prospects of one half of the human race living in friendship with the other half, namely biological females with biological males. Like all friendships, the possibilities for this kind of connection differ according to historical and sociocultural circumstances. The very idea of males and females being friends occupies a roiling intersection of diverse discourses concerning friendship, romance, marriage, family, individual will, relational practices, subjectivities, sexualities, femininities, masculinities, desire, permission, and narratives of the well-lived life.

Cross-sex friendships are reportedly more prevalent during the college years than at any other time in the life course (Monsour, 2002; Rawlins, 1992; Rubin, 1985; D. Wright, 1999). Seeking to explore this topic in relation to my students' accounts of their own lived experiences, for the past 15-plus years I have sponsored an informal debate about cross-sex friendship in each of my undergraduate interpersonal communication classes. The specific form of this debate was originally suggested to me by Kathy Werking, a graduate student studying with me at the time the discussions began and later the author of a note-worthy book, *We're Just Good Friends: Women and Men in Nonromantic Relationships* (1997). Here's how the debates proceed. Before class meets, the students read an essay I wrote concerning cross-sex friend-ship (Rawlins, 1982). Then, drawing on their own lives, familiar others' relationships, scholarly arguments and evidence, literary and popular media exemplars—any sources they find relevant—one half of the class develops all the arguments, conditions, and examples they can assemble to support the assertion, "Enduring, close, cross-sex friend-ship IS possible in our culture." The other half of the class works from the same potential range of sources their group identifies as pertinent to support the contrasting assertion, "Enduring, close, cross-sex friend-ship IS NOT possible in our culture." After spending a class period preparing their positions, the two groups present their cases to each other with me functioning as a moderator and commentator. The point of the exercise is to provoke the students' and my reflections on whether and how cross-sex friendships figure into our lives.

Over the past decade and a half I have taken careful notes in track-ing these discussions to engage with students' ideas in the classroom. Consequently, I have compiled an archive of some 25 interactive ses-sions asserting and challenging the possibility of enduring close cross-sex friendship. All of the classes met at two major universities in the midwestern United States. We should recognize from the outset that my re-presentation below is based largely upon predominantly white, middle class, young adults' discourses circulating in the midwestern United States in the late 20th and early 21st centuries. As such there are inevitable privileges, blind spots, and assumptions about social life inscribing the worldviews of their discourse. For example, there have been virtually no reflections about how class, racial, and ethnic differ-ences intersect with gendered ones in their discussions, and for the most part the students presume heterosexual identities.

Even so, in this chapter I read these students' exchanges as embodying enabling and constraining discourses that shape and reflect their lived experiences (or not) of cross-sex friendship. I have always been struck by the significant redundancies in themes and situations that have surfaced in their talk across the years. In the first half of this chapter I offer in mostly my words a composite re-presentation of the ebb and flow of a characteristic debate in an effort to display the issues that typically have emerged during their discussions. Just as I try to do in the classroom, in the last part of this chapter I will engage with, make some critical observations, and draw some overall conclusions about the discourses, conditions, and practices that facilitate and subvert cross-sex friendships as occasioned by these student interactions.

## ❖ DEBATING CROSS-SEX FRIENDSHIP

"One reason we know that cross-sex friendships are possible," the students often begin, "is that we have them. They are very common here at school." They admit such friendships are not easy but possible. Achieving them involves work not to be influenced by others who constantly question the fact that it is "just" a friendship. Other students argue no criteria dictate that friendship has to be same sex. They have same-sex friends and just as easily can have cross-sex friends. It's just a stereotype that cross-sex friendships are doomed to become "something else." The point is that friends can exert their will to be friends, actively resisting normative pressures and third-party judgments. I think it is important to recognize that across the years in these debates, many students have insisted on the presence, importance, and enjoyment of cross-sex friends in their lives. This pattern is consistent with extensive research documenting young adulthood as the life course period when cross-sex friends are most prevalent (Monsour, 2002; Rawlins, 1992).

### Differences Between Females and
### Males That Enhance Cross-Sex Friendships

The affirming students believe that males and females typically complement each other in ways that make cross-sex friendships special. Men and women each have their own strengths that are not available in same-sex friendships. For one, their communicative styles complement each other. Women make good friends for men because they listen better and are more sensitive; males can allow themselves to feel more vulnerable with female friends than male friends. Many men go to women to discuss emotional matters and relationship issues. Men can tell women things they can't tell men; they can be more open and let down their guard in front of women. By and large, their same-sex male friends don't respond in such understanding, caring ways with them.

However, men can also make good friends for women in several ways. Men like to do activities instead of going on and on about things. They shoot hoops and play video and computer games. They just hang out. Women don't need emotional outlets with men—male friends are more neutral, uninvolved, create less drama. Male friends are not petty with women like female friends can be; they actually make good friends for women because they aren't so sensitive. Females are more trusting of males because men are more laid back. While the men rely on women for emotional connection and support, the women like men because they don't take things too seriously. *Ironically, these students seem to incorporate some stereotyped images and practices of men and women in their portrayals of cross-sex friendships, which can mesh in ways that enable such friends to transcend stereotypical expectations of their relationship.*

In a word, the differences between females and males are valued in this context of friendship. The students maintain that cross-sex friendship is somewhat less judgmental *because* the friends are not the same. It is easier to open up and have that acceptance because neither person has to act in ways expected by persons of their gender. They argue that the differences between males and females alleviate competitive tendencies of either the male–male or female–female type within such friendships. Overall, there is less competition between cross-sex friends than same-sex ones. There is also a lack of competition for equal needs in the relationship; people can give differently and fit better. The competition that does occur in cross-sex friendships is about something that matters to both friends; it is competition that encourages each one to do and be better as a person. Between men and women there truly is friendly competition, which is more communication oriented. A male can protect a woman from undeserved disappointment in herself while a woman can empathize with man in similar ways.

One of the most frequently described benefits of cross-sex friendship derives directly from females' and males' contrasting worldviews. A member of the opposite sex provides an "insider's perspective" on the other sex. Students maintain that their closer, more intimate cross-sex and same-sex relationships are strengthened by such insight. Persons need that other sex's point of view. It is helpful to get a man's/woman's point of view, for example when trouble occurs in a dating relationship. Cross-sex friends get a male's perspective on relationship problems with a man and a female's perspective on relationship problems with a woman. Talking with a member of a different sex about issues involving a member of that sex is educational; persons learn from each other. You can't beat an opposite-sex mentor to consult about what to buy for Valentine's Day or your opposite-sex significant other's birthday. Cross-sex friends trade information concerning each gender's point of view. One female student observed if each person provides a different perspective on life, a man can see how a contemporary woman has to live and learn not to objectify women.

Additionally, people obtain insights into the other sex without competing for attention or dates from the opposite sex. They are more comfortable talking and sharing things with cross-sex friends about a potential romantic partner because they are not worried their cross-sex friend will go after this person. Finding a romantic partner is a key task of this period of life—what better friend to help with this pursuit than someone who understands how the other gender thinks and who is not competing with you for these persons?

A virtue of this dialogue between cross-sex friends is that it can allow participants to transcend narrow definitions of who they are. In some cases males and females blend their styles, with females enjoying activities they may not otherwise pursue and males learning how to care and converse about relationships and emotional matters. Some males want to communicate in feminine ways; some females want to communicate in masculine ways. They can do so less self-consciously in a cross-sex friendship. Males teach females to enjoy the surface; females teach males to get deeper. Without the pressure of being a romantic partner with a person of the opposite sex, individuals in cross-sex friendships are allowed to take on some behaviors not typically associated with their gender roles. As women try on "male roles" and males try on "women's roles" to varying degrees, stereotypical male/female roles lose some of their grip on persons' possibilities for being in relationships with others.

## Differences Between Females and Males That Undermine Cross-Sex Friendships

In contrast, the students arguing against the possibility of enduring close cross-sex friendship invoke discourses of human nature and social destiny. They assert that what happens between cross-sex friends is not merely a matter of will; it is human nature. Since people are supposed to reproduce, basic primal attraction can get in the way of friendship. It is natural to express cross-sex closeness sexually. Meanwhile, the social pressures for cross-sex friends to recognize "the true nature" of their relationship are also too compelling to be resisted. Most cross-sex intimate relationships start off as friendships, but cross-sex friendship will evolve into "something else" sooner or later. It cannot be avoided because of the natural course of close relationships between men and women.

Considered from this perspective, fundamental differences divide males and females. For one, the different modes of talking between males and females are seen to inhibit friendship. Basic differences in communication styles always create the possibility of misunderstanding, barriers, and frustration. There are also some things women don't feel they can talk about with a man, for example, "my new boyfriend," "my period," or "going to the gynecologist," but they could with a girlfriend. Basically, they feel uncomfortable talking "girl-talk" with a member of the other sex. Sometimes females don't open up because males don't understand their intentions; for example, a friendly confidence may be interpreted as an invitation to romance. Both males and females observed there are certain types of things they don't feel comfortable telling the other sex. It's hard to open up completely because of separate worlds of discourse. As a result, the women especially don't speak as freely or take as many risks with men as they do with their same-sex friends; they tend to hold back their friendship. How can persons really be intimate if they are guarded?

Further, men build relationships on mutual experiences and doing activities together. Women build their bonds on emotional sharing; to be best friends persons have to be able to share, and men typically don't do this to the same extent as women do. On basic emotional levels, men and women are also too different to be friends. Women become attached emotionally with their friends; men avoid involvement because they don't want to be vulnerable or one-down. Due to such differences, women won't get the emotional support they expect from a male friend. The fact that males and females like to do different things—men watch sports, fish, and hunt; women shop and talk—can also cause problems.

All told, a prime reason that cross-sex friendships don't work out is "the flat-out differences" between males and females. In addition to the natural tendencies toward sexual activity, different ways of talking, emotional outlooks, and interests make it difficult for males and females to be lasting friends.

### Mutually Defined Boundaries and Common Interests Facilitating Cross-Sex Friendships

Students advocating the possibility of sustained, close cross-sex friendship reject the notions of inherent differences dividing females and males as well as irrevocable propensities for sexualized relationships. In contrast, they argue that enduring cross-sex friends cultivate common interests and treat each other as individuals not defined by gender or sexual potential. For them, living in friendship involves sharing traits and breaking down stereotyped boundaries. Ways of speaking change; males and females communicate as individuals and determine common goals and interests. The students describe common interests—like music, campus politics, long-boarding, computers, sports, the outdoors, journalism—and the joy of having someone to talk with about them. They are friends with cross-sex others because of common interests, which promotes treating each other as equals with more freedom from stereotypes. As one student stated, "Friends will do things together and will have common interests; what they do together starts to circle back and blur distinctions." In short, such friends don't put the emphasis on sex. They view themselves and their friends as individuals, not as sex objects. They emphasize the person-hood of each other, saying in effect, "This is my friend." Regarding one another as really good friends, they focus on their commonalities versus their differences, and each other's singular humanity.

In doing so, these students maintain that it is crucial to communicate clear definitions and boundaries within the relationship. They acknowledge that many persons are drawn to the opposite sex and desire to be friends with them. Frequently there is some physical attraction, some sexual component, but expressing or acting upon it is not inevitable. Attraction can begin a relationship and create tension, but it can be viewed positively. Friendship doesn't negate romantic interest; physical and sexual attractiveness are simply aspects of cross-sex friendship that must be addressed if it is to remain a friendship.

For these students, the belief that sex is essential in a relationship between cross-sex friends or regarding sex as an uncontrollable drive is actually a part of socialization. Friends have to set boundaries that everyone must understand; they need to establish norms from the beginning. Cross-sex friends should talk about sex, address it. They should ask each other, "What do you want? What defines your understanding of friendship?" An explicit definition of the friendship that both people share establishes boundaries and clearly addresses the issues of sex and passion. As one student noted, "I have two friends; it's already been defined. There is no romantic friction; we have mutual understanding of our relationship's boundaries. Once we decided we're not going to be lovers, we emphasize other qualities." For such students, persons can't control what they think about, but persons can control what they do. They don't act on sex; they can even go on dates and just hang out. They deemphasize their sexuality. They consider this a mature basis for cross-sex friendship.

Even so, they recognize an ongoing need for open communication about the boundaries and definition of their relationships, noting there's always a point where persons have to state where they're at, to keep roles clearly defined. They may say, "I love you," but need to clarify, "But I'm not in love with you." Romantic feelings need to be kept in check; they can't slip into the boyfriend/girlfriend mode. It is an intimate relationship but not a sexual or romantic one, more of a deep friendship with a cross-sex person without sexual stuff.

However, actively communicating boundaries from the beginning is not the only way sexual matters are handled in ongoing cross-sex friendships. Physical attraction and sexual activity can play out in at least three other ways. First, sex is not always or necessarily an issue between cross-sex friends. If neither person finds the other physically or romantically attractive, sex just isn't an issue. The friends have a lot of things in common; they're just not physically attracted. Second, the friends may acknowledge their sexual attraction and romantic feelings for each other. They may actually explore these possibilities and decide it doesn't work, or that they both don't feel the same way, and return to a good friendship. Sometimes it's easy to do this and it may make the friendship better after they have gotten over the sexuality issue. The boundaries created after an initial crush make the friendship more comfortable. The third way of dealing with sex is to incorporate it into the relationship while still viewing each other as friends. This is sometimes called "friendship with benefits."

\* \* \*

I want to interject here that I believe that a more prevalent sexualization of friendship is connected with other trends occurring with this age group and emerging pop cultural discourses. In other words, I have observed one theme with important ramifications in the students' views change and take on more prominence over the past 15 years. In early discussions, the groups advocating enduring cross-sex friendship were almost uniformly adamant about how engaging in sex together risked altering the definition of their relationship as a friendship. They were vocal about the intrinsic values of friendship for friendship's sake between males and females despite the multiple challenges such friends face both internally and from third parties. Only on rare occasions were there allusions to what they termed "physical friendship," for example, where sex is regarded merely as another activity that friends do together.

However, I noticed their discourse begin to alter about the same time as Alanis Morisette's celebration of a "best friend with benefits" in the song "Head Over Feet" that appeared in her 1995 multiple platinum recording *Jagged Little Pill*. Along with her videos frequently appearing on MTV's rotation, the phrase "friends with benefits" began to surface routinely in our classroom discussions of cross-sex friendship. However, this song can be interpreted in different ways. On one hand, the song can be heard as attempting to celebrate a secure romantic relationship by saying to her lover, "You're the best listener that I've ever met; you're my best friend; best friend with benefits." On the other hand, it can be heard as celebrating sex as an added benefit between friends. In the past few years this latter interpretation of the phrase has even been taken up as a category of friendship in scholarly publications due to its circulation in multiple everyday cultural discourses apparent in research participants' discourse (Afifi & Faulkner, 2000; Hughes, Morrison, & Asada, 2005). For example, MTV devoted a widely repeated episode of their *True Life* series to friends with benefits. More bluntly in recent years a few students refer to "FtFs" or "friends that fuck." Reflecting the ongoing ambiguity and possible volatility of the option, *over the years "friendship with benefits" has been cited by students to support both the possibility and the impossibility of enduring close cross-sex friendship.*

As a further indication of the highly sexualized cultural context and social environment within which current students attempt to pursue their interpersonal relationships, I cite the practice of "hooking up" reported as popular by heterosexuals on college campuses (Lambert, Kahn, & Apple, 2003; Kirschner, 2004). Lambert, Kahn, and Apple (2003) report that "hooking up" refers to "when two people agree to engage in sexual behavior for which there is no future commitment" (p. 129). In fact, "The cardinal rule, according to students, is not to expect a relationship to develop" (Kirschner, 2004, p. 10). From my perspective, this practice is almost a caricature of the sexual objectification and use of others for personal gratification associated with uncommitted consensual sexism at its worst. Even so, I want to emphasize that I am not equating hooking up and friendship with benefits, but viewing them as interpersonal practices currently occurring in the cultural contexts of each other and heterosexual social life in college environments. I distinguish between friendship with benefits and hooking up while acknowledging that each arrangement likely involves multiple definitions across participants. I consider friendship with benefits to describe a cross-sex friendship of some duration that consensually includes sexual activities as contrasted with the lack of emotional involvement, casual promiscuity, and episodic contact associated with hooking up.

Granting this opinion, research reveals additional troubling aspects of the phenomenon of hooking up. First, Lambert et al. (2003) found that "both women and men reported less comfort with their perceived norm of hooking up than they believed was experienced by their same-sex peers. . . . In addition, both men and women believed members of the other gender experienced greater comfort with hooking-up behaviors than members of the other gender actually reported" (p. 132). The authors insightfully describe this unfortunate pattern of living down to inaccurately perceived expectations of their same-sex and cross-sex peers as "due to pluralistic ignorance" (Lambert et al., 2003, p. 132). They conclude, "It is likely that most students believe others engage in these hook-up behaviors primarily because they enjoy doing so, while they see themselves engaging in these behaviors primarily due to peer pressure" (p. 132). The students fail to realize the different degrees of comfort experienced by other persons engaged in hooking up. In the terms of this book, students perform the Primary Misperception of Participation in exaggerating the similarities between themselves and others and remaining unmindful of differences in perspective that could make a difference in whether they pursue this activity. In another study 75% of the sample reported at least one hookup with 33% of them having sexual intercourse "with a stranger or a brief acquaintance" (Paul, McManus, & Hayes, 2000, p. 84).

My overall point is that such widely reported instances of hooking up indicate a highly sexualized culture of interpersonal encounters among college students. It manifests some of the worst tendencies of heterosexist subculture, and it is antithetical to friendship as a committed, ethically informed, and other-regarding relationship. One of the main findings reported by Paul, McManus, and Hayes (2000) supports this contention. The authors conclude, "The more sexual involvement in hookup experiences, the more severe the alcohol intoxication symptomatology, the higher the fear of intimacy concerning the loss of individuality through relationships, and the less likely that relationship approaches were based on friendship or altruism" (pp. 84–85). Moreover, in another study Paul and Hayes (2002) report the prevalence of a sexual double standard for males and females in the heterosexist subculture of hooking up. Males brag about their hooking up experiences to their friends. In contrast, females explore with their friends how they will deal with encountering the male participant in the future. Despite the subcultural injunction to view the experience impersonally, women are more inclined to attach emotional significance to their hookups (termed "catching a feeling") than men are and to feel "confused and used" (Kirschner, 2004, p. 10). I return now to the students' debate.

* * *

In addition to clarifying the boundaries of their cross-sex friendships and deemphasizing sexual activities, a final practice effective for defining cross-sex friendships as only friends and nothing "more" is to employ discourses of kinship to describe one's friends. This terminology is used between the two friends as well as to portray the relationship to persons outside the bond. When persons describe friends as siblings, like a brother or a sister, they are clearly off-limits for sexual or romantic advances. In one female student's words, "The point when I know there is no possibility for romance is when they say you're like a little sister." Such friends look out for and take care of each other like brothers and sisters. Like siblings, sometimes they are fiercely protective of each other. Their mutual affection is interpreted as resembling family in depth and legitimacy. They may in fact be regular guests and regarded as family in each other's parents' homes.

The successful establishment of boundaries; avoidance of sexual and romantic tensions through various practices; and enjoyment of conversation, mutual sharing, and common interests, as well as the treatment of each other as equals, promotes mutual trust between cross-sex friends. Trust and respect are important components of such friendships. With sufficient trust developed in longer term relationships, there is a high comfort level. The friend is part of one's life. A person can be more intimate and talk about almost anything without second-guessing the friend's motives. It is easy to talk with such a friend about other relationships. Mutual trust continues to build when a person risks confiding and friends prove trustworthy.

### Desire and Inevitable Sexual Tensions Overcoming Spoken Definitions of Cross-Sex Friendships

In contrast, the group doubting cross-sex friendship's long-term viability presents compelling challenges to these optimistic images. First, these students maintain if both parties are heterosexual, inevitably there is going to be sexual tension that is either one-sided or mutual. Persons choose friends because there is something attractive about the friend; and even if their personality sparks the original interest, their looks can grow on someone. All cross-sex relationships revolve around underlying sexual needs and attraction. Physical attractiveness is important in any relationship, and so boundaries are too hard to define. Since physical love is the sexual counterpart of platonic love, physical attractiveness will eventually become sexual attraction even to people with whom a person is friends. Even if the attraction is not acted on physically, there will be sexual feelings and emotional tensions. Consequently, men and women can't be close friends indefinitely; underlying sexual tensions within the friendship will eventually ruin the idea of permanent platonic friendship.

These ambiguities are not easily or completely defined away. When a man and a woman start to spend a lot of time together, care for each other and feel attracted to each other, emotions get mixed and confused. It is difficult to define their relationship as friendship once it reaches that point. The rules aren't clear. People may say they only want to be friends, but they only think they do. Both persons' true feelings are never known even if they say clearly what they want. There also may be "attraction conflict" that clouds the friendship—one person wants romance, the other doesn't; or both are attracted romantically (Reeder, 2000). In the first case the person with deeper feelings will sometimes demand "all or nothing." If the other friend doesn't share these feelings and refuses, it often ends the friendship. Ironically, either asymmetrical or symmetrical romantic attraction or sexual desire makes long-term cross-sex friendship very difficult if not impossible.

Moreover, although the opening stages of friendship and romance are similar, participants can get confused if they have different expectations. When signals get crossed, it can end a friendship or start a romantic relationship. Both persons have to look at each other as friends in the same way. This is unlikely because motives and expectations may be different for a cross-sex friendship. Each sex seems to have incongruent definitions of relationships. For one thing, affection is misinterpreted by either males or females. "Intimate" to women typically means emotional closeness; "intimate" to men often means sex. Women are used to expressing emotional closeness with their same-sex friends. Men are not and are socialized to interpret caring from women as romance. As a result, men misinterpret motives (i.e., friendliness) more than women. Men have trouble keeping romance out; they can't be close with an attractive female without trying for "more." Women are more discriminating about their involvements. For women, there is always the underlying fear that the man is going to make a move. For both friends in some relationships that feeling of "What if?" never goes away.

Even if the friends mutually agree to try out a romantic or sexual relationship, it doesn't necessarily resolve tensions. It is hard to be friends after romance; it is hard to return to friendship once people have been lovers. In many ways it is too risky to go back to friendship after persons have admitted romantic feelings for each other. What if one person admits them and the other doesn't reciprocate those feelings? Once they cross that line, they will never look at each other the same. Friends may want to test it out, cross over—but once they try romance, they can't get the same friendship back.

### Other Relationships and Social Conditions
### That Facilitate Cross-Sex Friendships

Both groups remark that social circumstances and norms play a huge role in shaping the course of cross-sex friendships. Those arguing for enduring cross-sex friendships observe that it's culturally accepted now, as on television shows such as *Friends, Seinfeld,* and *Grey's Anatomy.* It depends on one's culture; times are changing and cross-sex friendships are seen as okay now. From kindergarten on, students describe participating in youth coed sports, for example. In the college environment, they may have many more relationships that are cross-sex friendships than they do sexual relationships, and they perceive such relationships as the best thing for them to do. They are forced to be friends with many people—in classes, residence halls, and student organizations. It is also easier when their peer group supports the friendship. The fact of more women entering the work force allows more common ground, hanging out, golfing, beer drinking. Productive working relationships insisting on business-only behaviors require cross-sex friendships; it doesn't pay to undercut effective cross-sex bonds.

A variety of other social conditions foster cross-sex friendships. Family connections enable multiple cross-sex friendships with diverse relatives, including brothers- and sisters-in-law, cousins, uncles, and aunts. While young, friendships with brothers and sisters, as well as girls' relationships with fathers and boys' relationships with mothers, provide a basis for cross-sex friendship early in life. Growing up with parents who have cross-sex friendship allows children to learn through watching their friendships, and students report developing friendships with some of their parents' friends. On that note, some students maintain that a large age discrepancy also allows for cross-sex friendship. Moreover, students invariably assert that cross-sex friendships are possible between homosexuals and heterosexuals. If either person is homosexual, this erases sexual attraction so that neither is attracted romantically to the other, and neither person will perpetuate a cycle of "What if?" The students suggest that gay men and heterosexual women are an especially good bet, since gay men can relate well to such women.

An important facilitating condition is when someone has a boyfriend or girlfriend and therefore is already committed romantically to another individual. When each friend has a significant other, it clarifies the focus on friendship between them. Sexual tension is reduced when someone is involved and content with a romantic relationship and those needs are already met. Even so, each friend plays important roles in making this situation work on an ongoing basis. First, if friends are involved with other relationships, each friend needs to respect the other's romantic relationship and not jeopardize it. It does no good for friends to make significant others jealous. However, some students argued that if boyfriends and girlfriends do get jealous, it is time to assert the importance of the cross-sex friendship. Romantic relationships do not fulfill all of a person's needs. One woman stated, "If you have a romantic relationship and you are looking for friendship. My best friend is male, and I want a guy that I can belch around and stuff that I don't do around my boyfriend—and he is not going to be the boyfriend. He is still a male; but he is my friend." Basically, it raises the question, how much does someone value each of the relationships, that is, the cross-sex friend versus the boyfriend or girlfriend? Will a person break off with a jealous significant other for his or her cross-sex friend? Will the person end a cross-sex friendship to appease a romantic partner? Perhaps the simplest circumstance is when neither person is in a romantic relationship. But that situation risks a whole other set of pressures from persons outside the friendship as well as within that relationship.

A particularly facilitative situation is when romantic couples make common friends. Couple friendships find a woman becoming friends with her boyfriend's buddies, and her own same-sex friends can become friends with her boyfriend. A male observed, "You can be friends with your girlfriend's friends—you would never breach that trust." Meanwhile, cross-sex friendships with a same-sex friend's boyfriend or girlfriend also are "honor bound." They are off-limits as potential romantic partners. In each case, one's loyalty to one's partner and one's friend is at stake. In general, ongoing cross-sex friendships are possible with a variety of people—including family members, co-workers, friends of cross-sex friends, friends of romantic partners, and romantic partners of same-sex friends. Cross-sex friendships are especially possible when they are not the primary relationship or a free-standing relationship.

## Other Relationships and Social Conditions
## That Subvert Cross-Sex Friendships

The skeptical group discusses the very conditions cited above for enabling cross-sex friendships as potentially constraining them. First, despite superficial changes and scattered media depictions, society still puts a damper on cross-sex friendships; they are not viewed as the norm. As a result, such friends experience numerous pressures. Cross-sex friends are pressured "to pair off" by those who love them, as well as those who don't necessarily. Parents and relatives automatically assume—say a person brings a friend to a picnic or family gathering—that person's relatives assume they are already together or that they are developing a relationship. There is pressure from family—especially older persons who see cross-sex friendships as against the norm—as well as from other friends to become a couple, pressure to be married. These outsiders say things like, "You have such a great relationship, why aren't you dating?" and "When are you going to admit your true feelings for each other?" If cross-sex friends are always seen together but as just friends, people won't approach and introduce themselves, which cuts down on each friend's possibilities for romantic relationships with others. Less caring third parties are also always suspicious, label the situation, gossip and continuously spread rumors. When they see a man and woman together a lot, they assume the two are romantically involved or having sex, and they constantly ask questions. Cross-sex friends get tired of having to explain themselves. Other friends don't have to; why should they?

Cross-sex friendships developed as a dimension of work relationships or different categories of familial relationships—such as with parents, siblings, in-laws—aren't truly free-standing friendships. The same limitation applies to befriending the spouse's best friend; getting married makes it more likely that persons will have couple friendships. Meanwhile, each spouse is more likely to drift away from the cross-sex friendships that they chose on their own and cared about before getting married. There is only so much time for relationships, and primary relationships such as marriage, family, and work come first. In work settings sexual harassment laws place an additional stress on the possibility of making cross-sex friends. Further, if a person has off-limits friends because of commitment to a boy- or girlfriend, and that commitment breaks down, the newly single person might become fair game. There is rebound potential, which could cause complications for the cross-sex friendship. If someone is involved with a romantic relationship that ends, what happens to the cross-sex friendships made through the romantic partner? How much were they the person's own relationships and how much merely an extension of the relationship with the boyfriend or girlfriend?

Jealousy is arguably the biggest issue affecting cross-sex friendships. Students frequently describe jealousy as "natural" and playing a large role in curtailing cross-sex friendships. If someone is in an established romantic relationship, the boyfriend or girlfriend is likely to become jealous of that person's cross-sex friends, especially if they are close ones. It is difficult for a partner to understand and allow much time and affection for a perceived competitor. Other persons may identify and talk about the friendship couple as more than friends, which also makes the partner jealous. Jealousy of either or both friends' significant others and/or competition for the friend's time creates tension and drives a wedge between cross-sex friends.

Jealousy takes other forms as well. Either person's same-sex friends may get jealous of the time someone spends with a cross-sex friend, prompting the question, "Why do you spend so much time with her/him and not us?" And the close cross-sex friend may become jealous about the time a person spends with same-sex friends. As a result, tensions may develop between the female friend versus his male friends as well as between the male friend and her female friends. There may be jealousy between the cross-sex friends themselves if one member starts to date someone else or that person's significant other gets jealous and successfully restricts the friends' time together. Friends also may have trouble dating their cross-sex friend's friends. According to one student, "You feel like they are off-limits." Multiple constraints on cross-sex friendships arise from societal norms and third party challenges ranging from relatives to friends to significant others.

❖ ADDRESSING STUDENTS' POSITIONS
   ON CROSS-SEX FRIENDSHIP

Sometimes when the students finish debating, they turn to me expectantly to render a verdict on the winning side of their debate. I emphasize that neither side defeats the other. Rather, in debating cross-sex friendship, both groups have voiced discourses at large in the culture with enabling, constraining, and mixed effects concerning the students' own possibilities for thinking about and engaging in friendship. Their spoken positions also presuppose their gendered identities, conceptions of romantic love, and sexual relations with other persons. *Focusing on the possibility of enduring, close cross-sex friendships reveals that all friendships are potentially sites of struggle due to the politics of sexual identity, enactments of gender, the relative importance of friendship versus romance, and the contingencies of social lives.* I argue that much of the commotion about cross-sex friendship inscribed in the students' exchanges arises in the pursuit and portrayal of such relationships in the context of a predominantly heterosexual culture. In the spirit of cultivating personal agency and expanded options for being friends with others, I explore with them how issues of sexism, gendered performances, and sexual identities—in conjunction with other selectively emphasized similarities and differences—influence descriptions of and participation in cross-sex friendships. I further argue that the positions we perform concerning these matters continually shape and reflect our own identities.

## Sexism, Gendered Performances, Sexual Identities, and Cross-Sex Friendships

By sexism I mean any outlook that privileges sexual activity as the root metaphor for our being-in-the-world. In Burke's (1969) sense, sexual striving constitutes our primordial vocabulary of motive, with selves and others consequently reduced to sex objects. Of course, Freud's writings emphasize precisely this outlook; in his view *all friendships* involve "aim-inhibited sexuality" (see Rangell, 1963). Now it is one thing to observe the importance of physical attractiveness in all types of social bonds and the notion that an individual's sexuality and desires are a necessary part of the total person, which may not be and probably should not ever be completely suppressed. But sexist vocabularies incorporated as part of any sexual identity can construct others primarily as naturalized objects of sexual desire, as opposed to social beings that may be known, befriended and/or loved for reasons and attributes that transcend sexual relations.

To a significant degree I perceive a heterosexist ideology with its required gendered identities manifest in the students' debates about cross-sex friendship I have re-presented here. Indeed, this seems to be the dominant system of signification and power under which they labor in forming their relationships and realizing their subjectivities. As a normative enterprise, heterosexism insists upon a naturalized binary division between genders based on biological sex differences; an assumed heterosexual orientation that rejects other sexual identities and orientations; and a privileging of heterosexual romance and marriage over friendship and other forms of loving. By and large, the challenges the students describe facing their cross-sex friendships transpire at dramatic intersections of sexist, heteronormative scripts encompassing both romantic relationships and cross-sex friendships. These scripts are inscribed upon male and female bodies with the students and others naturalizing these connections, prescriptions, and proscriptions. Taken seriously, cross-sex friendship productively troubles the naturalization of biological sex differences and romantic scripts through emphasizing participants' agency in fashioning their own gendered performances and relational expectations.

As Judith Butler (1990) has persuasively argued, there is nothing intrinsically natural about separating all human beings into two opposing categories on the basis of one physical attribute of their overall being-in-the-world. Rather than a static binary category for reductively sorting males and females, gender can be viewed as an ongoing array of activities, performances, and ideologies pervading all facets of social

life (Walker, 1994; West & Zimmerman, 1987). Gender functions ideo-
logically when people restrictively interpret the meaning of their own
and others' lives as well as their eligibility to think, feel, and behave in
desired ways solely due to their gender. In acting out stereotypical
beliefs about what males versus females are supposed to do and how
they are supposed to feel in close same-sex and cross-sex relationships,
we construct gendered contrasts on an ongoing basis (Reeder, 1996;
Walker, 1994; Werking, 1997). Preserving these gendered distinctions
obscures the diverse ways of being human occurring within each category of biological sex as well as the extensive commonalities performed across gender divides in various personal and social
relationships.

What assumptions are enacted about gendered identity—that is,
what it means to be a feminine or masculine woman, or a masculine or
feminine man—in our discussions and experiences of friendship? Does
being masculine (in gay, lesbian, bisexual, and heterosexual relationships) mean being assertive and initiating sexual activity, and does
being feminine mean wanting to get to know and care about a person
for who they are before or perhaps instead of pursuing sexual relations
(Nardi, 1992)? What performances and practices do persons use to
identify themselves and others as masculine or feminine within their
friendships? How are females and males required to act and feel in
ongoing relationships lived and breathed in extensively scripted cultural contexts for being a person and being-with-others? How gendered and sexual orientation identified are our judgments and
attributions about self and others in the contexts of caring relationships? To what extent do relational participants define themselves as
women or men according to sexual or other practices and participation
in normative scripts concerning marriage, procreation, and/or raising
children (Rose, 2000)?

What my students discuss as gender differences, complementari-
ties, and affinities negotiated between males and females in the context
of cross-sex friendships—for example, in speaking styles, instrumental
or emotional outlooks, and interests—also need to be addressed by
same-sex friends. This is true whether either or both friends are lesbian,
gay, bisexual, or heterosexual. Perhaps such issues do not arise as
noticeably between two masculine-identified homosexual or heterosexual males or between two feminine-identified lesbians or heterosexual females. However, consider a masculine-identified heterosexual
male developing a friendship with a feminine-identified heterosexual
male. Consider a feminine-identified heterosexual female becoming
friends with a masculine-identified heterosexual female. Salient issues

negotiated between the friends could be ones of gender identification, which could have varying consequences for how the friendships are conducted and experienced.

Will these persons experience subtle or overt pressure to alter the performance of their gender identifications and practices by their respective friends? Or will they voluntarily enjoy learning and performing some of the interests and ways of communicating of the other person's gender identity through spending time together as friends? If so, will these altered gendered practices carry over into the identities they perform in other relationships with family and at work? What could facilitate or limit such activities of being a person? How much support do they receive from others to be the more ambiguously gendered persons they take themselves to be?

On a different note, will these negotiations of gender identity between the friends become conflated with issues of sexual identity? If so, where is the impetus for this muddle? Does it arise through interactions between the friends, or will it more likely derive from judgmental messages received from outside of their friendship? A moment's reflection reveals that these cross-gendered same-sex friends may face similar exigencies potentially arising within their friendship and from their social networks as cross-sex friends do.

Such social exigencies and negotiations occur because understandings and ascriptions of gender are not discrete accomplishments. Gender interweaves with every aspect of human culture (Bateson, 1958). As Wittig (1992, p. 2) notes, "Masculine/feminine, male/female are the categories which serve to conceal the fact that social differences always belong to an economic, political, ideological order." Moreover, by and large the gender dichotomies assumed in the student discussions are continually constructed and enforced within "a heterosexual matrix in which heterosexuality is presupposed in the expression of 'real' forms of masculinity or femininity" (Butler, quoted in Allen, 2004, p. 473). This matrix supports a heteronormative gaze that envisions heterosexual romantic relationships and specific forms of segregated same-sex homosociality as the standard by which to judge all relationships (Kalmijn, 2002).

Informed by this outlook, cross-sex friendships are discussed as if similar predicaments do not occur in same-sex ones, for example, jealousy, possessiveness, physical and/or sexual attraction, and sexist attributions and injunctions by third parties. For example, Lorin Arnold (1995), who self-identifies as heterosexual, describes how her close, demonstrative same-sex friendship with another woman was constantly second-guessed as a lesbian sexual relationship by the males they worked with in a college town bar. Insisting that sexual relations were occurring between Lorin and her friend, these men badgered the women and asked if they could "watch" when the two women were alone. Consequently, these males performed a virtual caricature of the sexualizing and objectifying masculine-gendered identity often dramatized in heterosexist cultures and relationships. In doing so, they mapped their own world of constricted possibilities for friendship onto that of Lorin and Heidi.

Friendships between heterosexual males in middle-class North American culture are modally characterized by instrumentality and an activity orientation with limited emotional involvement or expression except in their closest bonds (Rawlins, 1992). Several authors argue that such men may be reluctant to express much affection for other men due to homophobia, a fear of being or perceived as homosexual (R. A. Lewis, 1978; Morin & Garfinkle, 1978). These concerns are more than functions of a predominantly heterosexual cultural setting; they also reflect men being taught to view most of their relations in a highly sexualized manner as an expression of masculinity (Abbey, 1982). In such a heterosexist setting, men may downplay their emotional feelings for other men and simultaneously feel that they should express similar feelings for women (e.g., their cross-sex friends) romantically and/or sexually. This is a pervasive script for performing masculine identity within a heterosexist worldview (Allen, 2004). By comparison, in a homosexist gay culture males may be urged to view other males initially or primarily as potential sexual partners. Reflective essayists in this setting have been concerned about the possibilities for "only" friendship between men who care about each other (A. White, 2006; E. White, 1983). It appears that gendered effects of certain versions of masculinity transcend sexual orientations.

Such masculinist tendencies come into sharper focus when compared with lesbian-feminist relationships. Lesbians tend to perceive love and friendship as transpiring on a continuum. The pronounced distinctions between romantic love relationships and friendships fade away for lesbians when they view friendship as a primary basis for forming romantic bonds and when they emphasize emotional closeness and companionship over sexual behavior across relationships (Rose, 2000; Vetere, 1982). Further, they also aspire to equal treatment of each other in a woman-identification that wants to supersede the brinkmanship, objectification, and power struggles they perceive in many heterosexual romantic relationships. Some lesbians hold that compartmentalized relationships derive from heterosexist culture with its emphasis on romantic ideologies and sexual activity over the affections of friendship on its own right and between lovers (Vetere, 1982). Consequently, for many lesbians deep friendships with other women do not necessarily threaten romantic partners. More typically they experience few problems "remaining close friends with ex-lovers" (Rose, 2000, p. 324), although tensions related to romance can occur (Kennedy, 2004; Vetere, 1982).

When the students maintain that close enduring cross-sex friendship is possible if either person is homosexual, they oversimplify the dynamics of sexual and gendered identities that I have been discussing. For one thing this possibility for friendship assumes that the complications produced by one-sided or mutual sexual attraction and activity are the most important problems cross-sex friends face. But it neglects the friends' gendered identities as well as other salient identifications such as race, ethnicity, class, or political involvement. Consider, for example, that a lesbian may have difficulties being friends with a masculine-identified heterosexual male primarily because of the woman's identification with feminist worldviews. These gendered convictions inform her disdain for masculinist worldviews with their characteristic focus on competition, unilateral power arrangements, and hierarchical relationships, irrespective of—though often played out in terms of—masculine sexuality (Connell, 1993). Because of his masculine-gendered identity, the male also may have difficulty self-disclosing or becoming emotionally available in a friendship. Whether he is gay or straight, to the extent that a man identifies with such masculine worldviews with their relational tendencies, it may be difficult for a woman-identified lesbian to entertain friendship with him. It may be more a matter of gendered and political identities than sexual orientation. On the masculine-identified heterosexual male's part, to the extent that he views a woman as cultivating a worldview that summarily marginalizes men, or inappropriately performs masculine-gendered identities or activities, he may avoid friendship with her. He may also feel threatened by a friendship with a woman who does not complement his masculine self-image.

Meanwhile, we need to keep in mind that masculinities and femininities (as well as sexual identities and conceptions of friendship and romantic loving) exist on a continuum of identifications, even though they have been discussed here in a binary fashion and with the risks of reproducing stereotypes in the previous examples. Moreover, in all cases the viability of given friendships will depend upon how the specific persons involved treat each other, the relevant identities situationally in play during their interactions, and the concrete circumstances of their friendship. For example, it is conceivable that the feminist lesbian and the masculinist heterosexual male considered above could form an alliance, become political or civic friends, and perhaps even personal friends, under circumstances where their shared participation in a worthwhile social cause with its associated identities allows them to perceive each other as similar or complementary in important ways that diminish the significance of other perceived differences. Their shared activities and alliances could trump individuated identities not directly relevant to concerted political action.

When the students suggest that gay men and heterosexual women are especially good candidates for cross-sex (as well as cross-sexual orientation) friendship, an array of identities, discourses, and practices frequently intersect to facilitate such bonds. First, the sexual identities and desires of gay men and heterosexual women typically remove potential sexual tensions and second-guessing of each other's affection from the relationship, although they still may find each other attractive. Second, in relationships involving feminine-identified gay men and heterosexual women, there are shared identifications with each other's lesser status in a masculinist, male-dominated, heterosexual world (Grigoriou, 2004; A. White, 2006). Equality is a significant aspiration of all friendships. Shared oppression can level the social field, providing an important basis for edifying identification with each other as friends. Third, the openness, trust, depth of disclosure, and emotional involvement arising from shared identification with feminine styles of communicating give these relationships a closeness and sense of comfort often associated with women's friendships. Fourth, in contrast to women's same-sex friendships, each participant also values the insider's perspective of the other sex. Meanwhile, they typically do not feel competitive about the men each may find sexually or romantically attractive as the woman might with her heterosexual same-sex friends and the man might with his gay friends (Grigoriou, 2004).

Through doing activities together, women friends may also connect gay men to the heterosexual world, the dominant social nexus ignored with difficulty and feelings of disappearance by gays (Tillmann-Healy, 2001). On their part, gay men provide women friends with male companionship without the risks, possessiveness, or involvements that occur in heterosexual romantic bonds (Grigoriou, 2004). Finally, in contrast to most other types of cross-sex friendships, well-known media texts like the television series *Will and Grace* and *Sex and the City* and movies like *My Best Friend's Wedding* actually dramatize this kind of friendship, rendering them more visible and normatively acceptable.

## The Comparative Significance of Friendship and Romantic Love

The challenges to cross-sex friendship voiced by these students also reflect the relative positions of friendship and romantic love in the heteronormative hierarchy of relationships in North American middle-class life. Heterosexual romantic love is widely encouraged, institutionalized, and positively sanctioned religiously and legally through marriage at this point in time. In contrast, friendship, as well as other forms of loving, occupies contingent, more tenuous positions (Brain, 1976). Romantic loving, with its exclusive commitment, possessiveness, and potential for sexual gratification, is often regarded as part and parcel of the march to marriage. Further, Greenfield (1965) argues that the "romantic love complex" (p. 364) instructs persons to fall in love in order to fill necessary positions in normative society as husbands-fathers and wives-mothers.

Despite their importance for emotional well-being, across young adulthood, friends increasingly take a back seat to the priorities of committed sexual relationships, romantic coupling, marriage, family, and work. In a sense, *all* friendships, not just cross-sex ones, must be permitted by this dominant heterosexual matrix if friends are to remain active parts of persons' lives. The added wrinkle of cross-sex friendships is their potential subversion of dominant heterosexualist scripts and the gendered identities they enforce. As the students suggest, cross-sex friendships can allow us some freedoms not found in romantic relationships in relation to enacting masculinity and femininity. Small wonder that so many discourses come to bear in restricting the perceived possibility of enduring, close cross-sex friendships between the young adult students in my classes over the years.

Indeed, the students voice several narrative imperatives produced by the ideology of the romantic, heterosexual institution of marriage. While friendship is described as the pinnacle of same-sex closeness, romance and marriage are regarded as the highest forms of cross-sex intimacy. As a result, it is considered inevitable that close cross-sex friendships will evolve into something "more than friendship," meaning romantic involvement and/or sexual activity. These narrative visions also join with a normative trajectory to heterosexual marriage. Once married, spouses embrace the "couple companionate ideal" in which each person is expected to meet all of the other's needs, including those for close friendship (Oliker, 1989). This vision further limits the possibilities for freestanding cross-sex friendship for either spouse. Not surprisingly, the greatest drop-off in the number of friendships, including cross-sex friends, at any point in the life course occurs during young adulthood when many persons marry (Rawlins, 1992).

Accompanying these discourses in the students' debate are ones that conspicuously tend to naturalize the practices of interpersonal relationships. We hear that it is *natural* for males and females who love each other as friends to want to take their relationship to "a higher level," to want "more," to have sex. Over the years one of the other common statements by students has been that jealousy is "natural" in romantic relationships. These locutions are apologies for versions of the status quo that picture romance as the be-all and end-all of inter-personal life, relegating friendship to second fiddle. In his comprehensive intercultural survey of human variations of loving, *Friends and Lovers,* anthropologist Robert Brain (1976) derides this hierarchy and the related notions that competition and conflict are "natural" features of the human condition. He asserts convincingly that cooperation and friendship are just as essential to human life.

But where do we hear that it is *natural* for men and women to be friends? If relationships are co-authored stories created within conventions and genres taught by our culture, where are the stories portraying close, enduring cross-sex friendship? I ask, what is *unnatural* about cross-sex friendship? In my judgment, most naturalizing discourse is used tautologically to explain practices that reduce humans to some essentializing common denominator like the sex drive or the instinct for aggression. Such discourses tend to be deployed as privileged vocabularies for masking mysteries or curtailing evolving practices of our being-and-becoming-with-others-in-the-world. They always serve somebody's interests and claims to power. Such discourses miss the point of our definitive abilities as symbol users and abusers in Kenneth Burke's (1966, 1969) view, that is, to fashion our own possibilities and impossibilities for loving and being loved, for caring and concern, for cooperation, and for sharing a planet.

Some friends preserve the platonic essence of their bond unselfconsciously through an absence of sexual attraction and/or activities. Other friends devote themselves to avoiding sexual expressions of affection, believing that such actions risk altering irrevocably the definition of their relationship as a friendship in their own and others' eyes. And other cross-sex friends enjoy sexual behaviors together as part of their activities as friends without assigning romantic significance to them. As mentioned above, such "friendship with benefits" seems to be emerging as yet another negotiated definition of cross-sex friendship that further blurs the boundaries among types of relationships (Afifi & Faulkner, 2000; Hughes, Morrison, & Asada, 2005). Perhaps cross-sex friendships of whatever stripe may be celebrated as alternatives to reductionist, heterosexist scripts and the naturalized march to romantic attachment sanctioned by the ideology of heterosexual marriage.

Meanwhile, cross-sex friendship ironically provides a strong basis for enduring affection within such normative scripts. People who have been friends before they become romantically involved tend to be kinder to each other during troubled times and nicer to each other if their romantic relationship ends (Rawlins, 1992). In my previous book, I asserted the desirability and ethical potentials of treating each other as friends within marriage. Here (cross-sex) friendship's person-qua-person regard for the other, negotiated mutuality and equality, and respect for each other's freedom compose humanizing supplements to the asymmetrical benefits, obligations, and role-based treatment of each other frequently occurring in "traditional" heterosexual marriages (Rawlins, 1992).

Friendships are permeated with ambiguities. Brain (1976) argues convincingly that they have lost their "ceremonial patterning and emotional expression" in Western capitalist cultures. How do persons know for certain that they are someone's friend? What private and public rituals do we have for registering friendship? When persons realize that they have formed a friendship that should last the rest of their lives, do they rent a hall, send out invitations, and gather their family and other friends to consecrate this commitment? On a different note, performing coitus typically and "traditionally" functions as the consummation of a heterosexual romantic bond (McPhillips, Braun, & Gavey, 2001). How are friendships consummated? More specifically for our purposes here, how are cross-sex friendships consummated? The lack of cultural scripts for performing binding affection in such relationships is part of the problem of sustaining them as friendships, especially in the context of unequivocal heteronormative romantic scripts. We need to develop grammars, discourses, and narratives that legitimize friendships of all kinds. It is likely that consummation and being joined together are not even the best metaphors.

Rake (1970) once observed that the exclusiveness and possessiveness of romantic loving produces the freedom-to-be-one in contrast to the practices of friendship, which create the freedom-to-be-two. In Conlon's words, "Friends share each other's experiences of the world; they see it in similar ways and enjoy it together. Lovers, in contrast, as the rhetoric of romance insists repeatedly, *are* each other's world" (1995, p. 297, emphasis in original). Perhaps the sense of union desired in romantic loving is a dubious counterpart to the sense of delight in each other's singular potentials offered in friendship. As such, cross-sex friends, indeed all friends, transcending enforced categories, must create and face together their own narrative openings and contingencies. The legitimacy of their stories will need to be recognized by third parties and enveloping cultural discourses.

## ❖ CONCLUSION

Pursuing cross-sex friendship takes us into an interlinked assortment of cultural myths, assumptions, identities, and positionings of similarities and differences between persons. Root images of mutually conditioning and mutually opposing otherness constitute femininities, masculinities, and sexualities that articulate the contingencies of cross-sex friendship in both edifying and unsettling ways. Strongly held binaries undermine the continuities, existential commonalities, and edifying distinctions among differently gendered and sexually identified people, as well as their relationships. Moreover, in these students' and other discourses, various subject positions—like those of race, ethnicity, class, and embodied abilities—are conspicuous in their absence from consideration (A. White, 2006). Taken-for-granted hierarchies of social relationships, including romantic love and marriage versus friendship, preferred and stigmatized sexual identities, and constructions of gender continually assemble the permitted modes of caring.

Close cross-sex friendships are merely one example of sustained human caring that subverts these pageants of allowed and disallowed relationships. Such friendships struggle for identity, both in finding names for the relationship that justify its otherness to third parties, and for the friends to legitimize their own practices and feelings for each other (Rawlins, 1982). Compounding the difficulties co-telling stories of cross-sex friendship is learning how to listen without prejudgment to other persons' narratives of friendship and loving and to hear them for who the friends say they are. This communicative work points to the very conditions for sustaining shared identities as friends in numerous situations of scrutiny and skeptical discourse. In short, cross-sex friendship challenges persons to position themselves among the intersections of an array of discourses with surpassing power to articulate for them the experiences and practices of their own relationships and subjectivities. Enduring is the issue. Realistically, how long can such freestanding friendships last, given all of the constraining factors we have witnessed, and usually living on borrowed time and secondhand language?

Talking with students, this chapter performs "discursive penetration." It is an effort to decipher and name the enabling and constraining discourses configuring their relationships' chances and complicities (Giddens, 1979). What normative discourses hold sway in composing the rationales for their relationships? What defines persons' identities and eligibilities as (cross-sex) friends? Is it their biological sex, gendered performances of self, sexual motivation, sexual orientation and identity, race, ethnicity, social class, interests and activities, abilities, speaking style? Some composition of these attributes? What configuration of these attributes does each person self-identify as? How much say do the friends actually have in identifying, negotiating, and celebrating the differences and similarities between them that matter across contexts? What social groups are the friends able to interconnect in light of their individuated configurations of self- and shared identities? What is each friend's stance toward their different identities, and how susceptible are these identities to commentary or even censure in emerging circumstances? How do friends avoid the reduction of each other and their friendship to others' categories based on stereotyped attributions? Recurring challenges of identity and social location shape and reflect the (im)possibilities of sustaining cross-sex friendships—indeed all forms of freely chosen caring relationships.

Differences and similarities are hierarchically arranged in social contexts. The differences modally associated with sexes and genders that we transcend through friendship are different differences to navigate than ones of race, social class, sexualities, or embodied abilities. In fact, many of the differences identified by these students in attempting cross-sex friendship presuppose a host of more fundamental similarities in life circumstances. For example, an array of privileges are connected with white, middle-class existence, including the opportunity to attend college (DeMott, 1995). Such oblivion is a potential shortcoming of their close dyadic friendships. *Individual similarities and personal differences incorporated into a dyadic relationship may consciously or unconsciously presuppose participation in another level of exclusion.*

Under what conditions are people allowed to care for each other? The case of cross-sex friendship reminds us that we are always acting within the discursively, culturally, and materially patterned opportunities and constraints of social positions. As with all friendships, it simultaneously depends upon the initiatives, choices, and negotiations—the praxis of the individuals involved. Blanket statements based on modal profiles potentially must answer to the voices, choices, and activities of individuals. To be sure, social circumstances and stratifications play crucial, often understated roles in the initiation, continuation, and demise of friendships (Adams & Allan, 1998; Allan, 1979; Kalmijn, 2002). In choosing each other as friends, we assume the ongoing responsibility to perform our choices together and to treat each other as friends to the extent our negotiated expectations and situations allow. When our friendships skirt conventional injunctions of gendered practices and sexual identities, we must be careful to avoid slippage into cultural scripts that deny the legitimacy of our mutually chosen practices and subjectivities. In doing so, we may face stringent contextual sanctions and need to take advantage of whatever facilitating conditions exist. All friendships—and certainly cross-sex ones struggling under the duress of marginalizing scripts—require individual agency, dyadic negotiation, and actively performed benevolence to become and remain part of social life.

# 6

# Pursuing Cross-Race Friendships in Personal, Sociocultural, and Historical Contexts

Two baseline conditions are required for friendships to form and flourish. First, social circumstances must provide opportunities for us to meet and communicate. As relationships develop, we must be able to play an active role in each other's lives to the extent that we deem appropriate. Great variance exists, however, across cultural circumstances as well as the life course in how available friends choose to be to each other and how much control we have over the time and space in our lives to share with friends (Rawlins, 1992). Despite the importance of individual initiatives, as discussed in Chapter 5 forces and discourses larger than friends pattern our social contexts and the very possibility of our friendships (Adams & Allan, 1998). There may be compulsory or restricted interaction with others.

A second condition involves the degree of shared meanings that we negotiate for our times together and apart. Wide variation occurs in the emotional significance assigned to the interactions and pursuits between friends. To a large extent becoming and remaining personal friends involves what Laing (1972) calls "co-inherence," that is, experiencing a similar friendship inside. Such friends perceive time together or messages exchanged in comparable ways, and they mutually assume that the other person shares these feelings. While civic or political friendships require dramatically less overlap in personal meanings to be effective, they often involve good will, coordinated actions, and convictions about common concerns. The possibility and continuance of friendships is susceptible to our concrete, socially conditioned opportunities to interact, and to the meanings each of us attributes to our activities and absences.

Both conditions point to the prevalence of similarity in friendships; friendships are typically homo-social versus hetero-social phenomena. Actual patterns of friendship in the United States reflect social stratification and economic disparities. Empirical studies repeatedly report the pronounced likelihood of friends being similar in race, ethnicity, age, sex, gender, sexual orientation, educational attainment, marital and career status, and socioeconomic level (Rawlins, 1992; A. White, 2006). Consequently, friendships are statistically more likely to reproduce macrolevel, palpable social differences than to transcend them (DeMott, 1995; Rawlins, 1992). The prevailing friendship practices of the U.S. middle class constitute trivial forces in presenting alternatives to the status quo or pursuing comprehensive social justice. DeMott (1995) argues further that the "friendship orthodoxy" of whites assuming underlying similarity despite perceptions of blacks' ostensive differences—what I term the Primary Misperception of Participation— is inimical to transforming race relations on social structural and interpersonal levels (Bonilla-Silva & Forman, 2000).

There are multiple structures, discourses, and organizational and relational configurations of racism in the United States (Ashcraft & Allen, 2003; S. Friedman, 1995). These systemic social forms also condition possibilities for constructing identities, friendships, and alliances within and across races, ethnicities, and cultural groups (S. Friedman, 1995). While there are many ways of constructing and discussing race, in this chapter I focus on friendships between individuals raced black and white in the United States. Most of the extant research concerning cross-race friendships addresses relationships between blacks and whites. Even so, notions of black and white take on particular meanings across diverse relationships and contexts. Clearly, many people do not identify themselves in a fixed manner as belonging to primarily any one race or ethnicity (De Andrade, 2000). Progressively embracing the dialectic of individuation and participation also contests dichotomous thinking about persons and groups who attempt to form friendships.

Cross-race relationships between blacks and whites typically face considerable challenges in both the circumstantial and intersubjective conditions facilitating friendship. Cross-race friendship scholar Mary McCullough observes, "Historically, racial difference is the single demographic characteristic most scholars find prohibits or prevents friendships from forming" (1998, p. 10). She registers the "systematically controlled availability" significantly curtailing interaction between blacks and whites and emphasizes "the structural origins of racially segregated networks as a first and lasting dimension of friendships, learned early in childhood" (McCullough, 1998, p. 12). While personal choice is involved in forming friendships, it is not free choice. Instead, it is constrained by the functional proximity of other persons, the likelihood that we will encounter and interact with them on a consistent basis in our daily lives (Jackman & Crane, 1986). Such sustained multifaceted interaction between blacks and whites remains comprehensively constrained in North American culture as does the statistical probability of cross-race friendship (DeMott, 1995).

In this chapter I first examine social circumstances and meanings constraining the possibilities of friendship between blacks and whites in the United States as portrayed in Toni Morrison's short story "Recitatif." Next I consider asymmetrical challenges and edifying practices that may arise when blacks and whites engage in friendships. Finally, I illustrate the ongoing accomplishment of cross-race friendships facing such exigencies with a published autobiographical example and two cases from dyadic interviews. The chapter closes with a discussion of the prospects for enriching cross-race friendships.

## ❖ CONSTRAINED CROSS-RACE FRIENDSHIP

The social contingencies and interpretive quandaries involved in a cross-race friendship pursued in circumstances stratified by racial differences are dramatized in Toni Morrison's (1983) short story "Recitatif." In the story one girl-then-woman is black and the other is white, but readers never know for certain each person's race. We are left to our own interpretive practices to construct these identifications. The discursive categories of friendship and race are two among several bases for inclusion and exclusion revealed throughout the narrative to be contingent, consequential, relational, and social matters. After being thrown together for 4 months in a children's shelter when they are 8 years old, these two women meet only by chance a few times over the courses of their lives in this story. During these moments they perform and interpret the past and present meanings of their relationship.

Since they were deposited by their own mothers at the orphanage, Twyla and Roberta are placed in a room together and excluded from the social networks of the other children at this facility, most of whom are real orphans. Due to their disvalued status identified as dumped off and as a biracial twosome, Twyla and Roberta spend most of their time at the shelter on the outside looking in, watching rather than joining the other children's activities. They both also perform poorly at school. Twyla appreciates the institution's food because it compares favorably to what she has experienced with her neglectful mother. Having been well fed at home, Roberta often leaves most of her food on the plate and doesn't mind if Twyla scarfs it up. Sometimes a group of older adolescent girls on the next floor who have run away from abusive households pick on them. These teenaged girls look tough and mean to Roberta and Twyla. Nevertheless fascinated by their appearance, they risk getting their arms twisted and hair pulled to spy on the older girls dancing together to their radios in the institution's orchard.

Identifying with each other through their shared exclusions, Twyla and Roberta develop some exclusionary practices of their own. They call their supervising nurse "The Big Bozo" (p. 243). Because her omnipresence and mercurial moods embody the common oppression of the place for the girls, she becomes a fearful inside joke for them. They also objectify the older girls upstairs, referring to them as "the gar girls" based on Roberta's mishearing of a reference to creepy decorations on medieval buildings in one of their classes. They identify the gar girls as the ones they do not want to become—much older, still at the facility, painted up, mean. Meanwhile, Twyla and Roberta find their own person to pick on in Maggie, a kitchen worker at the orphanage whom they once memorably see fall down and get laughed at by the older girls. Maggie is excluded on many accounts for she is identified by her physical features, clothes, and carriage as disfigured, disabled, mute, old, of ambiguous race, and lower working class. After 4 months together, Roberta returns home, leaving Twyla and a legacy of shared exclusions, common struggles, and tender feelings.

Eight years later Twyla encounters a much-changed Roberta while Twyla is working as a waitress. Barely acknowledging Twyla, Roberta makes fun of her job and shares private laughter with her two male companions. Twyla feels conspicuous, marked, and unwelcome in her waitress uniform. Roberta doesn't introduce Twyla to her companions and derides her hurtfully for not knowing about Jimi Hendrix. Excluded and identified as "other" by her onetime friend, it's a numbing encounter for Twyla after almost a decade with no contact.

A dozen years later Twyla still lives modestly in the same city and is happily married. On a whim she visits an upscale food store in an area of town currently being gentrified by the moneyed IBM crowd. An expensively dressed woman accosts Twyla using her first name. When Twyla doesn't recognize her, Roberta mimics their childhood experiences lampooning their former overseer as "The Big Bozo" in trying to connect with Twyla across time and diverging circumstances. Twyla has remained in the same town for two decades; she is very comfortable with her fireman husband and son. Roberta has recently moved to a nearby suburb, marrying a widower and adopting his four children, though she barely seems to know what her wealthy husband does for a living. Obviously impressed by Roberta's chauffeured car, Twyla exclaims, "Oh my. If the Big Bozo could see you now" (p. 252). Her matching allusion to this key figure from their shared past brings them happily into the present: "We both giggled. Really giggled. Suddenly, in just a pulse beat, twenty years disappeared and all of it came rushing back" (pp. 252–253). Indeed, an important task for friendship is making the passage of time between reunions disappear—standing outside of time. Pensively, Twyla continues:

> We went into the coffee shop holding on to one another and I tried to think why we were glad to see each other this time and not before. Once, twelve years ago, we passed like strangers. A black girl and a white girl meeting in a Howard Johnson's on the road and having nothing to say. One in a blue and white triangle waitress hat—the other on her way to see Hendrix. Now we were behaving like sisters separated for too long. Those four short months were nothing in time. Maybe it was the thing itself. Just being there, together. Two little girls who knew what nobody else in the world knew—how not to ask questions. How to believe what had to be believed. There was politeness in that reluctance and generosity as well. (p. 253)

What does "just being there, together" mean to these two women? How does their time together then and the intervening times bear upon their time together now? The women seemingly have to negotiate these questions during every encounter. Twyla reflects upon the presents of their onetime friendship—and "presents" has at least two intertwining meanings. As a span of time we live as an opening between the past and the future, it is our ongoing experience of now. It flees from us even as it tempts us with possibilities, and we fill it with our choices and experiences. Second, between friends a present is a gift—that which is being granted to us through the potentials and actualities of friendship. It can be an offering of oneself to another—a sharing of worlds.

As mere temporal intervals, "Those four short months were nothing in time." But the actual "being there, together" involved valued practices stemming from their shared sense of isolation and desires to be a self—to be someone who belonged somewhere. In these circumstances it was generous to respect each other's vulnerabilities, "to believe what had to be believed," and not to question or press for hurtful details from someone already experiencing enough scrutiny and pain. Within the confines of their shared exclusion such "politeness" allowed space and performed respect for each girl's important differences. Under these conditions sharing food and avoiding questions reflexively composed mutual unspoken understandings.

As a gift and a jointly lived span of time, friendship composes a presence in our lives. While we are experiencing it as thriving, it is unfinished, a story we are writing together. We don't think of it as ending while we are in it and feel the presence of a friend in our lives. When friends are separated, the memories of friendship become the substance of friendship. In recalling our shared moments individually, we each weave together the meanings of events that may be disconnected in time and certainly not all pleasant. How we do so together during any subsequent and unfolding "now" will shape the friendship's future possibilities.

The two women catch up on the intervening years. Treading lightly at first, they disagree about the time they saw Maggie, the kitchen worker, fall down at the orphanage. Twyla wants to revisit and clarify Roberta's brush-off of her at Howard Johnson's. Enveloping social discourses seem to cloud and color their recollections of the snub. Roberta attributes her actions to "how it was in those days: black—white. You know how everything was" (p. 255). But Twyla perceives those times in an opposite manner. From her vantage point in Howard Johnson's she saw "busloads of blacks and whites . . . students, musicians, lovers, protesters" traveling together. She recalls that "blacks were very friendly with whites in those days" (p. 255).

Each woman speaks in contrasting ways about how she viewed race relations at that time. In each case it is difficult to know for certain if she actually saw things that way then or instead has come to speak about those times now. What were Roberta and Twyla to each other during the unplanned encounter 12 years ago? How much were each woman's actions toward the other informed by the social currents that immersed them? And what kinds of allowances do their present circumstances offer their connection with each other? Dare we say their friendship? How different are these women? What do they share? As the women leave the coffee shop, they promise once again to stay in touch.

Their relationship is buffeted further by external forces when plans are announced to bus junior high schoolchildren between the inner city and the suburbs. Twyla narrates that "strife came to us that fall" (p. 255), begging the question, who is *us?* Is she speaking about her family or her race, whose children will be bussed to the suburbs? Is she referring to her connection with Roberta and its supposed standing as an interracial friendship, now repositioned in a larger network of palpable racial tensions? Or does this "us" more inclusively describe the greater metropolitan community?

The two women meet face-to-face when Twyla accidentally encounters Roberta picketing in protest at the nearby school slated for integration. A testy exchange ensues about the legitimacy of her actions with Roberta observing, "They want to take my kids and send them out of the neighborhood. They don't want to go." Twyla replies:

"So what if they go to another school? My boy's being bussed too, and I don't mind. Why should you?"

"It's not about us, Twyla. Me and you. It's about our kids."

"What's more *us* than that?" (p. 256, original emphasis)

At issue are the distinctiveness and interdependence of Twyla's and Roberta's actions and identities as individuals, friends, mothers, and members of different races and social classes. Also at stake is the very possibility of separating their friendship from a contemporary controversy involving their children. In this context who does each woman self-identify as and with? Who are they identifying each other as and with? What hierarchy of connections and divisions identify them as mothers but with opposing groups of mothers? Is it primarily a racial, ethnic, or socioeconomic class divide, or is it all three? Does their membership in these categories take precedence over their common identities as mothers? What bearing do their intermittent times and activities of friendship have upon their respective identities now? Can their friendship be individuated from their participation in family and political life without damaging its integrity?

A few seconds later Twyla initiates an exchange with Roberta who responds with identical language. Their words mark a crucial quandary in this would-be friendship's narrative:

"I wonder what made me think that you were different."

"I wonder what made me think that you were different." (p. 256)

What are these women saying to each other? There are multiple possible interpretations of their words, given the personal, social, and historically conditioned contexts of their relationship. Despite speaking identical words and their individual life circumstances, these women voice asymmetrical positions as raced beings in the United States. The black woman speaks from a historical position of oppression, the white woman from one of privilege and taken for granted opportunity. Their identical locutions are drenched in contrasting cultural histories always shaping in undeniable ways the bodies, beings, and meanings of the persons uttering them. As women and mothers, they unavoidably state contested "common differences" (Joseph & Lewis, 1981).

While acknowledging these cultural disparities that persist despite their identical words, other possible meanings arise. For one, spoken from the mists of childhood friendship and spawned by the present conflict, the "different" each woman wonders about here seems to imply a compliment. Yet rendered in the past tense, it suggests that this positive perception of difference no longer applies. Since both women state the same sentence, it appears to be a mutual recognition. Precisely how was or is each girl-now-woman "different"? We know from Bateson (1972) that difference is a relationship. It does not inhere in either person being compared and contrasted.

For me an array of possible differences is registered in the matching sentences, "I wonder what made me think that you were different." The possibilities include:

- You were different toward me than others of your race have been—a race of persons that I perceive as categorically different from me in ways I have not heretofore primarily identified as you.

- You were different from numerous types of people throughout my life who would judge and exclude me (and by extension those whom I care about). Poignant examples from our past are the real orphans, the older girls, and The Bozo.

- You were different from other persons I have known well because you were markedly excluded as a young girl, just as I was excluded.

- You were different from that generalized category of others in my life that I have not considered to be my friend, however briefly or long.

- Each and all of these differences made me think you were *different from others* in significant ways, which is to say *similar to me* in valued ways, or perhaps sharing an existential domain of appreciated similarity—enough so that I could identify with you, if only when we shared that mutual dwelling place.

These edifying differences individuating the other person also composed a basis for participating in friendship when joint circumstances enabled or perhaps compelled it. Consequently, each woman also may be saying:

- I thought you were different as in unique, singular, one-of-a-kind in my life. You were different in the sense that you understood I felt that way about you and that I understood you felt that way about me.

- I thought you were different in that you defy easy categorization and that you in turn allowed me to defy categorization. This mutual perception of singularity was unspoken.

- Perhaps I initially thought you were different *now* from whom you once were—now a mature woman with a past shared with me who is able to engage *this* trying present with courage and an understanding of who we have been together, are now, and can be together, that is, as friends.

- Perhaps I thought you were even "the wholly other," which Benhabib deems "a regulative principle of hope" (1995, p. 30). I thought that knowing you would allow me to become someone totally different from who I was before I met you. You would give me a chance to transcend the limitations of my life. Perhaps your difference would even allow us to rise above the racial divisions of this moment.

What does it mean that each woman expresses this complex array of possible recognitions ambiguously as a statement that can be heard as a question? As she speaks, is she realizing that she thought these differences from others were valid and now believes they are not? Does this realization find her admitting that she (may have) incorrectly perceived ways in which her former friend was different from others and therefore similar to herself? Perhaps she now identifies the other woman as just like those various categorical others and consequently significantly different from her own self? Could it be that she was wrong ever to have identified with her? These questions emphasize that we are always in a process of self-formation vis-à-vis others. Constrained by stratified cultural moments, we reflexively construct the relevant selves and the relevant others—who we are identifying with and who we are self-identifying as.

At another level, they *both* make this exact same statement about possibly misperceiving the other woman as significantly different from others and therefore as being a kindred spirit. As such, they are participating in a moment of mutual realization *and* disappointment (which possibly embodies for each of them any or all of the unspoken ambiguities mentioned here). To compound matters, if this is a disappointment, it is a disappointment based on a previously held regard, a keenly important array of identifications-with. As such, it is a moment of identically worded statements freighted with paradox.

So Twyla and Roberta may also be saying to each other:

- In wondering what made *me* think *you* were different, I am simultaneously meditating about myself in the past and the present, you in the past and the present, and our relationship to each other in the past and the present. How was it that our differences constituted a basis for identifications with each other during these stretches of time? How were we able to participate in sporadic times together as friends?

Moreover, Twyla and Roberta are making this statement right now, thereby ironically performing profound similarities and bases for identification with each other under intense social pressures and scrutiny. In a sense they are saying:

- We know we have changed and grown apart in ways that probably cannot be transcended except in our shared recognition of the meaning of this moment. But do our present racially charged circumstances and identifications prevent our acknowledging this fact and therefore preempt our friendship?

Twyla tries to get Roberta to stand with her by identifying the other protesting women as "Bozos" (p. 257). Both women have used this reference in the past to connect. This figure embodies joint oppression in the orphanage and a basis for identification with each other transcending this situation. Subverting the allusion, Roberta looks at Twyla "out of some refrigerator behind her eyes" and says, "No, they're not. They're just mothers" (p. 257). From Roberta's standpoint, they are not oppressors; they are *just* mothers, a word that simultaneously connotes "merely" mothers and "fair-minded" mothers. In identifying them *as* such mothers, is she identifying *with* them? Do these identifications exclude Twyla? When the women begin to rock Twyla's car, she reaches out for Roberta, who fails to grasp Twyla's hand as she would have when others threatened them in the orphanage. Contemporary events reveal their once loyal bond to be a thing of the past. The women part angrily, their discourse reduced to name-calling, their times spent together unmasked as coincidences determined by larger forces than themselves and not by their choices as friends.

Toni Morrison's story about Twyla and Roberta's relationship dramatizes the jagged edges and contextual susceptibilities of a would-be cross-race friendship. Dumped together at the orphanage, the two girls' racial differences are less significant than their shared segregation and joint rejection of other persons in defining their friendship. Growing older in contrasting social circumstances, they experience limited opportunities to compose shared lives and identities. Interacting more by chance than choice, they only intermittently and accidentally recognize their mutual significance in the story of each woman's life. Yet their face-to-face encounters depict the ongoing salience of negotiated memories and stories between former friends. How memories are shared and contested over time has much to say about the identities that are permitted to flourish within relationships. Twyla and Roberta's friendship seems unable to transcend the patterning of racial divides outside the shelter of the orphanage. Altered social positions magnify their differences over the years and become lived bases for exclusion despite their shared history as friends. Their "salt and pepper" (p. 244) childhood friendship seemingly must answer to the comprehensive social stratification of raced relationships in North American culture.

❖   BLACKS AND WHITES ENGAGING IN FRIENDSHIPS:
    ASYMMETRICAL CHALLENGES AND EDIFYING PRACTICES

If structural conditions and individual initiatives do engender cross-racial friendships, members continually must address a complex array of deeply ingrained existential outlooks and social practices at odds with friendship. A history of slavery, economic exploitation, and servitude composes a caustic backdrop for cross-race relationships between blacks and whites in the United States. Consequently, negotiating viable cross-race friendship requires continually overcoming historical injustices and contemporary conditions divergently articulating participants' subject positions. From the outset, most whites and blacks experience contrasting awareness of racialized consciousness. By and large white persons have difficulties even seeing themselves as racialized beings. Speaking of white women, for example, Frankenberg (1993) described power-evasive practices of white privilege, which allow them to sidestep the distresses of dealing with real differences. Without full awareness such persons live an ideology of white denial that wants to preserve illusions of equality, the comforting myth for systematically advantaged persons concerning material and social conditions that "we all are in the same boat" (DeMott, 1995).

In contrast, black persons have had to be cognizant of racial markings and barriers. As the dominant majority, whites are an ineluctable part of the generalized other of black persons. They constitute a judgmental, demanding, and denigrating audience lodged in black consciousness in tandem with the very awareness of being black. At the turn of the last century, Du Bois (1903/1997) described this "dual consciousness" and acute vision emerging from the standpoint of "radical marginality" in the unfavorable juxtaposition with (white) America (Unger, 2000). Hall and Fine (2005) argue, "The externalization of the self via the assumptions and stereotypes of the majority culture created a distorted self-perception, painting a people of compromised abilities and aptitude" (p. 177). Meanwhile, despite demeaning treatment by this dominant other, developing "dual consciousness" allows blacks simultaneously to take pride in their own cultural heritage (Hall & Fine, 2005). Most whites have not faced the same injunctions to know their race and relative place in order to recognize themselves. At the same time, this fundamental existential privilege of unencumbered and unprovoked racial self-recognition is taken for granted by most whites and only realized in consciousness-producing situations of racial and cultural contrast (if then).

For example, I once asked a class of predominantly white students about the race of the person they assumed they were addressing when they visited a new Web site or chat room on the Internet. Whom did they envision themselves addressing? All of the white students *and* the black student stated they imagined they were addressing a white person, to everyone's surprise except the one person of color in the class. When we then listed our favorite sites to visit on the Internet, the white students were further astonished (while the black student was not) that there was virtually no overlap between their own and the black student's sites. Popularly held conceptions, that is, myths, of an Internet oblivious to the races of its users transmuted into yet another stratified reminder of unreflectively assumed white domains by white people. In contrast, it is always necessary for persons with less power and/or in the minority to be watchful. McCullough (1998) states, "Whites knew and know little about Blacks by comparison; this is a necessary component in the dehumanization process that permits racial oppression." She continues, "The negotiation of this particular tension, both in celebrating differences and in struggling with the legacy of pain they represent leaves us with important communicative issues not found in other diverse friendships" (p. 160). Differences in positionality and their resulting subjectivities must be addressed on ongoing bases by cross-racial friends.

Thus, one of the first tasks facing any attempt at cross-racial friendship is to acknowledge the presence of racism informing their relations, that everyone is potentially racist (Smith & Nickerson, 1986). The closely related second task according to cross-race friends and co-authors Althea Smith and Stephanie Nickerson is "to realize that racism takes different forms" (1986, p. 15) in the everyday lives of blacks and whites. Asymmetrical perceptions abound. Black racism involves loathing whites and can involve self-loathing displayed by accepting mistreatment from whites and distancing oneself from other blacks. Blacks view whites stereotypically as exploitative, condescending, mostly insincere, and untrustworthy. On their parts, whites presume their superiority over blacks as well as black inferiority—a stance doubly degrading for blacks (Smith & Nickerson, 1986). Unexamined awareness of these perceptions manifests itself as "White guilt and Black shame" (McCullough, 1998, p. 161).

As already noted, the internal landscape of black indignity is complexly wrought through dual consciousness, the "simultaneously objective and subjective life experience of being both inside and outside of the dominant group—that is, on the margin" (Hall & Fine, 2005, p. 177). The disparaging gaze of white persons is always already part of how blacks see themselves as they exchange words and looks with whites in actual interaction. Whereas whites believe they can take actions to expiate their guilt and moral discomfort, black shame derives from viewing oneself as inherently flawed (McCullough, 1998). Further, due to lives of relative advantage, it is easier for most whites to assume the potential for benevolence toward themselves on the part of others. This attitude is essential for forming friendships, however unfounded it may be with respect to blacks. Routinely oppressed and excluded by a white world, it is easier for blacks to assume malevolence on the part of whites, a stance inimical to friendship. These contrasting stances are magnified by persistently lopsided sociocultural affordances and barriers (DeMott, 1995).

Meanwhile, blacks know considerably more about whites than the reverse, further complicating the possibility of comparable orientations toward friendship. Black persons have had to develop such knowledge due to the demands of dwelling simultaneously in both white and black worlds. Most white persons only need to understand and live in a white world. This reality was dramatically performed by a black student in an undergraduate course I taught a few years ago about friendship. After reading the assigned chapters on children's friendships from my first book, she disagreed with my discussion of the age-related achievement of reciprocal perspective-taking skills often considered essential for the mature negotiation of friendship by children. Associating its emerging accomplishment by 9- and 10-year-olds, I had written:

> Such perspective-taking ability is necessary for children to pursue a "two-way" approach to friendship, whereby the friends coordinate and adjust their actions in an attempt to fulfill or reconcile each other's expectations, rather than either friend simply assuming that the other should live up to his/her own standards. (Rawlins, 1992, p. 31)

The student observed that this depiction simply did not apply to her experiences growing up as a black child in a white neighborhood. She reflected that as far back as she could remember—and certainly much younger than 9 or 10—she was comprehensively aware of being observed and perceived as different by white people and needing to adapt her behaviors and speech to their expectations. She had to be able to judge her own actions from a white person's perspective regardless of whether they could or would adopt hers. Only when she returned home could she relax, even though she was also careful to drop the airs and distinctive enunciations of white talk required outside around her own family.

During the ensuing class discussion I remarked on how eye-opening her observations were for me and how importantly they contradicted the normative presuppositions and cultural limitations of developmental theories. After class I complimented her again on her candor in helping us recognize the inaccuracies in my book and thanked her for transforming my understanding of these issues in such a compelling manner. I encouraged her to share all such perceptions with us in the class when she noticed them. While it wasn't necessarily her primary intention, she taught me another significant lesson. She said, "I probably won't do that because I am weary of having to make white professors and students aware of so many issues of black experience in most of my classes. I would rather focus on the material I need to learn than on having to teach these issues over and over." Acknowledging this second epiphany for me, I encouraged her to participate in whatever ways were meaningful for her learning and engagement with our course material. I thanked her for alerting me to this pedagogical responsibility that I was unreflectively foisting on her. Cross-race friends also must avoid such an asymmetrical requirement for the black person to educate the white person about the truths of their cultural world, in Audre Lorde's words, "to bridge the gap between the actualities of our lives and the consciousness of our oppressor" (Lorde, 1984, p. 114).

A crucial third task for cross-race friends is to confront together the implicit obligations and privileges pre-woven unequally into the tenuous threads of emerging friendship. Within the web of misgivings and asymmetrical perceptions described above, our talk is further hampered by the fact that both of our identities are reflexively implicated in our discourse about the issues at hand. Each of us understands our identity largely in light of the same racialized structures and discourses that our friendship hopes to transcend. We can't address our differences apart from our individuated embodiment and performances of them. In doing so we risk conveying misplaced pride, oblivion, resentment, stereotypical associations, and/or hypocrisy. As a result, unfounded presumptions of similarity by white persons as de facto members of the dominant cultural group may find them unconsciously assimilating black persons' experiences and denying radically different experiences of shared situations. Or whites may exaggerate their differences from black persons based on their white privileged outlooks and overcompensate for their own guilt by consciously accommodating blacks in ways of speaking or actions that ironically reinforce these misperceptions of differences or lack of commonalities. Black persons may attempt to carry themselves in ways that minimize their distinctive qualities to assimilate with white practices, making accommodations in speech patterns or activities to resemble the dominant culture and sacrificing crucial bases for self-recognition in the process.

Whether it is one- or two-sided, too much assimilation or accommodation mutes the differences that animate edifying individuation and inspiriting participation in cross-race friendship. A vital ongoing practice in pursuing friendship is to recognize and accept one's own and the other's differences as a concrete basis for connection. Neither person's worldview should serve as the privileged benchmark or scapegoat. One gift of friendship is to be perceived by our friends in ways that confirm our sense of self. A friend must be seen as a singular person—neither reduced to a token of race nor expanded into a nondescript representative of the human condition. Audre Lorde (1984) remarked, "Too often, we pour the energy needed for recognizing and exploring differences into pretending those differences are insurmountable barriers, or that they do not exist at all. This results in voluntary isolation, or false and treacherous connections" (p. 533).

Such "voluntary isolation" derives from the Primary Misperception of Individuation, exaggerating the significance of our differences and refusing to regard *this* black or white person *as* a total person. At the same time, denying the existence of important differences enacts the Primary Misperception of Participation, overlooking the salience of the other's contrasting experiences. It is crucial to see our cross-race friends as persons just as we are persons *and* as different from themselves and us in meaningful ways. As one of Mary McCullough's interviewed black participants in a cross-race friendship stated, "You have to like me *and* the fact that I am different from you. Not just one or the other" (1998, p. 165). For authentic friendship we all must retain our self-recognizing identities.

Such practices are evident in Althea Smith's expectations for a good cross-race friendship, "I would rather have friends who are comfortable in their own ethnic identity and are not trying to take over mine. At the same time, I prefer friends who appreciate and celebrate my differentness and don't forget I'm black" (Smith & Nickerson, 1986, p. 16). Such outlooks foster edifying individuation. She also describes experiencing equal treatment, reciprocated candor, and the absence of condescension for being black as requirements for cross-race friendship. Her friend and co-author Stephanie Nickerson in turn desires "tolerance for my white mistakes, my interpersonal cultural blunders. I want an attitude of 'Let's explore racial issues together.'" (p. 16). She also wants acceptance "as a white person" (p. 16). Both women's expectations involve reflexive accomplishments in cross-race friendships in which the means for addressing each other and transcending enculturated outlooks simultaneously presuppose those outlooks. Dialectically, this situation constitutes ongoing challenges.

## ❖ RECOGNIZING MEANINGFULLY WHOLE PERSONS AND CONTINGENT IDENTITIES

Cross-race friends understand that our respective identities involve multiple facets whose meanings are never permanent and may be constrained, subverted, or enabled across contexts. Our identities further shift specifically in relation to each other. Each of us occupies sites of intersecting differences with respect to others and the situations we face. These differences include race, gender, ethnicity, sexual identity, socioeconomic status, abilities, and talents. Commonly held situations may highlight these characteristics as well as numerous other personally and culturally emphasized attributes. Despite contrasting, potentially fragmenting aspects, we can respond to our friends and ourselves as meaningfully integrated wholes. Confirming responses arising in moments spent together foster edifying individuation. When a trusted friend dignifies our holistic experience of our self as a decisive agent in the face of contrasting situational demands, it facilitates our sense of personal integrity.

Our self concepts, our overall image of ourselves, compose an ongoing confluence of the multiple roles or identities we perform in relational contexts (Villard & Whipple, 1976). These various identities can be described in four ways (Villard & Whipple, 1976). First is the *saliency* of the identity. How central or important is this identity in composing our overall self-concept? How crucial is this identity to our self-recognition? Certainly racial identity may become especially salient in a situation when we are conspicuously in the minority. Despite its potentially contingent effects, experiencing our racial identity as a and perhaps *the* salient feature of our identity is far more common for black persons than white persons in North American culture. In contrast, the unacknowledged salience of whiteness for white persons derives from its unmarked omnipresence. Nonetheless, the racial identities of friends may shift in salience across circumstances.

The second aspect is the *stability* of the identity. How much support or confirmation from others do we require to sustain a specific identity as a significant part of our self-concept? Alternatively, how rigidly is this identity imposed and enforced by others? Individuals take certain identities for granted, for example, the privileges of a white person or constraints in being black. It requires significant and/or persistent interactions with others to unseat such understandings of self—and it ultimately may require social change. By comparison, we may need considerable support from others to sustain our identity as a singer, administrator, or thinker, while requiring little confirmation from others for our math abilities or religious convictions. Meanwhile, our identity as an administrator or as a person of faith may be a highly salient identity for us regardless of the amount of support from others needed to sustain it.

Third is the *valence* of the identity. How positive or negative is this identity for us? Being black or white has changing valences across the social situations of one's life. Even so, what is the overall valence of racial identity in composing our identity? Is it a comprehensive source of pride or shame? How is the valence developed, sustained or altered? Concerning more activity-based identities, what is the primary valence of our identity as a teacher, mother, father, administrator, wage laborer, or math whiz? To what extent do we experience these as positive or negative identities? What circumstances or relationships promote these experiences?

The *utility* of our identity is a final consideration. How congruent is this identity with our short-term and/or long-term goals in specific situations? For example, how useful is it to perform a role as a "results-oriented administrator with little patience" in a situation demanding careful attention to the nuances of another's story about an emotional, tangential matter? What are the administrator's short- and long-term goals here? Some of us are willing to suffer short-term affronts to a salient identity in the interests of longer term or broadly relevant goals. *The salience, stability, valence, and utility of the multiple identities composing our always contingent self-concepts remain subject to relational and situational determinations* (Villard & Whipple, 1976).

What aspects of our identities do friends highlight as significant? What experiences are shared, witnessed, and confirmed between friends? What differences separate and what commonalities connect us? In cross-race dyads McCullough remarked upon "a balance of friendships holding some parts of the self as shared and validated and some parts that are to be explored as different and subsequently understood and possibly appreciated" (1998, p. 84). The dialectic of judgment and acceptance (Rawlins, 1992) critically frames such discursive activities between cross-race friends. Airing significant differences provides a basis for accepting each other's actions and outlooks on that person's terms in light of the specific tradition of meanings shaping them. Even in this accepting context, the necessity for judgment of friends by friends may arise. In judging a friend, a chief risk is to apply inappropriately our own standards. Yet there is also the risk of not using our vantage point as a differently cultured and raced other constructively when the situation warrants it. Disconfirmation is embodied in our reluctance to judge honestly a friend, suggesting we do not take our friend seriously enough to judge him or her.

Our distance and difference from the friend, our familiarity with cultural circumstances alien to our friend may underwrite the potential value of our evaluation. Cross-race friends wish each other well for their own sakes from significantly different yet mutually respected subject positions. Accordingly, we may develop together nuanced standards and appropriate times to apply them based on negotiating our distinctive worlds. Compassionate objectivity may emerge through enduring events in the world, growing older, doing things together, and discussing our reactions to incidents and the reactions of others. In doing so, we must remain attuned to asymmetrical oversights born of unquestioned privileges, habitual deference, arrogance, and anger—differing power and points of view across diverse cultural settings.

In these pursuits co-constructing personal narratives are crucial resources and pleasures of friendship. Telling and carefully listening to stories is a vital way to learn about each other across cultural divides. When we narrate our own experiences, our friends have the opportunity to perceive us in the contexts of our own life stories as opposed to categorically. Taken for granted features and normative coordinates of social life give way to the details our friend relates as significant. Stories enable us to identify viscerally with our narrating friend's embodied experience of intersecting structural conditions. Leveling abstractions vanish. Gone is the blithe assumption of similarity when a white person hears first-hand about vividly contrasting experiences of oppressive conditions and prejudice from a black friend. Gone is the blanket stance of righteous indignation when a black person hears a white friend relate unsettling accounts of vulnerability to violence and injustice.

Reciprocal, mutual storytelling shapes and reflects dialogue between friends. Our stories can compose instructive moments in the ongoing dialogue of our relationship. They dramatize fundamental differences but also important similarities in our life experiences. Meanwhile, this ongoing dialogue addressing the moments of our lives also helps constitute an emerging co-authored story of our friendship. Our individual stories feed our dialogue, and our dialogue together nourishes the evolving story of our friendship. Such exchanges attest to racially aligned possibilities and impediments from the inside out as well as the outside in across private and public circumstances. Friends externalize, objectivate, name, and own issues through listening and sharing stories in their dialogues together versus unmindfully taking them for granted. If either friend accommodates too much to the other's worldview, both lose the chance of witnessing genuine differences in concrete experiences and outlooks. By resisting pretenses of empathy, friends achieve heightened awareness of our contrasting lives as well as our jointly humanizing consciousness.

No learning of consequence occurs within cross-race friendships without changes in the persons involved—and there is no meaningful change in people without integrating new knowledge into our lives. Active learning with friends promotes confidence to self-reflect and provides the relational context to try to live differently and become noticeably different persons. Cross-race friendship provides a forgiving space to learn, practice, and hear ourselves addressing issues of deep personal and political concern that divide and alienate people. McCullough maintains, "There is an active learning process that is ongoing and involving appreciation for the self and the other in these friendships" (1998, p. 166). Even so, she observes importantly that "not all learning is positively viewed and incorporated into the friendship as a new and wonderful thing; some differences are noted and respected, but not necessarily liked by the partners" (1998, p. 167). This is the space and freedom of friendship; we don't have to be the same people to be valued. We can still value each other without agreeing with or liking everything about each other.

While we continue to teach our friends about our respective worlds through our actions and discourse, it is neither friend's sole responsibility to educate the other or to be converted wholesale to that way of thinking. We must remain mindful of the ways in which contrasting worldviews show up in our discourse. Unlearning racism is a lifelong project (McCullough, 1998). Cross-race friends must continually address encrusted structures perpetuating white privilege and black discontent. In Laing's words, "Unless we can 'see through' the rules, we can only see through them" (1972, p. 105). The ongoing challenge is to perceive each other as a provisionally complete and integrated being, a meaningfully whole self performed in this situation with (an)other self. Each person's identity is simultaneously being constituted in this moment as a potentially skewed intersection of cultural discourses *and* in relationship to the friend.

In this process, friends regard each other in ways that encourage an integration of self with respect to the contingencies and risks of the moment at hand. There are pronounced differences between a dispiriting gaze and an affirming regard. In our workaday life we may perceive someone as objectified pieces, functions, and disconnected parts in light of our specific needs in situations. In friendship we regard someone as a whole person from the standpoint of our own activated personhood in the context of a co-evolving narrative. A mutual endeavor of living in friendship is for each person to perceive and be perceived as a meaningful yet contingent whole—a provisionally complete human being open to unfolding possibilities.

## ❖ ACCOMPLISHING CROSS-RACE FRIENDSHIP

**Nathan's Story**

Nathan McCall devotes a chapter of his autobiography, *Makes Me Wanna Holler: A Young Black Man in America* (1994), to the story of his friendship with a white man, Danny Baum. Routine encounters, as well as conscious efforts by both parties, are necessary to achieve their relationship. He describes meeting Danny when the latter joins the newsroom of *The Atlanta Journal–Constitution* and occupies a reporter's desk near Nathan's. Initially wary, but nonetheless curious about Danny due to his genuine friendliness, Nathan observes him closely for several weeks to get a better bead on him and what he is about. Nathan decides there is "something different" (p. 333) about Danny. He is forthright, exhibiting an unselfconscious "childlike honesty" that Nathan does not experience "with most other white people" (p. 333). The positive ways Danny differs from other whites are refreshing. Talking with him further while on the job, Nathan notes they have arrived at similar conclusions about "the white mainstream" (p. 333) and the corporate rat race in America. They share disdain for those who posture and pander to the newspaper's management. He is impressed when Danny demonstrates the courage of his convictions by violating company policy and participating in a public protest against racism in the predominantly black district where Danny lives.

Later, Danny invites Nathan for dinner on the weekend. Choosing to do things together that are not required constitutes a significant precursor to and practice of friendship. Such an invitation to behave as possible friends always risks rejection. And indeed Nathan is reluctant to spend time with white people outside of the compulsory interactions with them shrouding his life. He reflects, "Thinking about it, even *considering* spending my free weekend time at a white person's house, was a major leap for me" (p. 334). Deciding to go, he enjoys the evening with Danny and Danny's girlfriend Meg and notices distinctive qualities of their conversation with him. Nathan reflects:

> I didn't feel like Danny and Meg were judging me by their standards all the time. They didn't pretend there were no differences between us, like everybody else I knew. They celebrated our differences, and we joked about contrasts in the way blacks and whites talked, cooked, dressed, danced, and everything else. (p. 334)

The evening's exchanges lay the foundation for engaging together authentically in the dialectic of judgment and acceptance across racial

differences. Reconciling the interconnected bases for judging and accepting one another is an important ongoing challenge in robust friendships
(Rawlins, 1992). For one thing, Danny and Meg do not commit the
Primary Misperception of Participation and assume that their standards
apply to Nathan's world. There is no pretense at color-blindness. The
myth of sameness between races may be well-meaning in given cases but
also can function as a disguised basis for ethnocentric judgments perpet-
uated by some members of a dominant white culture when it serves their
interests. The three persons acknowledge and even spoof selective differences that matter in shaping their respective cultural experiences. They
foster edifying individuation on each other's parts. Soon after, Nathan
reciprocates the invitation. Danny and Meg meet Nathan's wife and children and take pleasure in dinner and an extended evening of animated
conversation with Nathan and Debbie. Nathan remarks they are the first
"white people" (p. 335) his family has ever entertained at their home.

Danny and Nathan choose to do more things together inside and
outside of work. Like many emerging friends they develop offbeat
nicknames for each other. They continue to discuss issues of race at
length. Without apology they raise tough questions and express personal perspectives about whites and blacks that take each of them
beyond stereotypical assumptions. Danny's ignorance about Nathan's
anger for being reminded of his race every day at every turn and
Nathan's inability to fathom Danny's privileged life without racial constraints are repeatedly addressed. In doing so, they straightforwardly
develop better informed judgments about each other based on growing
acceptance of both their unique backgrounds and common aspirations.
Making efforts to learn is what friends do. Nathan considers:

> Danny was the first white person I met whom I actually saw trying
> hard to understand. It meant a lot to me that he tried because he
> wanted to and not because he had to. By the same token, he helped
> me see the world through white eyes and helped me better
> understand the fear and ignorance behind prejudice. (p. 337)

Devoting the effort to understand others of different races, ethnicities, and cultures on their own terms in a spirit of good will is exercising the will to friendship. Nathan closes his narrative with personal
recognition tinged with societal regret observing about Danny and
Meg, "Of all the white people I know, they are among the very few I
can call friends. It's sad, this gulf between blacks and whites" (p. 339).
This autobiographical narrative depicts shared exercise of the will to
friendship with particular others, to engage differently raced and
cultured consciousnesses in forming personal cross-race friendship.

To hear the voices of actual pairs of cross-race friends, we turn now to a brace of interviews made available to me by a colleague. One interview involves two female and the other two male friends. Undergraduate students conducted these interviews with the participants, who granted informed consent that their words may be used in my published work with their identities protected. I am especially grateful to be able to listen to and learn from both parties in a friendship, instead of only hearing one person's perspective as often occurs with interview discourse. These two conversations feature the friends speaking together with a peer, giving them added richness and vitality.

In presenting these interviews I acknowledge the distressing images of inner city black life in the United States that appear in them. In that sense the two black participants' life circumstances displayed here could be read as reproducing negative stereotypes of African Americans although that is not my intention in sharing their words. While both persons are college students, they come from single parent households. The young black woman became a single mother during her later teen years. The young black man's older brother was murdered in drug-related circumstances, and he plays basketball in college on scholarship as a way out of the ghetto. I present their candidly offered words as embodying their individually lived experiences. I witness and share their stories respectfully as performing their perspectives from their singular lives—yet I do so also in a spirit of social critique. These young persons' accounts personify the deeply troubling statistical social structural patterns associated with blacks and whites in the United States. There are persistent, striking disparities in income and educational opportunities (Ohlemacher, 2007), and a greater likelihood of black children being raised in single parent homes ("Shifting Attitudes," 2007). Homicide is the leading cause of death for black men 15 to 34 years old in contrast to the third cause for white males in the same age range (Heron, 2004).

Recognizing the abundant insights their discourse provides, I present extended unedited excerpts here (except for using pseudonyms and altering other identifying factors) with only interspersed commentary.

## Felmonia and Tina

*Mindy:*    Thank you for agreeing to sit down and talk to me about the friendship you have with each other. I guess we can start by giving a little information on each of your backgrounds, like where your hometown is, your age, and what you are currently doing with your life.

*Felmonia:*    As you can see I am an African American female and I am twenty-one years old. I am currently a college student. I attend Temple University in Philadelphia, which is pretty far away from where I grew up. I grew up in New York City. I would say I grew up in a bad neighborhood. My senior year of high school right after graduation, I had a baby. I named him Felmon. I am not currently with the father of the baby anymore or with anyone else at the present time. My baby lives at home in New York with my mom while I am going to college, which is hard but I manage. My parents are divorced and I don't really talk to my dad that much. I actually only see him about twice a year. I have one sister named Kayla.

*Mindy:*    How about your background, Tina?

*Tina:*    I am a Caucasian female and I am also twenty-one years old. I still live in Brooklyn, which was where I grew up. I never moved once. I am currently attending Brooklyn College and I am in my fourth year, but I am not going to graduate just yet. I had a little trouble majoring in accounting so I decided to change my major to history. I am good at writing. My parents are still together and I have one brother who is a senior in high school this year.

*Mindy:*    How did you meet each other and when did you meet each other?

*Tina:*    I met Felmonia in my freshman year of high school at Bishop Ford in Brooklyn. We met through cheerleading. She was my first black friend. I loved her when I first met her. I thought she was the funniest most down to earth person I have ever met. She was different than the friends I had and she was definitely louder!

*Felmonia:*    Yeah, just like Tina said, we met through cheerleading in high school. When I met Tina, she was this little perky white girl with a long ponytail. She definitely wasn't like my other friends. All the friends I had from grade school were pretty much just like me. They were either African American or Puerto Rican. One thing I loved about her is she came out of her group in cheerleading and started talking to me. Tina and her friends were white, would be in one group during practice and me and like two other African American girls would be in another group. I mean, don't get me wrong, they were never mean to us or anything, there was definitely no hostility, but Tina went beyond just saying hello to me. She actually started talking with my friends and I more often at practice and during school hours. During lunch in the cafeteria, we started sitting at each other's tables. It was cool. I'm glad I met her! I'm glad we met Tina!

*Tina:*       Aw, me too!

*Mindy:*      You guys are so cute. Okay, well when you first started hanging out with each other outside of cheerleading and school hours, were your friends accepting of this, because you both had said you were pretty much friendly with mostly people of your same race?

*Tina:*       I can remember the first time I asked Felmonia to come out with me and my friends where we hung out. Felmonia got a ride to my house and then we both went out together to meet up with my other friends. They knew I had invited her out with us. They were definitely nice to Felmonia, but it was almost like they were jealous or mad that I had brought someone out who wasn't in our group of friends. It was almost like, 'Who are you to bring someone out to hang out with us? That isn't cool. Are we not good enough for you?' That was the impression I received even though I know that isn't what they were trying to act like. That is just the way my friends were. To answer your question, I guess you could say that they were accepting of Felmonia, but I don't think they were happy about me trying to include Felmonia in our group of friends. Let me tell you something, my group of friends actually gave ourselves a name. We called ourselves, "The Emeralds," which is ridiculous. We were extremely cliquey.

*Felmonia:*   Yea, I think my friends were accepting of Tina, but I don't think that they wanted me to bring Tina out. They looked at her as like a stuck-up white girl, even though she is not! It was hard to please my friends though. It didn't help the fact that all my friends were in the Pep Squad, which was like a rival of the cheerleading team. I think they were actually mad at me for wanting to be on the cheerleading team. Whatever, I did what I wanted to do and I don't care what people think about me. I was also on the Pep Squad, but that is beside the point. I think my friends accepted the fact that I wasn't going to not be friends with someone just because they were white or of some other race than African American. That is one of the reasons why I loved Tina. She didn't care if her friends were all about sticking in their emerald group or whatever they called themselves, she was going to be friends with who she wanted to be friends with.

When they met through cheerleading 8 years earlier, Tina and Felmonia were immediately attracted to ways each other differed from friends of her own race. Both young women say their existing friends were "accepting" of the other during their initial efforts to befriend this girl of another race. This acceptance seems superficial, however, since they also describe their friends' thinly disguised resistance to having a cross-race student join their exclusive groups. Felmonia was especially impressed that Tina made the effort to emerge from "just saying hello" with her segregated, arrogantly self-named group and "actually" begin talking with her. Both girls chose to eat at each other's tables in the cafeteria and to hang out together beyond overlapping school activities. Felmonia celebrates their determination to become friends despite the judgments of their respective racial in-groups.

*Mindy:*    I know that you both attend college and that you both attend colleges that are quite a bit away from each other. You have obviously kept in touch over these past four years of college but is it hard on your friendship, and does it put a strain on your friendship in any way?

*Tina:*    Considering the fact that I still live at home, and Felmonia goes to college in Philadelphia, our friendship has definitely changed over the last four years. It is different than the friendship we had in high school, different in a good way though. It made us realize that we can go off and do our separate things but we always will be there for one another no matter the distance between us. Even though Felmonia may be away at school, I still go over and visit little Felmon and Felmonia's mom. We got so close that she is like my second mom.

*Felmonia:*    I know for me, our friendship only got stronger over the past four years. Tina knows that even though I am away at school I will always come home to visit with her. I've met people here at college but the friendships I have with them aren't really like the friendship I have with Tina. Me and Tina know each other so well that it would be hard to find someone who relates to me better. We have been friends this long, I don't think now is the time to stop being friends.

Both women celebrate the positive changes in their friendship during their college years. Their accounts reflect their cherished exchange of the "conjunctive freedoms" that are vitally important in ongoing close friendships across life (Rawlins, 1983b, 1992). On one hand, they exercise their freedom to be independent, respecting each other's differing life choices and circumstances. At the same time, they perform their freedom to be dependent, continuing to grow closer through ongoing voluntary visits with each other, including Tina's with Felmonia's mother and child while she is away at school.

*Mindy:*     Has anything stuck out about the differences in race between you two?

*Felmonia:*   Well Tina's house has a lot of chandeliers and mirrors. I think it might be an Italian thing. I'm not very sure. Just kidding. In relation to our friendship compared to my friendships with my African American friends, I have noticed a slight difference. If I have a problem with a boy, I like to go to Tina for advice. She seems to listen to both sides of the story, referring to my side and the boy's side. My African American friends will automatically say, 'Dump him, he's a dog!' Tina is more open to listening rather than jumping in right away with some advice. I just feel more comfortable talking to Tina.

*Tina:*     Felmonia tends to tell me the honest truth more than my other white friends. She doesn't simply tell me what she thinks I want to hear. She will actually tell me I look stupid in this outfit if she thinks I look stupid. My other friends will most likely let me go out of the house looking like a total freak! I like that about Felmonia. She helps me to be more like that as well, which is something I want to be. I want to be able to speak my mind more often than not and she encourages me to do just that.

Felmonia celebrates Tina's ability "to listen to both sides of the story" in contrast with her other friends' knee jerk reactions to problems with men. On her part, Tina values the candor she has experienced and is learning from Felmonia in contrast with her other friends. The two women seem to have developed shared conversational practices that transcend those of their prior friendships.

Mindy:      I just want to maybe talk about the fact that you are a mother Felmonia. I was just curious if that has any effect on your friendship with Tina.

Tina:       I think if Felmonia had the baby when she was a fresh-man in high school, we might not have been friends due to the fact that she might have stopped going to school to take care of the baby or something like that. She had the baby at the end of the senior year of high school. It was actually right after we graduated. If anything, I think it brought us closer because I help her out a lot whenever she needs me to. I see her more than I might if she didn't have a baby. I think we have different priorities that come first. For example, Felmonia has school and Felmon to think about. I just have school that is my number one pri-ority right now. Felmonia does well with balancing it all out.

Felmonia:   I think that Felmon has changed some things in my life, but for the better. He opened my eyes up to reality and I see things differently. I love all the people in my life who have been there to support me through that. Having a baby at an early age is not an easy thing. Tina has been there to help me out with so much along with my mom. Although one night when Tina will be out hanging out with friends, I may be in with Felmon when I am home from school, it doesn't matter. Our friendship is still strong. If anything he makes it stronger.

Mindy:      Are there any other things you want to add?

Felmonia:   I just want to add that I think all people should try to become friends with someone of a different race. You can learn so much from someone who is different from your-self. If you stay around people who are the same as you that is all you come to know.

Tina:       Well said. If you meet people different from you, you come to an understanding of things as a whole rather than just seeing things your way.

Both women celebrate the differences and caring connections composing their lives as friends. Beyond their racial and cultural differences, addressing their contrasting salient identities and life exigencies with Felmonia a single mother and Tina childless has strengthened their friendship as they each attend college. Both believe that they have gained significantly more encompassing perspectives on life through being involved cross-race friends.

We turn now to Tim's conversation with Brad and Tyrone.

## Brad and Tyrone

Tim:      Well, first of all let me ask you guys individually what was it like growing up? Like what was the demographic of your neighborhoods? What were your homes like? And what did your parents do?

Brad:     My school was predominately white. As a matter of fact, there were only like a total of 10 black kids out of my school of 1500. My dad owns his own construction company and my mom teaches elementary school. We weren't rich, but we were pretty well off. I don't think we were any different than most of the kids in my school. I would say the normal suburban family. I lived in a single home. I have a pool in my back yard and I live right by the school. I have an older brother and sister. We're all in college right now.

Tyrone:   Okay Dawson, did you have a creek by your house too?

Brad:     Actually I did. We used to jump off the rope swing all the time in the summer.

Tyrone:   Well, our stories are like night and day. I grew up in New York City and went to an all black school. My house was nice. My mom always provided for us. She did what she could. She worked a lot so she wasn't home too much. My older brother took care of my sister and me. My school was like a jungle. We ran the school. I remember sometimes we used to throw paper at the teacher if we didn't like him. We would sometimes go through like three teachers a year in one class alone. There were fights every single day in school. My homies didn't have pools in their back yards. They didn't have back yards. The streets were where we learned our life lessons. A lot of my boys saw no way out of the hood. They said college wasn't for them so they sold drugs and made fast money. Real fast. Everyone lived in a mediocre to low income house with the nicest cars and clothes. My brother was one of the biggest drug dealers in the city until someone shot him in the head in front of his baby. When he died, I was 15. That was so devastating to me, but I couldn't let those in my hood see me sweat. If they saw my weakness, I might be next. I knew after that though I wanted to get out of the hood and do better for my family. I picked up a basketball because I had an uncle that told me I had a ticket out and that ticket was college and a degree.

The stark differences in Brad and Tyrone's stories truly do read "like night and day." Their opening accounts vividly personify disturbing contrasts between the comfort, safety, privilege, formal educational opportunities, and prosperity living on the white side—and the struggle, violence, deprivation, forced street smarts, and long-shot hopes living on the black side of the color line dividing much of the U.S. population. Equally striking is what is taken for granted. For Brad, living with both of his parents who also are employed (with his dad owning his own business), a pool, and two other siblings in college constitutes "the normal suburban family." That these circumstances are not considered "rich" by him, merely "pretty well off," speaks volumes about his expectations from life. Tyrone jokingly addresses Brad as a character in the sheltered white family from the U.S. network television show *Dawson's Creek*. Even though he may already know the answer, Tyrone's question about a creek near Brad's house portrays wry astonishment at the idyllic home life his friend just described, which Brad reconfirms in describing the rope swing.

Tyrone's contrasting narrative includes his mother who "did what she could" and provided a "nice" house though she couldn't be home much of the time. Yet he also describes a chaotic "jungle" of a school with daily fights and beleaguered teachers, "mediocre to low income houses" without back yards, much less swimming pools. Perceiving "no way out of the hood," many of his peers made "fast money" by selling drugs. This included his older brother, who had taken care of Tyrone and his sister while his mother worked. Devastated when this brother is violently murdered, at 15 years old Tyrone takes his uncle's advice and decides to earn a basketball scholarship to college as a "ticket out" of oppressive conditions. The interview continues:

| | |
|---|---|
| *Brad:* | Wow! I didn't know any of that. |
| *Tyrone:* | You knew where I grew up, Dogg. You know how the hood is. |
| *Brad:* | Yeah, but I didn't know your brother got shot. |
| *Tim:* | You made it though, Dogg. That's what's up. |
| *Tyrone:* | I didn't make it yet. I am still in school. I don't feel like I made it until I can give my mom something. |
| *Brad:* | My bad, Ty. I feel like I just rubbed my neighborhood in your face. |
| *Tyrone:* | It's nothing. Don't even worry about that. I appreciate the fact your parents did well by you. |

Brad's spontaneous heartfelt reactions reveal just how little he knows about Tyrone's world despite some understandings achieved in their friendship. He is learning about this pivotal life-changing event for the first time in the context of the interview. He apologizes to Tyrone, realizing how oblivious he was in flaunting the good fortune of his own privileged white world in front of his friend. Tyrone graciously accepts the apology and expresses dignified appreciation for "the fact" of his friend's upbringing. Seemingly taken aback and wanting to comfort Tyrone using nicknames and street vernacular, Tim, the interviewer, acknowledges that Tyrone has "made it." Tyrone responds with another reality check. He has only succeeded in getting to college. As a black man he cannot take anything for granted like these white men apparently do. He will only feel like he has "made it" when he can materially benefit his mother—"until I can give my mom something."

| | |
|---|---|
| *Tim:* | Well, how did you guys meet? |
| *Brad:* | Well, I first met Tyrone at our recruiting visit up here. He is one year ahead of me, so when I came up here I was assigned to him. He was my host. |
| *Tyrone:* | Yeah I took the young boy under my wing. He was a Doogie Howser type guy and he came up here tryin' to be all cool. I liked him though and he made me laugh. |
| *Tim:* | For those that don't know, what do you mean recruiting visit? |
| *Brad:* | Well, we both play basketball and when a school offers you a scholarship, they let you come up to the school and visit |

first. The visit is called a recruiting visit. Tyrone was already here so he was assigned to show me a good time.

*Tim:*    Okay, so you guys have been friends since you came here Brad?

*Brad:*    Well at first we weren't really friends. We were just team-mates. Actually, I didn't really like Tyrone too much because I was a freshman. I had to do little stuff like carry his tray in the cafeteria and stuff like that. I thought he was picking on me, but I later realized it was all in tradition.

*Tim:*    Well, when would you guys say you actually became friends?

*Tyrone:*    Well, it all started at practice one day. Brad was on our side during a scrimmage and one of the other guys on the team was playing kind of tough and pushed Brad down. I immediately jumped in and defended him. After that we just started hanging out and stuff.

Simply being assigned to each other did not make Tyrone and Brad friends. Designated his host, Tyrone initially perceived Brad as a rather typical white guy (expressed once again using a character from mainstream U.S. media)—likable, funny, nevertheless "tryin' to be all cool." Brad didn't like being one down to this ranking team member. A path toward friendship emerged when Tyrone stuck up for Brad during a practice and they chose to spend time together "hanging out."

*Tim:*    Do you guys think that being two different races affects your friendship? Do you do the same type of things with your friends as you would with each other?

*Tyrone:*    I think it is a little different because of the difference in cultures. Like sometimes Brad wants to hang out with me on the weekend, but we have had clashes. I remember Brad wanted to take me to one of the frat houses on Green Street. I decided to bring some friends from home with me, of course, all black. The guys at the door took one look at me and my friends and said they were not letting anyone else in the house. We stood around the corner for a good half an hour and watched about 20 other guys walk in. There's so many examples of stuff like that. I remember when Brad and I went to one of his dad's golf tournaments. I felt like

I was on display the whole time. I was the only color in the whole country club.

Brad:    Yeah, well, can you remember the time I went with you to the Uncle Luke concert and I was the only white kid in the whole club?

Tyrone:    Yeah, but the girls loved you.

Brad:    Yeah, but the guys hated me.

Tyrone:    I also remember that time you came home with me and we went to the black frat party down at Queens.

Brad:    Yeah, I just felt really out of place and uncomfortable. I mean I can't dance. I dress differently and frankly, I am scared to death!

Tyrone:    We do have differences and we have had some instances, but we hang out all the time and instead of focusing on our differences, we enjoy the things we have in common.

Both men are aware of raced differences, circumstances, and reactions by others that striate their friendship. Even so, Tyrone has experienced more extensive prejudice and exclusion, remarking in passing "so many examples of stuff like that." He is used to being singled out in white settings, "on display the whole time" as the "only color" in a white world. By comparison, Brad's brushes with black settings sound like identifiably exotic visits by him as opposed to Tyrone's more continuous experience as the marked other. While aware of their differences, Tyrone says they are not the primary "focus" of the friendship, observing, "We enjoy the things we have in common."

Tim:    Well, have you learned anything from each other in the process of your friendship?

Brad:    I've learned and experienced a whole lot from being cool with Ty. He's my first black friend. I remember I went over to his house on Christmas night last year and I had all types of great food that I never had before. Even the foods that I was already used to eating were seasoned so differently so they had a different taste to them. You know what they say; variety is the spice of life.

Tyrone:    I've learned never to go to a Catholic Church service. I went about two weeks ago with Brad and it was the most boring thing I've ever been to. I felt like I was in some sort of cult movie when they were singing in Latin.

Brad: Ha, ha. Yeah, when we switched churches you had the Reverend Jesse Jackson up there dancing all around the pulpit.

Tim: They both sound like interesting experiences. So, what are some of the similarities that you guys have in common? What have you drawn or picked up on from one another?

Brad: I've picked up a lot of Tyrone's slang and recently some of his style. He helps me with the latest gear because I've never cared too much about that kind of stuff.

Tyrone: Well, Brad has me listening to some of his music and he has introduced me to a whole new set of friends that I don't think I would have had before. He has even introduced me to some of his white female friends. They are a lot different than black girls.

Brad: Yeah, Tyrone can't be so aggressive with white girls. He has to change faces a little or he might scare some away.

Tim: Do you guys still think racism is prevalent?

Brad: I never realized it until I started hanging out with Tyrone. Sometimes my friends make black jokes and stuff, but I never really thought anything of it. Now I get offended. I think racism is extremely prevalent and will always be there.

Tyrone: Of course. White people will always be wary of black people. I think it's because we really don't understand each other.

Tim: How would your life be different if you two never met each other?

Brad: I think now that I met Tyrone I've become more diverse in every aspect. I've become able to see culture from both sides and I've been able to have a better understanding of friendship without boundaries.

Tyrone: I don't know. I think because the world isn't just all black or all white. Brad has helped me learn how to communicate better with people of a different race. He has also taught me different norms and terms associated with his culture. I think that without Brad I would not be as well rounded.

These two men enjoy each other and can acknowledge and joke about their differences in a mutually well-intended spirit. Their friendship has been eye-opening for Brad in a number of ways and has expanded his sensitivity to blatant examples of racism. Yet how deeply he is able "to see culture from both sides" remains an important question. I hope it is fair to say that he still seems to presume one (read that normative white) culture that needs to be grasped "from both sides" instead of multiple cultures, radically contrasting lived predicaments, and divergent worldviews. Like many of us, Brad's friendship with a significantly different person only begins to educate him about our respective boundaries. It doesn't make those boundaries and privileged uptakes disappear. By comparison, the differences this friendship has made in Tyrone's life are more measured. In general he envisions no end to white people's wariness of blacks, noting that "we really don't understand each other." In addition, he observes "the world isn't just all black or all white," implying a multiplicity of differences. For him life is an ongoing project of learning to communicate with persons of different cultures and races. His friendship with Brad has taught him some contrasting aspects of white culture and helped him to become more "well-rounded."

## ❖ MAKING CHOICES, LEARNING LESSONS, AND SERVING SOCIAL BECOMING THROUGH CROSS-RACE FRIENDSHIPS

In the context of historical injustices, persisting social disparities and impediments, and asymmetrical perceptions of each other, developing friendships between blacks and whites involves concrete ongoing effort and mutual recognition by most participants in the United States. Acknowledging these conditions, some might say the positive stories presented in this chapter constitute small beginnings at creating social worlds where such narratives are commonplace—and to a degree they would be right. But if they dismiss such beginnings as insignificant, I believe they miss the point. Shining through these stories is integrity, learning, shared pleasure and affirmation, and pride in the name of friendship against the odds. At the same time we witness in their words the vibrant combination of ease *and* effort that characterizes the life of many friendships regardless of diverse racial and ethnic composition and other differences.

Differences loom large and weave possibilities in such relationships. Cross-race friends continually witness and engage with deeply etched differences from one another. But they also experience the

other-raced person as differing in singular ways rather than categorically different from self. Sharing such differences finds others resembling self in meaningful ways, as does the mutual refusal to be less than
they can be as friends. Making the choice to spend time together
enables situational intersections of valued identities and the discovery
of common differences (Joseph & Lewis, 1981). In contrast to Twyla and
Roberta, these persisting friendships also negotiate sites of intersecting
and potentially anxious differences—in race, ethnicity, cultural traditions, socioeconomic status, gender, ability, talents, parenting status—
where common purpose and mutual regard carry the day. They
continually must compose their identities as friends with respect to
others as well as the situations they face singly and together. What
aspects of their lives and their identities do friends choose to recognize
as salient to their lives and times together? How do they support each
other's valued identities that may be destabilized and undermined in
certain situations? Or negative identities insisted upon through ignorance and fear in other circumstances? What utility do their negotiated
identities hold for accomplishing personal and social goals?

Friendship and learning go hand in hand. Making the effort to
understand specific others of different cultures, races, and ethnicities
on their own terms in a spirit of particularized caring and individual
regard is exercising the will to personal friendship. I believe that our
practices for cultivating personal friendships offer chances to enhance
ourselves and to learn as individuals throughout our lives. These are
worthwhile practices in their own right. Even so, stratified conditions
still segregate blacks and whites in large measure. Historically
unequal educational and economic opportunities to a great extent
choke off the structural possibilities for meeting and choosing each
other as friends. Witnessing these constraints bespeaks the tight connections between the possibilities of personal and political cross-race
friendship in the United States. Each form of friendship can work to
facilitate the likelihood of the other. In this context making the effort
to learn about and engage with multiple diverse others on their own
terms in a generalized spirit of good will is exercising the will to civic
friendship. Our active, collective practices for developing civic friendships and political alliances with progressive goals create the possibilities of improving the social conditions detrimental to cross-race
friendship.

Aristotle (1980) wisely observed that among friends there is no
need for justice, but with justice there is still a need for friendship. I
believe that one kind of justice still in need of a friendship ethic
employs a revamped vocabulary of "color blindness" to address issues

of social justice. This need arises because the very character and conse-quences of that color blindness have mutated. For an extended period of the 20th century, aspirations to color-blind justice embodied the morally upstanding goal of avoiding the Primary Misperceptions of Individuation. Such errors occur when raced and ethnic differences such as those marked by skin color are unjustly emphasized to the detriment of the persons thus categorized as other—as in the historical, systematic discrimination against and subordination of blacks prac-ticed in the United States. In attempting to protect dominant white interests, however, color blindness can embody the Primary Misperception of Participation where important differences in histori-cal conditions and opportunities are ignored as making a significant difference in contemporary peoples' lives. Instead, the same standards of judgment are insisted upon as applying equally to everyone because "we all are in the same boat and deserve the same treatment." How might a stance of friendship intervene in this knotty and consequential predicament? It is one where legitimate claims may be voiced for just social practices on both sides of the historical unfolding of these mean-ings of color blindness.

The spirit of friendship avoids both of the above misperceptions. It attempts with good will to create spaces where both the meaningful differences and commonalities between friends are honored. Personal and political friends must consciously manage the dialectic of judg-ment and acceptance in constructing and applying standards of evalu-ation that judiciously reconcile significant individual differences with common hopes and goals in given cases. We have witnessed personal friends practicing edifying individuation in their treatment of each other. In ongoing ways, they acknowledge their differences as raced persons and in circumstances transcending their time together. They respect the differences that make them who they are individually and in relation to each other. In doing so, they treat each other as meaning-fully and provisionally whole persons—persons with integrity subject in particularized and unequal ways to changing circumstances. At the same time they accomplish edifying participation together—an ongo-ing co-creation and celebration of their important similarities. Their friendships involve ongoing negotiation of a coordinated frame of ref-erence for understanding and evaluating their actions in the face of contrasting and exploitative traditions.

Multiple consciousnesses and subjectivities are at stake. Black per-sons' dual consciousness derives from poignant historical knowledge with incessant reminders of concrete disparities and barriers. Many white persons take for granted privileges and notions of place in their worlds that fuels their optimism. A simultaneous lesson, aspiration, and practice of friendship is making the effort to learn about differences instead of judging others by our own standards and assuming that differences don't make a difference. Such practices of friendship are deliberately embraced and performed. The activities of edifying individuation and inspiriting participation contextualize each other in these friendships. Cross-race friends dignify each other in realizing them.

# 7

# Embracing
# Ethical and Political
# Potentials of Friendship

Throughout this book I have alluded to ethical potentials of friend-ship. Focusing on dyadic friendships in Chapters 3 and 4, I explored the possibilities of their dialogue and storytelling for addressing their similarities and differences, and for making choices that facilitate worth-while individuation and participation. Even so, I have not directly addressed the unique ethical profile of friendship. What are the special moral potentials of friendship? How and to what extent can friendship provide ethical guidance in our lives? The initial section of this chapter addresses these questions in the context of personal friendships.

In Chapters 5 and 6 I then discussed cross-sex and cross-race friend-ships as markedly embodying the susceptibility of all friendships to enveloping forces. Such bonds are revealing sites of intersecting social positions shaped by culturally charged discourses and ascribed identities. Examining these two specific types of friendships disclosed the capacities of all friendships to serve human freedom and affirmation. But we also witnessed the vulnerability of friendships to lived circumstances, histori-cal and structural constraints, material conditions, discursive closure, and foiled imaginations. These prospects raise questions concerning the political potentials of friendships. How extensively can friendship contribute to the moral practices of larger social systems? How far can the practices of friendship extend into public life to facilitate social justice and achieve social change? What is the potential political efficacy of friendships? I consider these issues in the chapter's later sections.

As discussed in Chapter 1, Aristotle (1980) anticipated important aspects of these questions in his conceptions of true (dyadic) friendship and political friendship. Many of the authors I discuss in this chapter have drawn upon Aristotle's thinking on these matters. It is difficult to consider the ethical and political values of friendships in western civilization without encountering his ideas in some form. Yet, a troubling irony is that his insights derived from a position of privilege in a society where slavery was practiced, where only property owners could vote, and women largely were confined to households with no role in public life (Hutter, 1978). Despite their value, Aristotle's ideas reflect the limitations of their original homogenizing context. While acknowledging Aristotle's enduring influence, the account I present in this chapter also considers authors and circumstances that extend our understandings of ethical and political potentials of friendships. The final section directly challenges the broad applicability of primary Aristotelian assumptions about political friendship.

## ❖ ETHICAL PRACTICES OF FRIENDSHIPS

Friendships do not just happen to us, and people cannot be compelled to be friends. Instead, *becoming and remaining friends with others is an ongoing voluntary achievement that involves the continual exercise of moral will by each friend* (Blum, 1980). Our finite, embodied existence in space and time necessitates and limits our choices of friends (Meilander, 1981). Our choices of friends are constrained significantly by our geographical and social locations, available discourses, and material conditions. The contingencies of our lives place us in functional and existential proximity to some people and distant from others. We encounter some persons routinely because of how our lives are organized. We cannot and do not respond to everyone in the same ways; in making distinctions, we simply feel closer to certain others. In this process our overtures of friendship are not merely emotional responses; they also involve our motivated perceptions and reasoned ordering of possibilities. According to Pakaluk (1994), "Aristotle holds that the love found in friendship is not merely an emotion. Rather, the core element pertains to the will, to a rational desire" (p. 201). Thus, we keep in touch with friends who live far away, we make the effort to learn about our coworkers, and we find time amid our family and romantic obligations to be with our friends. However constrained and enabled we are by where we live at this moment in time and our place in society, our feelings and thoughts work together to inform our active choices to live as friends.

Choosing friends implies preference and qualified freedom in responding to the differences and similarities that individuate others and make them appealing as possible friends (Meilander, 1981). Our choices of friends and ongoing actions with them express our moral being (Blum, 1980). The necessity of choice implies the necessity for ethics, moral guidance in our actions with others (Meilander, 1981). Our actions together as friends further define permitted conduct with each other. We establish shared standards for our relational behavior that may differ in important ways from those of larger society, thereby constituting a private morality. Because of its essentially voluntary nature despite situational encouragements and constraints, friendship persists only as long as we fulfill each other's expectations as friends and behave in accordance with our shared "norms of propriety" (Paine, 1969). If either friend violates the private morality of friendship, negative repercussions between the friends follow and, depending on the severity of the infraction, the friendship could end. The voluntary, negotiated bases of friendship are important features of its moral composition (Annis, 1987; M. Friedman, 1992; Paine, 1969).

*Second, friendship involves mutual concern for the other's well-being for that person's own sake* (Aristotle, 1980). As friends, Jack wants what is best for June in recognition of the very person she is, and June has the same regard for Jack's thriving. Intrinsic caring for other persons for their own sakes is considered morally good and a defining ethical feature of authentic friendship (Annis, 1987; Blum, 1980; Thomas, 1989). This generous regard for the other *as* other is *mutual* in friendship (Aristotle, 1980). It constitutes the relationship and is not reducible to the logic of economic exchange with a ledger of balanced reciprocity or an independent contractor maximizing gains and minimizing losses. Self-interested, short-sighted "giving–to-receive" is contrary to the generosity occurring between friends. Blum (1980) argues, "In fact, friendship is a context in which the division between self-interest and other-interest is often not applicable" (p. 76).

The giving of friends is also not a matter of self-sacrifice—a denial of our self and our well-being in helping our friend. The giving of friends simultaneously reflects self's and other's interests. Through her generosity to him, June becomes more of the person and friend she already is in her friendship with Jack. Giving is a way of realizing herself as his friend even as she aids his own individuated becoming. Marilyn Friedman explains:

> In my partiality for those who are, in this way, near and dear to me, I show a moral attitude that is neither egoism nor self-denying altruism. The flourishing of loved ones promotes my own well-being, yet my motivation to care for them does not require me to compute how their well-being will further my own interests; I simply am interested in them. (1992, p. 69)

Friendship does not require June to impose her outlook on Jack or to annex his distinctive life projects and identities as her own in order to be friends with him. By comparison, when Kate says, "In helping Kyle, I basically am helping myself," she does not acknowledge his distinctive initiatives. Viewing Kyle as simply an extension of her self, Kate commits the Primary Misperception of Participation. Altruism paradoxically becomes an undertaking of "extended self-interest" (Blum, 1980, p. 75). In giving to Kyle primarily to enhance her own pleasure, Kate is still self-centered. We do not "live through" our friends (Blum, 1980, p. 76), we live *with* them. Kate's self-serving altruism contrasts with June's genuine other-regarding offerings to Jack for the very person he is within the unfolding narrative of their friendship (Cooper, 1980). The generosity of friends involves the ongoing mutual affirmation of self as self and other as other, the shared enjoyment of their distinctive subjectivities and potentials. Choosing to give freely to a friend for that person's own sake serves the self-recognizing integrity of both friends. It contrasts to giving offered solely as a response to receiving benefits from others or in order to create obligations. Thomas (1989) argues that "friendship is the vehicle of social interaction through which we come to have the degree of autonomous altruism that morality requires" (p. 132).

Such "autonomous altruism" (Thomas, 1989) derives from the mutual gifting of two freedoms living at the heart of authentic friendship (Rawlins, 1983b). In becoming close friends, I contend that we offer each other the freedom to be independent and the freedom to be dependent. In effect, we say to one another, "Because you are my friend, I will support in any way I can your freedom to become the person you can be and to pursue your own projects. However, as you pursue your dreams, if and whenever you need my assistance, please feel free to call upon me. I am always with you in spirit." Through mutually granting and performing these freedoms, friends at once live up to their potentials as individuated persons *and* as participants in their friendship.

As a self-recognizing person, June takes on projects that cultivate her own talents and express her moral being. She does so with Jack's encouragement and awareness. She does not act alone with only individual consequences. The mutual regard of the friends means that she also is answerable to Jack for her actions because he cares about her. Meanwhile, when June calls on Jack for assistance, she offers him the opportunity to help, to realize himself as a friend. June also dignifies Jack when she seeks his judgments about her plans. The mutually gifted freedoms to be independent and to be dependent constitute "conjunctive freedoms" allowing for both the edifying individuation and participation of friendship. The liberties connect friends in freedom. Even so, the contradictory and contingent demands placed on each friend make the ongoing achievement of these mutual freedoms a situated, dialectical, and ethical challenge for friends (Rawlins, 1983b, 1989a, 1992). In fact, we must accomplish all of the ethical practices of friendship continually in concrete circumstances. The call to serve friends is both redemptive and tragic—inviting us to demonstrate our best qualities or to fall selfishly short. Friends' ethical responses are not givens but must be performed in each situation, which enhances their potential as moral actions.

*Third, special practices pursuing equality characterize friendship.* Friendships presuppose and create a space—a shared project, interest, or basis for the relationship. This shared concern transcends the particular individuals and functions as a leveler. Friends treat each other as equals with regard to their common pursuits. But such equality does not necessarily mean similarity. Friends may differ from each other in numerous ways—talents, insights, life experiences, speaking styles, social or institutional statuses, physical attributes or abilities, age, race, ethnicity, sex, gender, sexual orientation, religious creeds. Some differences resist direct hierarchical comparisons, such as measuring one person's singing against another's cooking ability, or one's physical against the other's social courage. Yet differences can be mapped painfully (and arbitrarily) onto hierarchical social scales and life chances. These socially charged differences can occur in cultural contexts regarding our age, gender, race, class, ethnicity, educational attainment, sexual identity, and embodied abilities. We do not countenance the reduction of our friends' value to categorical judgments. We respect each other for the particular person that each of us is.

Despite differences, for political or personal friendship to thrive, as C. S. Lewis (1960) maintained, "Friendship must be about something" (p. 66). Lewis clearly endorsed Aristotle's (1980) notion of a common good or interest connecting friends. Lewis insisted that friends orient themselves around something besides the relationship itself—some thing, idea, or endeavor that we care about or enjoy doing together, something from which we both derive pleasure or learn. These shared interests, from sports to movies, constitute something between us that does not belong exclusively to either friend. This "something" beyond creates the space between us that allows us to draw upon our differences to stand as equals vis-à-vis our shared interest, mission, or passion (Hansot, 2000; Murphy, 1998).

Our equality as friends is demonstrated by our respect for each other and *in relation to* our common concerns and activities—not by direct comparisons of our individual abilities or attributes (Murphy, 1998). For example, as friends we may treat each other as equals in our enjoyment of music, excitement about learning, our shared pursuit of justice or environmental action irrespective of our particular musical ability, intellectual accomplishment, or political acumen. In contrast to romantic love, which often collapses the differences separating lovers in our attempts to merge and become one, both civic and personal friendships enliven the space between persons and preserve our freedom to be different. At its best, friendship demands and serves responsible freedom. This freedom animates the space between friends, connecting us as individuated participants who regard ourselves as equals in relation to the common interests constituting our friendship. Because inequality is opposed to the spirit of friendship, we must settle issues of power that threaten our just treatment of each other (Fisher & Galler, 1988; Hutter, 1978).

*Fourth, an ethical requirement of friendship involves ongoing learning about each other.* Even though some of us may respond positively to each other from our very first meeting, close friendships take time and interaction to develop. Initially, we seek to know more about others in deciding whether we would like to or could be friends. Getting to know someone as a friend subsequently involves spending time together voluntarily across a variety of settings and communicating about personal and shared interests. By experiencing each other in different circumstances, we learn specific things that matter to each other, personal cares and enthusiasms, hobbies, habits, quirks, issues of pride and perhaps regret.

Becoming friends pulls us out of ourselves. In coming to care about our friends, we try to understand what is important to them, how we might contribute to their happiness, and what identities they cherish (Annis, 1987). For our friendships to remain meaningfully responsive, we engage in continuous processes of learning about each other.

Creating understandings and ongoing learning is a relational and ethical necessity to remain connected and to meet our friends on their own terms where they are in their own lives. Shared knowledge enables the particularized caring and responses of friendship (Annis, 1987). What do our friends go through on any given day to be the persons they are, to anticipate and cope with life's big and little changes? Successes, failures, family quarrels, romantic involvements, physical changes, poor sleep, creative breakthroughs, domestic danger, recovering health, new tools or possessions, births, deaths, sufferings, joys— feeling trapped, beautiful, strong, ignored, angry.

Knowledge about our friends has ethical implications. For example, speaking as friends who live with differing abilities, Fisher and Galler (1988) observe, "But the very process of becoming friends brings up the meanings of social values such as justice, fairness, and reciprocity, to be struggled over and figured out in the course of our daily lives" (p. 187). As friends we want justice for each other within our friendship as well as in our everyday lives transcending our bond. Understanding our friends' changing needs helps address our demands for justice and persists as a crucial ethical component of our discourse. Over the years, we watch our friends change their hair and clothing styles while searching for meaningful work and lasting romance. We also see our friends get sick, lose jobs, change romantic partners, mourn family members, and grow older. We live and change and age together.

Cross-examining mundane and significant issues involves ongoing dialogue and storytelling between friends. Carefully listening to each other's positions and stories, we deal with principles and concrete events as we perform the dialectic of judgment and acceptance (Rawlins, 1989a, 1992). In light of our acceptance of each other as friends, we reflexively establish shared standards that we use to evaluate each other's statements and actions. That means "unconditional friendship is . . . an oxymoron" (Swanson, 1992, p. 175). Friends have ethical expectations for each other. Learning with affirming friends promotes courage to reflect on our self and to cross-examine the moral basis of our choices. Part of the beauty of friendship is the chance to have conversations we can't have with anyone else (Thomas, 1989). Friends allow us to facilitate the development of each other's moral judgment and understanding.

*Fifth*, interwoven with the ethical qualities of voluntary mutual regard, equality, learning and knowledge, *friends behave in trusting and trustworthy ways with each other.* Announcing myself as a friend embodies a promise that I am going to be who I say I am, and that I am going to do what I say I am going to do with respect to our friendship. To the extent that I do these things, I am trustworthy. To the extent that I am trustworthy, I hope that my friend(s) trust me. Accordingly, I act in ways I am expected to act by my personal friends—with whom I have negotiated these expectations (Grunebaum, 2003). Our actions together and apart continually create the encompassing narrative, values, and identities experienced through our friendship.

As friends we appraise each other's actions and hold each other accountable to our negotiated moral standards and trustworthy practices. This robust ethical composition of friendship demands the widely celebrated loyalty of friends. Betrayal is indeed the sin against our friend (May, 1967). Even so, friends continually exercise judgment in upholding moral visions and monitoring each other's actions. In this witnessing, June's loyalty to Jack may be strained by Jack's actions that violate June's ethical convictions, or by his actions that compromise his own moral character (Thomas, 1989). Granting freedom, trust, and loyalty, we hold each other to the ethical standards of our friendship.

To achieve trust, *sixth, friends practice respectful honesty in our discourse with each other.* We must be able to share vital truths with personal friends. We expect our friends to speak their minds, sharing with us their actual thoughts, perceptions, and feelings. We have to be able to state tough truths to each other, and we have to be able to disagree. These are the ways we come to understand our personal concerns and potentials. Honest statements are foundations of robustly forged, co-constructed knowledge and worthwhile thinking together.

In speaking truthfully as friends, we must also consider the potential impact of our words on our friends (Rawlins, 1983c). Discretion must accompany our honesty; we must respect our friends' privacy and sensitive issues. Our opinions may simultaneously convey hurtful sentiments that disrespect our friends' convictions, self-esteem, and valued identities. These statements risk violating our indispensable trust in each other as personal friends. Our knowledge of matters that risk the affections of our close friends or undermine the good will of fellow community members derives from our ongoing ethical commitment to learn about and with our friends. We need to be similarly measured in attributing hurtful intentions to our friends. The dialectic of expressiveness and protectiveness encourages June and Jack to talk freely while simultaneously guarding the best interests of the other. Building and preserving the assumption of benevolence between friends is closely connected to behaving in trustworthy ways and practicing respectful honesty.

*Seventh,* in living up to these ethical values *friendship is a conscientiously interested relationship.* Friends perform distinctive moral outlooks with mutually caring practices. Blum (1980) celebrates "the concern, care, sympathy, and the willingness to give of oneself to the friend which goes beyond what is characteristic and expected of people generally. The caring within a friendship is built up on a basis of knowledge, trust, and intimacy" (p. 67). We are partial toward our friends. We regard and treat them in special and thoughtful ways as they do us, which creates a distinctive "ethical pull" (Annis, 1987, p. 353; Koehn, 1998). Friends' special ethical responsibilities contrast with the impartial treatment of anonymous others. Annis (1987) states, "I should be impartial all things being equal, but not all things are equal with special duties" (p. 353). Friendship resembles family, marital, and parenting relationships in the caring involved. Additional moral demands are posed by such relationships (Thomas, 1989). While admiring devotion to the good of all humankind, Blum (1980) endorses the particularized caring of friendship, observing, "These relationships involve a deeper identification with the other's good than is customary in their absence; and it is entirely proper that they do so" (p. 81).

Human finitude typically limits our concrete opportunities for devoted service to particular others (Meilander, 1981). However, treating one's friends well does not necessitate intentionally harming others or undermining their abilities to flourish. In fact, our dedication to friends becomes ethically objectionable when it leads to deprivation of others. Thoughtfully attending to the well-being of our friends should not actively exclude or hurt others, or diminish their opportunities out of exclusive regard for our friends (M. Friedman, 1992; Meilander, 1981). Blum (1980) agrees, "It is important to recognize that genuine devotion to a particular group—family, neighborhood, ethnic community, ethnic group, club—is in itself morally good, and becomes morally suspect only when it involves a deficient stance towards others" (p. 80). In discussing the political potentials of friendship I will return to friends' conscientious interest in each other, which Friedman endorses as friendship's "substantive partiality" (1992, p. 54), as an ethical political practice.

To summarize, authentic participation in friendship involves significant ethical practices. Each friendship practice shapes and occurs in the context of the others in composing an ethics of friendship. First, friendship is *negotiated voluntarily* within limits between friends and not imposed from outside. This quasi-voluntarism constitutes an important quality composing the moral fiber of friendship (M. Friedman, 1992). Second, friends *care about each other's well-being* for the person's own sake. In doing so, friends achieve expanded, other-regarding, relational selves. Third, friends *respect each other as equals* in relation to their common pursuits. Fourth, mutual respect and recognition of their identities as continuous achievements find friends *engaging in ongoing learning* about each other as an ethical requirement of their relationship. Fifth, performing the ethical practices of friendship *engenders trust* between friends. Sixth, friends further ensure trust communicatively through *practicing respectful honesty* in their dealings with each other. Seventh, in light of these mutually achieved ethical qualities, friendship is a conscientiously interested relationship. We *give special attention to* our friends' needs and desires.

An ongoing expectation of friendship is to respond to our friends as provisionally complete and integrated beings. We thoughtfully regard our friends as persons who work to achieve self-recognizing identities in concrete moments. We realize they do so in the face of conditioning cultural discourses and power arrangements. Their identities also arise in relationship to our own actions regarding them. Through the ethical practices of friendship, we strive continually to hear our own and our friends' voices—what we are saying and what others are saying to and with us. We achieve the ideals of friendship to varying degrees across differing existential, practical, and material circumstances. Accomplishing these ethical practices in diverse social situations with variable support, personal friendships are micromovements of political involvement. As such, friendships can inspire and contribute to broader political activity.

### ❖ POLITICAL PRACTICES OF FRIENDSHIPS

In considering ethical potentials of friendship, I have focused primarily on private dyads. In contrast, politics is a public arena for ensuring justice for all citizens. It is also a public realm of antagonistic disagreements about access to power, identity recognition, and resource distribution—all of which typically require impersonal procedures to protect the rights of vulnerable groups and individuals (Mansbridge, 1975). What can the ethics of friendship contribute to such a realm? I argue that, within limits, the substantive ethical practices of dyadic friendships can inform political friendships. I also maintain that the conscientious interest in others cultivated through personal friendships and friendship networks can provide an ethical pull toward broader political activity.

Striving to treat friends justly is the soul of all friendships. Acknowledging this potential, Deneen (2001) with Aristotle (1980) argues that friendships should not be considered merely private relationships "but rather as relations ideally located within a civic context and, in fact, a necessary basis for civic trust and true justice" (p. 48). The edifying individuation occurring between friends—their recognition of the meaningful differences shaping their distinct possibilities—promotes authentic justice. In Deneen's words, "Justice in its 'highest form' considers the particularity of each individual, ceases to be an abstraction, becoming substantive and individuated justice" (2001, p. 53). Participation in actual friendships facilitates moral learning and concern for particular others (Bukowski & Sippola, 1996). It is important to avoid the Primary Misperception of Participation, which can result in faceless ethics and anonymous political involvement. All individuals have a personal responsibility and moral obligation to make their values known (Morson & Emerson, 1989). For Bakhtin concrete recognition of actual persons grounds an ethical approach to politics: "There is no person in general, there is me, there is a definite concrete other: my close friend, my contemporary (social humanity), the past and future of real people (of real historical humanity)" (quoted in Morson & Emerson, 1989, p. 20). Significantly, a definite concrete other and one's close friend are cited as bases for reaching out to others in ethical political action grounded in concern for real people rather than abstractions.

Within the constraints and resources of their sociocultural situation, friends voluntarily negotiate private moral visions and alternative spaces for performing social lives. Motivated by such shared outlooks, they may decide to join with or invite others to effect changes in the conditions shaping their possibilities (Hutter, 1978). First, *the voluntary exercise of moral will in participating is an ethical touchstone of political friendship.* We must continually decide to do what we believe is right for and with our friends. Celebrating the move in ancient Greek politics away from inbred kinship ties and privileges, Deneen observes, "A form of friendship coextensive with civic ties, based on voluntary commitments, provided a more benign model for political relationships" (2001, p. 50). We retain self-interests but voluntarily recognize more general goods as necessary for and arising from political participation (Swanson, 1992). Political activity in a spirit of friendship always presumes voluntary participation. We continually choose to do what we can in seeking justice for ourselves and recognized others.

Second, *pursuing common goods despite citizens' differences in a spirit of good will is a contingent aspiration of political friendship.* When I asserted a second ethical practice of personal friendship involving mutual concern for the other's well-being for that person's sake, I combined Aristotle's (1980) two definitive features of true friendship. These two features are concern for the other for her or his sake and mutual well-wishing. Concerns for our self become mediated by our concern for the well-being of our friend(s). Even so, giving to another within friendship is not sacrificing self, just as June did not sacrifice herself for her friendship with Jack. Enhanced subjectivities arise in the mutual giving and affirming of friends as well as in sharing interests. Aristotle (1980) expands the reach of these ethical practices in describing political friendship. The concern for specific individuals for their own sake becomes a generalized *good will* extended to the members of our political community. The mutual well-wishing of dyadic friends transmutes into a concern for the *common good* implicating all participants in our polity.

Pursuing political goals in a spirit of good will is an ideal aspiration of political friendship according to Aristotle (1980). Of course deeply held antagonisms and stark disparities in power and material conditions cause senseless human suffering. Demonstrating good will by the persons suffering is a ridiculous idea in such settings. In many circumstances, however, we can engage with others with good intentions in our commonly occupied political space. We can be willing to hear others' differing perceptions of the matters at hand, or at least refrain from open hostility. The spirit of good will performed in political friendship renounces self-sealing, dispiriting individuation. Lena and Luis don't have to agree with each other, but they have to be willing to hear one another. Good will celebrates reaching out to others, the possibility of hope, and the chance to break down barriers to our shared humanity.

Seeking to identify and accomplish the common good is a second way that Aristotle's (1980) ethical image of personal friendship informs the practices of political friendship. Pursuing the common good is another way to challenge narrow views of self-interest in political activities. Friendship always involves considering our interests in the context of others' interests and vice versa. As Kahane (1999, p. 269) notes, political friendship constitutes "a model of citizenship outside of the zero-sum game of sameness-difference." Accomplishing the common good involves ongoing, coordinated endeavors among citizens addressing shared times, places, and consequences. It requires edifying participation.

Critics of Aristotle rightly note the hegemonic potential in this conception if it involves a monolithic Good (with a capital G) foisted by those with the most power on vulnerable citizens with differing needs. However, ethical aspirations of political friendship can work to undo such totalizing conceptions of "The Good" (Deneen, 2001, p. 54; Pakaluk, 1994; Swanson, 1992). Deneen (2001) lucidly describes such ethical political practices:

> Aristotle suggests that agreement, arising simultaneously from different perspectives that are nevertheless subordinated to a willingness to engage in conversation, is precisely the kind of friendship that will characterize the best relations between citizens. . . . Aristotle did not propose to separate people from one another and thereby guarantee political stability, but rather recommended an alternative and explicitly political theory of friendship based on a goal of common good that even citizens motivated by different interests might achieve. (p. 56)

Political friends readily admit that others may perceive things differently. Through dialogue, deliberation, working together, and sharing stories, they strive to establish feasible goals and bases for cooperation (Kahane, 1999; Pakaluk, 1994). To do otherwise violates the aspirations to justice of political friendship (Swanson, 1992).

Some conceptions of friendship and alliance formation do not presume common goods or good will to accomplish social change in contested, public, political spheres (Arendt, 1968; Dill, 1983; Disch, 1995; Scott, 1998). Instead of focusing on good will between political friends, oppressed persons are seen as marked participants in political activity. Dominant factions charge marginalized group differences with deviant status as essential bases for oppression. These marked attributes become "political facts . . . without which one cannot appear in a public space" (Disch, 1995, p. 293). Having our identity essentialized through ascribed categories—such as female, male, black, white, Protestant, Moslem, Jewish, Catholic, heterosexual, homosexual, lesbian, gay, unemployed, employed, legal, illegal, salaried, wage earner—presents "false choices" for identifying ourselves within the "divide and conquer" strategies of dominant regimes (Dill, 1983, p. 136). In Emerson's words, each of us is "huge" and contains "multitudes." But pejorative and restrictive identities impose discursive closure on the multiple, intersecting categories of identity that we draw upon to construct our sense of self and our interests in political participation (Scott, 1998). Such dispiriting individuation falsely emphasizes the differences between (and similarities within) designated categories of human beings.

In other circumstances these participants may have little in common and much to dislike about each other, but contingent events are harming them all in related though distinctive ways. Disch (1995) holds such situations call for "articulated solidarity." Working with Arendt's (1958, 1968) ideas, she explains:

> Rather than defining *what* we believe in or declaring *who* we are, we now need to assess *how* we are implicated in a worldly event. This is the task of articulating solidarity: constructing the "facts" of a contingent situation in a way that makes possible a coordinated response by a plurality of actors who—apart from that contingency—may have more differences than affinities. (Disch, 1995, pp. 287–288, original emphasis)

Hannah Arendt argues that articulated solidarity requires "vigilant partisanship" (Disch, 1995, p. 293). Friendship has a distinct meaning for feminists and Arendt in volatile and fragmented political contexts. This friendship inherently recognizes multiple worldviews on events affecting actors. It constitutes a space between citizens for disputing a plurality of interests arising from diverse locations. "Paradoxically, then," Disch concludes, "the 'between' that sustains Arendt's conception of friendship is not a common moral framework of identity, but distance" (1995, p. 304). In divisive circumstances viable friendships and political alliances recognize multiple positions and contingent bases for identity that do not merge or transcend themselves in working to address concrete challenges and facilitate social justice.

Political friendship is not a totalizing outlook. Its practices attempt to mediate public and private lives. Even so, there are limits to the reach of its good will and the degree of differences it can embrace in striving for the common good. Consequently, political friendships continually must work to constitute themselves around shared and divided concerns. This ethically minded political activity attempts to create flexible (if fragile) third spaces for addressing differences. In performing these spaces, political friends step away from dispiriting participation or assimilation that oppressively discourages differences. Meanwhile, political friends step out of self-sealing individualism or ethnocentrism to participate in the tenuous solidarity of political friendship as self-recognizing beings with valued distinctive qualities. The third spaces of such friendship are spaces of contingent positionings of political friends responding to lived exigencies. The ethical spirit of friendship resists binary thinking about others and selves. Instead, we view our actions and identities across meaningful possibilities within the particular events of our lives.

Third, *practicing equal and respectful treatment among friends is an ethical principle as well as a political goal in less than ideal worlds.* Political conditions that separate us in hierarchical power relations jeopardize our respectful treatment of each other as equals. Consequently, respectful and equal treatment of others is an ongoing ethical requirement and objective for would-be political friends in alienating contexts. The "double agency" of friendship can enable us to facilitate each other's well-being and sense of belonging across our private and public lives (Rawlins, 1992). Friends recognize each other as provisionally whole persons. Confirming self-perceptions in private interaction facilitates personal integration. In projects transcending public and private realms, aspiring political friends respect each other's potentially different yet equally relevant contributions to the common political activity. Thus, Lena and Luis's involvement doesn't have to be exactly the same to be viewed by both of them as equal.

In personal friendship facilitating happiness and belonging are individual matters of supporting someone's self-esteem. Our personal friendships draw sustenance from the special confirmation we communicate to a particular other person. June looks to Jack to value her as a person. However, in political friendships we experience varying degrees of solidarity with others as contributing members of *this* political community that is trying to achieve *these* goals together. We acknowledge our shared presence, commitment, and work. Political friends must communicate respect for fellow citizens despite individual differences, antagonisms, or lack of closeness—even if and especially if we disagree. This type of friendship is not about closeness or affection. Lena and Luis don't hang out together or with each other's friends on a regular basis. Political friendship is actually about co-creating a space of freedom and justice that allows for the recognition of persons' differences as contributing to the common projects of community life. Invoking Aristotle's political friendship, Arendt (1958) wisely observed, "What love is in its own, narrowly circumscribed sphere, respect is in the larger domain of human affairs. Respect, not unlike the Aristotelian *philia politike*, is a kind of 'friendship' without intimacy and without closeness; it is regard for the person from the distance which the space of the world puts between us" (p. 243).

Political friendships continually involve a mixture of equal needs and varying interests (Deneen, 2001). Acknowledging our differential motivations while preserving a stance of equal respect presents continual challenges to us as political friends. Accordingly, Pakaluk (1994) argues that political friendship requires embracing a "common scheme of cooperation," that "constitutes justice for that community" (p. 205). We understand that diverse tasks must be performed in order to achieve the political goals of our community. Despite different activities, all members are accorded equal respect for their work for the betterment of all "as a *consequence* of their accepting the terms of coop-eration for that community" (Pakaluk, 1994, p. 205, original emphasis).

Meanwhile, we do not necessarily share identical interpretations of the meanings of our common activities. As a result, it is vital to negoti-ate a shared frame of reference that comprehends the differences among political friends and dignifies their particular reasons for par-ticipation (Kahane, 1999). Kahane proposes "symmetry" of orienta-tions within and across groups of political friends to the value of differing perspectives about common concerns. He observes, "In both cases, a shared set of reference points (interpreted from different per-spectives) can provide a reason for regarding the relationship as sig-nificant, and for experiencing a bond with others" (p. 283). Civic friends who draw their identities from deeply contrasting traditions—and may live with starkly contrasting privileges—face ongoing chal-lenges in attempting to interact respectfully as equals. A key requirement is to craft together a common frame of reference that simultaneously affirms their individuated identities as members of sig-nificantly contrasting social groups. Lena and Luis don't abandon their individual differences when demonstrating their respect for one another while working for combined political objectives. This negoti-ated frame must enable edifying participation in a political undertaking with shared consequences.

Despite well-intended efforts, strains always can arise from salient differences among political friends. This is especially likely when citi-zens' identities or contributions are valued differently in public cir-cumstances. Maybe Lena's public comments aren't as valued as much as Luis's in certain public discussions because she's a stay-at-home mom. Maybe Luis's public comments aren't as valued as Lena's because he speaks accented English. In such cases the ethical practices of equal respect in friendship collide with political realities (Mansbridge, 1975).

Fourth, *political friends continuously learn about the others' circum-stances and viewpoints to appreciate their identities, co-construct frames of reference, and coordinate activities.* Continuous learning about political friends is not only an ethical requirement but also a practical necessity for such friendships to exist. Ethically speaking, when we make the effort to learn about others, we achieve an enlarged sense of how others live and what matters to them and why. We enlarge our conception of the circumstances we may share but actually experience differently. Lena and Luis learn how the lack of public transportation in their neigh-borhoods differently affects each other yet motivates their joint political involvement. We develop insights about our friends' self-perceptions and the ways in which they perceive us (Goering, 2003). Political friends try to see the world from the other's perspective and with genuine concern for the other's experience (Kahane, 1999). Through this process we develop substantive knowledge about others' life chances, identities, and circumstances—their worlds.

These learning activities tangibly remind all of us that there are multiple conceptions of the "common good" and the desirable actions to achieve it. Of course, people in deprived or vulnerable circumstances usually do not need such reminding. Moreover, we must remember that it is not others' responsibility to teach us about their worlds. While friendship involves actively seeking to learn about and with others, it does not include demands to be taught (Rawlins, 2003). Forcing people to educate or learn about others doesn't automatically make us appreciate their differences. Learning arises through thoughtful attentiveness to others' actions, assertions, and stories addressing individual and shared circumstances. Cultivating knowledge about our would-be political friends carefully attends to their actions toward us on their own turf and in their attempts to find a place to stand in the world we also think of as ours.

Through collective activities, storytelling, respectful dialogue, and resolute debate about salient concerns, political friends work to perceive others within the contingencies and narratives of their own lives. Practically speaking, learning about the ways our political friends differ from us and how they orient toward shared and divergent concerns enables us to coordinate our efforts meaningfully. Such learning enables our co-construction of workable frames of reference that recognizes the distinctive stakes in our common political activities seeking justice (Kahane, 1999).

While learning about each other can broaden our outlooks and enhance our capacities for taking each other's perspective, it does not guarantee trust between political friends. In some cases increased knowledge of others diminishes our trust in them as we learn more about their longstanding disdain for us or objectionable tendencies in their way of life. Fifth, *while significant for constructive interaction, trust is a tenuous achievement and matter of degree; it must be earned continually between political friends.* Trust does not easily arise between potentially antagonistic persons or collectives in political affairs. We cautiously observe the actions of others in personal and political activities that bear on our own and others' well-being. We look for (in)consistencies between what others say in private versus public contexts about us and how these others actually treat members of our group. In short, we skeptically scrutinize the degree to which potentially opposed others actually live up to their overtures of political friendship. Luis and Lena are always negotiating the trust in their political relationship.

In many ways this continual checking for fidelity of speech and action by others resembles any context of everyday life (Goffman, 1959). Even so, as personal friends become emotionally close, we develop mutual assumptions of benevolence and usually give friends the benefit of the doubt. Through enjoyable activity together, revealing conversations, and caring responsiveness to each other's needs across time and personal circumstances, close friends typically develop "deep trust" in each other (Putnam, 2000). This trust functions as a type of "bonding social capital" we can draw upon in managing everyday interdependencies of our lives.

In contrast, this degree of trust is much less likely to arise between persons whose worlds and activities minimally overlap. We may develop looser connections based on more sporadic, less emotionally involving interactions. As members of groups aspiring to political friendship, however, we also may behave in dependably positive ways toward each other. We may cooperate on mutually beneficial tasks and do what needs to be done together to accomplish work or broader community goals. Behaving reliably with (though in some circumstances without) good will in these capacities can establish the "loose ties" and "shallow trust" that help to produce "bridging social capital" (Granovetter, 1973; Putnam, 2000). These actively accomplished connections and enhanced perspectives of one another facilitate working trust and political friendship.

Sixth, *political friends communicatively accomplish trust through respectful honesty in our dealings with each other in private and especially in public settings.* In our deliberations as community members, we are straightforward with each other but not to the point of offending fellow citizens. Political friends must be able to engage potentially divisive issues that matter to us as part of our common activities. At the same time these discursive actions implicate the speakers' identities as well as group members who identify with them. Respectful honesty acknowledges the tensions between encouraging the expression of necessary truths, while being discreet about sensitive matters that might upset them or threaten their good standing as community members. Thoughtfully managing these contradictory activities can engender trust in both the honesty and discretion of speakers. It recommends such speakers as potentially valued persons with whom to deliberate and form judgments. Respectful honesty continually shapes and reflects discursive trust in political relationships.

Seventh, *the conscientiously interested practices of friendship can compose an ethical pull toward political involvement.* We take seriously our friends' concerns and do what we can to ensure their happiness. This substantive partiality of friendship may include only a restricted group of people (M. Friedman, 1992). Yet the ethical practices of friendship— including voluntary participation, good will toward others for their own sakes, equal respect, continual learning about other persons, trustworthy actions, respectful honesty, and desires for justice—may hearten us to reach out more toward others. Pursuing positive associations with others and making diverse types of friends through various kinds of interactions inherently broadens our outlook (Goering, 2003). Learning about others' worlds in the spirit of equal respect modeled by our personal friendships, we can begin to identify with their specific needs for justice. As a result, we can experience an ethical summons to extend the compass of our concern for political friends to include formerly excluded others. Political friendship builds on the interested, other-regarding stance of all friendships to act on behalf of those whom we have come to understand as deserving just treatment. Learning about others, identifying with their circumstances, and choosing to ensure spaces for voices to be heard in a spirit of equal respect and justice can create ethical calls to political action.

## ❖  FRIENDSHIPS AND SOCIAL CHANGE

Our social lives are inherently political. In the micropolitical actions of everyday life we can shape each other's experience of ourselves (Laing, 1968). In every waking moment we can affirm each other's sense of self and cherished identities. We can enhance our potentials to feel joy, to be proud of who we are, and to pursue our dreams. We can address and empower each other as equals. But we can also undermine each other's sense of self, disregard or destroy identities. We can do whatever it takes to glorify ourselves, sustain our privileges, and reign over others. In numberless ways we can make others miserable, keep them in their place, and prop ourselves up. The personal *is* political. Our daily actions can promote freedom and justice in small and large ways, but they can also perpetuate oppression. In every instance to some degree we choose whether or not and how to act (W. James, 1991).

But we may have precious little choice in the actual range of our available choices. This is another way that the personal is political. Each one of us embodies the enabling and constraining structural possibilities of our place in the society where we live (Giddens, 1979). We may enjoy abundant opportunities to fashion a life of relative ease and happiness. Our opportunities also may be severely constrained through systems of domination that prevent us from earning a living wage, render us susceptible to disease and starvation, and/or conscript us into violent circumstances where we are always in danger. Our identities may be demeaning, categorical "political facts" (Disch, 1995) foisted on us by others with little say by us about how we are treated. In light of these ascribed identities, our differences may be essentialized as deviant, causing us to be ignored or disrespected. The discourses of dispiriting individuation used by nearly everyone we encounter make it extremely difficult to envision our selves and our choices otherwise.

Friendships arise within and across the destitution and privileges of these diverse circumstances. Just as there is no known culture without hierarchy (Spence, 1978), there is no culture in the world without a notion of friendship (Brain, 1976). Friendships transpire across complex continua of associations between people. In some cases friendship is a primary bond pursued as an end-in-itself between two mutually devoted persons. In other instances friendships develop as a dimension of family, work, recreational, community, religious, or political relationships. Friendships differ greatly in their dependence on shared activities for continued existence, as well as their degree of common interests, mutual caring, regard, and involvement. There are practical limits on the number and quality of personal friends we may develop. It takes time, effort, availability, and interaction to become and remain friends with other people. Moreover, social stratifications may overdetermine the extent to which any friends are able to share their lives (Allan, 1979).

Even so, the flexibility of friendship can sponsor positive relations between people in a variety of circumstances. Friendships provide multiple opportunities for political activity. The very idea of friendship involves persons paired in the same role, that of friend to friend (Paine, 1969). Standing as equals embodies a challenge to hierarchical social structures. The tendency of friendships toward equal treatment is therefore a fundamental political potential. Because of this capability, people in power often discourage friendships between persons from differing statuses in the social structure (Hutter, 1978). Numerous businesses have rules against supervisors becoming friends with employees. Under these conditions merely becoming friends can be a measure of freedom (Naegele, 1958) and constitutes significant political activity (Ackelsberg, 1983). It flies in the face of the status quo.

Friends with differing privileges recognize and discuss the injustices of situations faced by the oppressed friend as well as others. With one of the two friends requiring a wheelchair, Fisher and Galler (1988) encountered and conversed in depth about inexcusable barriers to persons' mobility in a variety of settings. The women recalled their growing involvement during the early years of the disability rights movement: "But an understanding friend helps take the sting out of the injustice and their friendship feeds the spirit of resistance" (Fisher & Galler, 1988, p. 191). As part of the private morality of their friendship, such friends develop shared conceptions of necessary changes in prevailing social and power arrangements. Ackelsberg (1983) asserts, "While generally treated as falling within the 'private' sphere, friendships can be intensely political. They can form—and have formed—the basis for radical political association" (p. 351).

Friendships serve social change in multiple ways. Using a language of friendship to characterize relationships avoids the restrictive connotations of marriage, family, and kinship (Ackelsberg, 1983; M. Friedman, 1992). These relationships typically prescribe natural and traditional hierarchies among their participants with membership sanctioned through historical traditions, legal rules, and religious authorities. In contrast, personal and political friendships create communities of choice from dyads to larger groups (Ackelsberg, 1983; M. Friedman, 1992). Friends negotiate the terms and goals of their association. Recall the discussion of the subversive potential of cross-sex friendships in Chapter 5. Invoking an ethic of friendship between males and females liberates us from the injunctions of heterosexist institutions. Insisting on cross-sex friendship challenges the sexual objectification of partners, the privileging of romance over friendship on the expected march to marriage, and the enforcement of heteronormative and gendered scripts for female and male relationships. More broadly, cross-sex friendships challenge presupposed sexual identities and how we perform our selves. They interrogate a broad spectrum of taken-for-granted practices and power relations. The private moral visions that we negotiate with our friends can provide alternative templates for social relationships and for public morality (M. Friedman, 1992).

Discovering common perceptions of deeper social injustices with others despite initially apparent differences enables edifying participation in political activity. In Goering's words, "Friendships can *motivate* valuable social change" (2003, p. 406, emphasis added). We need to learn about and identify with others to involve ourselves politically on their behalf (Nardi, 1999). We develop our sense of obligation to support causes that do not directly implicate us through our identification with and concern for specific other persons—such as family members, work associates, colleagues, neighbors, and friends. Though certainly not the only basis for identification, typically the closer the relationship, the more we will identify with someone else's plight. Even so, it is one thing to identify with others; it is quite another to involve ourselves in public political activity supporting them. Putting our safe, privileged, or vulnerable identities on the line through public action on behalf of less favored or persecuted friends with whom we identify are risky authentications of our political commitment. Sometimes, for example, men don't want to speak up on behalf of women for the fear of being perceived as being controlled by women. And women may not want to speak up on behalf of men for the fear of being seen as betraying other women.

Friendship networks have been especially important bases for political movements challenging the status quo. Mutual trust, shared judgments, and dedication to specific friends can inspire persons' participation. Consequently, many political movements grow out of an initial group of close friends (Hutter, 1978; Nardi, 1999). Referring to progressive feminist action, Ackelsberg (1983) contends, "The strength of the movement, both during the nineteenth century and in the contemporary period, has been at its base, not in family ties, but in friendship networks" (p. 339). She notes friendships' similar importance for men's political groups: "Male friendships, as well, have provided important sources of support for those who participate in them. It seems no accident that early associations of workingmen, which provided the basis for unions, were called 'friendly societies'" (p. 344). The value of "interpersonal networks of friends" for mediating communications, linking associates, and mobilizing groups of participants in political endeavors on behalf of gay and lesbian rights has been noted (Nardi, 1999, p. 201). These preexisting communities of choice and belonging (M. Friedman, 1992)—these friendship networks—simultaneously confirm individual identities and connect them with larger "cultural and political communities" (Nardi, 1999, p. 206). The double agency of friendship serves both personal and social integration in political involvement.

In his book *Gay Men's Friendships: Invincible Communities*, Peter Nardi (1999) details the interrelated roles of personal and political friendships in accomplishing civic changes enabling gay and lesbian rights. At the outset he describes pockets of personal friends socializing individuals into the gay lifestyle, introducing them to other friends who can provide moral support for their identities and give them courage to shed closeted self-understandings, out themselves, and perform their gay identities publicly with pride. Nardi (1999) observes, "Friendship networks, thus, become the primary site where the daily lives of gay men and lesbians are carried out and shaped" (p. 192). Co-telling and listening to narratives with friends helped persons to consolidate their senses of personal identity and community belonging.

The onset of political, commercial, health, and residential development activities by gays and lesbians linked networks of loosely connected friendship groups. The "bridging social capital" developed through such civic engagement with political friends of diverse ethnicities and lifestyles worked to create the community spaces and neighborhoods for everyday gay life (Peacock, Eyre, Crouse Quinn, & Kegeles, 2001; Putnam, 2000). One of Nardi's research participants aptly called it "a dialectical process between gay friendship and gay social action. Each promotes and begets the other" (1999, p. 197). Nardi (1999) emphasizes the dynamic interconnections among gay identities, personal and political friendships, and active participation in community life:

> For many of those who get involved in collective actions, gay identity acceptance and friendships precede mobilization; for others gay identity and friendship networks are developed, reproduced, and maintained through participation in the institutions of a gay community, including organizations, bars, and social movements. (pp. 200–201)

Establishing "communities of identity and equality" in a spirit of friendship strongly affirms individuals' self-conceptions and feelings of social integration (Nardi, 1992, p. 192).

A recurring dynamic emerges with such amalgamated efforts at community formation by groups who otherwise differ in significant ways. Identifying with other groups in pursuing common interests enables the edifying participation of political friends. In the case of gay and lesbian rights various dissimilar groups cooperated as equals to advance the common causes of persons with sexual orientations challenging the normative social order. However, the groups began individuating themselves in light of their other salient identities. Nardi (1999) relates that "a politics of difference emerged, and concepts of community as a single, homogenous, and egalitarian category collapsed, especially since sexual orientation is distributed through a variety of class, racial, and gender groups" (p. 192). Participants derive their identities from multiple group memberships. Sexual orientation may suffice initially as a basis for political friendship under conditions of shared oppression. But historical injustices, material disparities, and unequal recognition by enveloping cultures work to highlight other identities as more salient "political facts" (Disch, 1995) for self-recognition and separate group identities (Peacock et al., 2001). Differently raced and/or working class gays may no longer identify with gentrified white gays. Gays identifying with unprotected sexual practices feel judged and excluded by a gay mainstream identified with condom use (Peacock et al., 2001, p. 198). An ongoing dialectic transpires between the identities considered central and those marked as marginal by the mainstream. Persons with marginalized identities begin to gather around them as newly acknowledged bases for group identification and community formation (Peacock et al., 2001). In cases of falsely essentialized differences and simmering hostility, opposed identities may become sufficiently charged to render former political friendships no longer possible.

## ❖  LIMITATIONS OF POLITICAL FRIENDSHIPS

The ethical aspirations of political friendship are constrained by stark realities of politics. There are troublesome limits to the political compass of friendship at both ends of the spectrum of private and public life. Friendship with specific persons puts faces on issues, allowing us to identify closely with their fates. Within our powers we seek justice for those whose needs we understand. But the ethical pull of particularized caring within personal friendships can lead to subjective decisions and unjust favoritism. Affection for our special friend may find us ignoring our judgments' questionable fairness and consequences for a broader community. M. Kaplan (2005, p. 447) argues that when focused solely on dyads or personal cliques, "even as individuals cultivate the capacity for judgment, they do so not as citizens but as members of an affective, rather than political, community." Instead of fostering participation in genuine politics, such friendships can be privatized retreats. Kaplan rightly criticizes such practices of friendship as "citizenship's alibi" constituting "a zone of private intimacy as the privileged site of [personal] authenticity and moral judgment" (p. 436). Harbored within our personal friendships we may become too complacent for political participation. As long as the needs of our specific friends are met, we feel no need to enhance the lives of unknown others.

Political collectives cleaving to narrow definitions of the common good in the name of civic friendship fare no better as ethical models. Problems arise from excessive partiality toward our like-minded political friends and selfish regard for the special interests of our community. Political activity and community participation that derive from restricted identifications with similar friends promote exclusionary activities. In seeking justice, we must be watchful about the bases for the common goods we espouse. This is because the shared identities and solidarity of political friendship too easily can turn into sanctioned prejudices and insularity. For example, the celebrated friendships among citizens in ancient Greece were responsible for as much discord between city-states as stability within them (Hutter, 1978). Moreover, these civic friendships presumed considerable homogeneity among privileged citizens with women excluded from public life and most non-Greeks living as slaves (Hutter, 1978).

Broader, divisive political arenas involve further constraints on civic friendship. Certain limitations derive from the sheer size of the polity. The informal practices of friendship for recognizing another's concerns, protecting that person's autonomy, and ensuring equal respect do not readily convert to formal public procedures involving numerous people (Mansbridge, 1975). Larger numbers of citizens increase the differentiated bases for identification and the possibility of coalitions (Burke, 1969). Significantly, pursuing the common good despite differences and participating in a spirit of good will—the fundamental watchwords of Aristotle's vision of political friendship— become substantially strained in political settings involving intractable differences and multitudes of people.

Deeply contested visions of the common good sharply challenge the very meaning of shared aims for enabling political friendship. There are practical limits to the extent of differences among citizens that political friendship can embrace. Some differences in living conditions and life chances are too great for any pretense of commonality. Moreover, unforgivable actions by others or certain "ideological divides" "eliminate the possibility of mutual respect and trust" (Goering, 2003, p. 405). In such circumstances it is politically naïve or patronizing to assert the possibility of political friendship based on the common good. Facilitating the capacity of citizens to judge together and address political matters with shared consequences is an important goal of civic friendship (Beiner, 1983). However, as M. Kaplan (2005) warns, "A theory of action that privileges the faculty of judgment is dangerously myopic if it marginalizes the constitutive role ideological motivations and constraints play in determining the scope and modality of judgment" (p. 437). We must interrogate embedded ideologies and structural inequalities. They can sharply partition interests and make empty charades of appeals to the common good (Giddens, 1979).

There are related limits to good will in political situations. Asymmetrical power relations among social groups often results in sustained resentment and hostility. Around the globe people occupy highly contentious positions of entrenched opposition over scarce resources, sacred sites, political power, and fundamental freedoms. Viewing such disparities as endemic to the human condition, authors share Hannah Arendt's conception of "politics as the proper sphere of social antagonism" (M. Kaplan, 2005, p. 431). According to Kaplan, political activity is defined by "that antagonism which bears on fundamentally contrary conceptions of the common good" (2005, p. 432). In these circumstances Aristotle's image of political friendship clearly lacks traction.

Performing good will can be a luxury of those in power and cynically viewed as an exercise in mystification. Those who operate from privileged positions can extend good will to subordinates to salve inequalities and sustain unjust power relations. Jackman and Crane (1986) observe, "Intergroup friendship increases the bonds of affection with subordinates, but it does not undercut the discrimination that defines the unequal relationship between the two groups" (p. 482). We critique good will when it focuses merely on enhancing social relations to the detriment of addressing power disparities and exploitative social structures (M. Kaplan, 2005). Ethical political activity in the name of friendship serves justice through tackling these conditions and extending the range of human choices.

In my judgment, certain ethical aspirations involving friendship can inform a range of human practices across private and public contexts. Whether we speak of dyads or larger groups, bridgeable human differences or those unable to be crossed, temporary arrangements or sustained relationships—practicing friendship implies reverence for humane and edifying individuation and participation. In the final chapter I will examine the compass of friendship in this spirit.

# 8

# The Compass of
# Friendship

The destinies of selves, others, and our associated groups are always interrelated. We are co-dwellers of a planet that shrinks in size every nanosecond as communication technologies instantly impact the ideas, beliefs, and actions transpiring in distant places. Meanwhile, geometrically multiplying populations, migrating peoples, and dwindling natural resources give lie to fixed notions of the earth's size and the spaces between cultures. Languages, ways of life, and what and who people worship may differ markedly, but matters like the warmth of nurturance—and the gut-wrenching tragedy of *any* child's untimely death—do not. As human beings throughout this Earth, we share the times we are alive. We encounter our diverse traditions through each other's actions in the present. We bequeath the legacies of our interactions now to present and subsequent generations. We are involved in the making and the unmaking of humanity's world and all people's worlds.

In Marai's novel *Embers* (1942/2002), Henrik ponders how differences construct "otherness" during his final conversation with Konrad. Close friends in their youths, he contemplates the disturbing separation of their adult lives:

I do not understand, I still don't know what being different means . . .
It takes a long time, many lonely hours, to teach myself that it is

always and exclusively about the fact that between men and women, friends and acquaintances, there is this question of otherness, and that the human race is divided into two camps. Sometimes I think these two camps are what define the entire world, and that all class distinctions, all shades of opinion and all variations in power relations are simply variants of this otherness. (pp. 192–193)

Selves do not exist without other selves. And selves *as* selves and others *as* others do not exist except in dynamic juxtaposition and inter-action—in relationships. These possibilities for selfhood and otherhood arise both within and between human groups. For better and for worse, the notions of me and you, we and they, Self and Other, Us and Them, arise within and between dyads and human collectives of every size. These notions take on their significance, both hopeful and tragic, for every living being through the incessant co-creation of meaning(s) with others. Our fate as human beings is to assign meanings to the moments we are alive. What we experience individually as conscious-ness depends upon interaction, symbolic activity, communication with other human beings. Communication with others is essential to our humanity—to continually being and becoming human beings.

Friendship matters to people everywhere. It is a redemptive, liber-ating potential of human relational existence. Yet friendship is not with-out demands, contradictions, limits, or failings. In this book, I have explored *the compass of friendship* in two interrelated senses. First, I have considered the *scope* of friendship through the dialectic of individuation and participation. What does it mean to communicate as friends? What special practices characterize our treatment of others in friendship? How far can the praxis of friendship reach in spanning human differ-ences across private and public contexts? How encompassing are the ideals and sentiments of friendship? What constraints do friendships encounter in concrete settings and discursive formations? In a second sense, I have focused on the ethical *guidance* provided by friendship. How do the communicative practices of friendship facilitate judging and making choices? How do friends help each other to find moral direction in our lives? Questions concerning the scope and guidance of friendship's compass entwine as we examine the interconnections among negotiating contexts, making meanings, and co-creating indi-vidual, relational, and collective identities as friends.

We need to believe that our lives matter, our personal actions make a significant difference to somebody, and that we belong (Gans, 1985; Laing, 1969). We desire both self-assertion and self-transcendence. We must act singly and collectively to achieve social continuities and changes. Yet meaningful individuality and community arise in the context of each other. Our choices in creating meanings and crafting our identities inherently respond to the similarities and differences composing each of our worlds. *This dynamic continuum of self/other identity formation necessarily involves dialectical interrelationships of individuation and participation.*

*Individuation* describes our experience of self and others as separately embodied individuals. Every one of us occupies a radically distinctive physical time and place across the moments of our lives; each human being is singular. At the same time, from birth we only understand ourselves as individuated persons through our communicative links with others. This *participation* incorporates self with others and identifies each of us as a relational being connected through interaction with others. Participation emphasizes significant similarities of a self among other selves. In analogous ways, human groupings of various sizes individuate themselves through emphasizing the similarities and differences they share as commonly recognized participants. They accomplish this profile of participation and member self-recognition in contrast to the composites of similarities and differences they ascribe to other groups. Meanwhile, the same composites may or may not be used by members of these other groups to identify themselves.

Our identities as individuals and groups are simultaneously individuated and participatory. I argue that individuation and participation occur in edifying and dispiriting ways. *Edifying individuation* embraces responsibility for the unique potentials of each of our singular, embodied, self-recognizing existences. We make choices thoughtfully as individuals (and groups) within the perceived, tangible possibilities of our circumstances. We respect the comparable potentials of other persons (and groups). Because we value our own and others' singularity as human beings, we may decide to stand with and stand up for others when they face adversity. On the other hand, if we are too impressed with ourselves as a special being or group, we may exaggerate our distinctions from others and practice *dispiriting individuation. The Primary Misperception of Individuation* is to overemphasize our differences and uniqueness to the neglect of significant similarities shared with others. Disavowing our interdependency with others, we may impose sharp, if arbitrary, borders between our concerns and theirs. We must be careful not to let individuation become merely alienating, self-serving individualism. Despite our salient differences, there always are vital ways in which we resemble others *and* aspects in which others are similar to us.

*Edifying participation* capitalizes on our meaningful similarities in building connections with others. We communicate in ways that include others and facilitate their belonging. The authentic solidarity accomplished through edifying participation requires that included persons and groups retain their unique, self-recognizing identities. *Dispiriting participation* involves exclusionary practices that erase or devalue meaningful diversity in human beings. *The Primary Misperception of Participation* is to insist upon our similarities with others while disregarding their significant differences. Because acknowledging others' values may threaten our perceived purity, out-groups may suffer, excel, or identify themselves in ways we refuse to recognize. Despite significant commonalities, there are always consequential ways we differ from others *and* vital ways they contrast with us.

We accomplish edifying individuation by recognizing our and others' distinctive qualities in the face of mutually identified similarities. At the same time, we achieve edifying participation by acknowledging our common humanity in the face of jointly recognized differences. Motivated by the shared regard of friendship, these valued ratios of acknowledged differences and similarities can evolve constructively over time in concrete situations. *It is in the spirit of both personal and political friendship to facilitate edifying individuation and participation through communicative action.*

I argue that *friends serve their singular and shared identities through the communicative practices of storytelling and dialogue.* In *telling stories* we relate meaningful events of our lives in ways that demonstrate our particular points of view. This narrative activity simultaneously involves us as co-participants. It calls for careful listening to recognize the personal issues and sociocultural circumstances at stake for the teller of the narrative. We also portray valued identities and images of ourselves as community members in our stories. Moreover, how we describe the temporal connections among events in our narratives demonstrates how we live and perceive time. How scheduled, rushed, calm, or chaotic are our lives? What configurations of demands concurrently bear down on us? How much choice and constraint in shaping our own lives do our stories suggest? *Practicing dialogue* is vital for friendship as well. Through dialogue, we actively exchange, question, and respond to our points of view on issues of concern. Our conversation embodies pronounced respect for ourselves and for other(s). We acknowledge that our individual identities involve salient similarities and differences that are historical, contextual, and relational accomplishments. We actively and mutually engage in dialogue; we are present to each other. While adhering to our convictions, we remain open to other viewpoints. We also realize that our dialogue can demonstrate intractable positions and concrete constraints on our relationship. We may come to understand limits to our understanding (Gurevitch, 1989).

Narrative and dialogue interweave in the discourses of friend-ship, vividly revealing the worldviews of friends. Both discursive activities welcome the participation of others and emphasize the cre-ative, ethical, and mutually affirming significance of engaged listen-ing. Moments of dialogue and storytelling among friends encourage expressing ourselves and hearing our voices. These activities may arise as ends-in-themselves for the enjoyment of time passed in each other's presence. At the same time dialogues and narratives exchanged among friends constitute moral visions. They dramatize and question our conceptions of well-lived lives. As friends we envision possibili-ties and co-construct choices through narrating stories and pursuing dialogues together.

Chapter 4 examined how the afternoon conversation between two longtime women friends embodied *the ongoing communicative achieve-ment of friendship as a dialogue of narratives and a narrative of dialogues.* Indeed, these braided activities can animate friendship's potentials for co-creating understandings. Every person's life is comprised of many stories. In telling the events of our lives, we portray our own characters and our encounters with people we admire and disdain. We describe mundane happenings, challenges, happy moments, worrisome dilem-mas, and tough decisions. We describe circumstances when we felt strong and when we were vulnerable. We relate choices we are proud of and situations we could have handled better. We keep the past vivid to help us deal with the present and anticipate the future. All of these narrated moments reflect our values, self-perceptions of our capacities and limits, our hopes and fears.

As we live and exchange our stories with friends, we compose *a dia-logue of narratives.* Sometimes we swap narratives about incidents with comparable issues at stake. Sometimes our stories passionately clash in their portrayals of occurrences or the meanings of actions. We listen carefully, waiting for the climax, punch line, or moral. The stories of our individuated lives draw breath and recognition from our participation in the ongoing dialogue of our friendship. The dialogue of our narra-tives becomes more active as we cross-examine the positions embodied in our stories. We may question any aspect of the narratives we share as friends. The meanings, points of view, identities, cultural circumstances, values, choices, and pace of lives featured in our stories can spawn out-right dialogue between us. We may tell other stories to clarify or sup-port our contentions. We question the existential positions embodied in our stories. We may also examine the moral positions embodied in the questions we ask each other. Why are these issues so important to us? Would you please explain to me why this is so upsetting to you? How is what you've just described a good thing? Is there any way I can get you to consider a different position? What can we do together to change the situation you are facing? Or we may fail to see the humor in a story, pointing out troubling social conditions our friend assumes without thinking or ignores. Either way, it's time for more talk. How could you possibly see *this* as funny? Tell me. Hearing your reasons for telling the story, I learn more about where you are coming from. I also learn about myself and perhaps some of the unrecognized conceits motivating my cross-examination of your story.

Our friendship embodies a *narrative of dialogues* that we pursue together. What kinds of conversations characterize the story of our friendship? Much of our talk may be playful banter, shooting the breeze, passing the time. Many interactions are simply back and forth exchanges about the events of the day or planning future activities. But as ordinary as our talk might seem, it takes on gravity when troubles occur. Maybe we've been hurt by a romantic partner or treated unjustly at work. Our talk with friends changes when danger, hunger, health problems, prejudice, or barriers to our abilities to accomplish basic needs threaten our everyday existence. Our daily dialogues as friends now constitute a narrative of continuous coping, mutual support, and working to co-create possibilities in constricting conditions. If we share the narrative of these dialogues with other members of our community, they may begin to identify with us. They may have grappled with comparable issues. We may perceive how the individuated events of our lives relate to our common participation in oppressive political conditions. Despite our differences we may decide it is time to do something about it.

Practicing friendship invites us to belong with others at the same time that it values who we are as individuals. Negotiating friendship involves creating discursive space between friends that recognizes and supports our singular qualities *and* brings us together for meaningful participation in a shared life. Interweaving narration and dialogue shapes and reflects this flexible, responsible, and responsive freedom. Both dialogues and narratives resist discursive closure in conceiving of others and their possibilities for action. Dialogue entertains multiple meanings simultaneously revealed by any situation. It refuses either/or thinking by collaboratively opening up new vistas between initially perceived options. Narrative envisions human predicaments and possibilities occurring contingently across time. Storytelling knits together the events of time and place and refuses to see our potentials separate from actual and possible contexts. *We try to perceive our friends within the narratives of their own lives.* Even so, our past experiences do not have to be repeated in the present. Who we were before does not dictate who we are now and who we can be in the future. Linking narrative and dialogue, friends cross-examine meaningful turning points in their stories. How could things be different? Friends decide what matters now and how we might achieve it. Friends support our opportunities to make choices. Likewise, we want our friends to have as much say as possible in shaping the stories of their lives.

Personal friends develop shared private moral visions through stories and dialogues. But we must live out our conceptions of right and wrong actions in broader social contexts. Cross-sex and cross-race friendships reveal the potential vulnerability of all dyadic friendships negotiated in cultural networks of power relations. Culturally marked friendships are susceptible to socially sanctioned hierarchies and categorical divisions between persons based on arbitrarily emphasized differences. In heteronormative situations, enduring cross-sex friendships question femininities, masculinities, and sexualities governing the accepted practices of cross-sex and same-sex affection. Strongly held binaries undermine the commonalities and meaningful variations among differently gendered and sexually identified people. Taken for granted hierarchies of relationships, such as privileging romantic love and marriage over friendship, in conjunction with favored and stigmatized sexual identities and constructions of gender, regulate socially approved modes of caring. Intersections of ethnicity, race, and class further condition possibilities. Demonstrating the flexibility and fragility of all friendships, enduring cross-sex friendships both align with and subvert these arrangements.

Cross-race friendships such as those between blacks and whites also engage in sustained human caring that confronts cultural orders prescribing and proscribing relationships. With a background of historical injustices, persisting social obstructions, and asymmetrical perceptions, developing cross-race friendships involves continuous effort by most participants in the United States. These friendships challenge us to position and respond to each other within intersections of caustic historical discourses and concrete conditions that threaten our subjectivities and shared experiences. Negotiating friendship is difficult when each of us understands our identity largely in light of the same racialized structures and discourses that our friendship hopes to transcend.

Cross-race friends understand that our identities involve multiple aspects that fluctuate across contexts. Our identities further shift specifically in relation to each other. Common situations may highlight personally and culturally emphasized attributes. The ongoing challenge is to perceive each other as a provisionally complete being, a meaningfully whole self performed in this situation with (an)other self.

Each person's identity is simultaneously constituted in given moments as a potentially skewed intersection of cultural discourses and in relationship to our friend. *Many friends find it worthwhile to emphasize commonalities **and** each other's singular humanity.*

Discourses with enabling, constraining, and mixed effects configure the likelihood of friendships (Giddens, 1979). What defines our identities and eligibilities as friends? Is it our biological sex, gendered performances of self, or sexual identity? Is it our race, ethnicity, or social class? Is it our embodied abilities, occupational status, religion, or political party? Is it our height, weight, body type, hair or eye color, or dietary preferences? Is it some specific composition of these attributes? What configuration of personal and cultural attributes does each of us value in constructing our own identities? How much say do we as friends actually have in identifying, negotiating, and celebrating the differences and similarities between us that matter across contexts? What social groups are friends able to interconnect in light of individuated configurations of self- and shared identities? What is each friend's stance toward the differing identities, and how susceptible are these identities to commentary or even censure in emerging circumstances?

What capacities do cross-sex and cross-race friends have for expanding the compass of friendship? For one, they enact and provide models of radical inclusiveness and reaching across (sub)cultural divides. Oppressive structural conditions should not rule out such interpersonal striving. Acknowledging enabling and constraining factors, *every single person and every friendship can make a difference in contributing to positive social action and humane changes.* Friends also can participate actively as links between formerly disconnected social networks (Nardi, 1999). Yet at every level it may be asked: What and whose good is this particular participatory framework, this friendship, serving? The challenge for friends concerned with social justice is to work together with ever more inclusive groupings to confront the higher order exclusions that divide and degrade people. This is part of the labor of progressive political friendship and alliances—to create and sustain other possibilities for human flourishing.

Cultivating friendships, moral visions, and justice are related activities. Important ethical practices characterize personal friendship (Aristotle, 1980; Blum, 1980; Brain, 1976). Conditioned by our circumstances, we exercise our moral will in voluntarily developing and sustaining our friendships (Blum, 1980). Significantly, we continually choose to do right by our friends. We practice mutual altruistic concern for our friend's own sake (Aristotle, 1980). Doing this enlarges our notions of selfhood as we become relationally concerned selves. We respect our friends and seek equality in our common activities. We continue to learn about our friends as an ethical requirement of living in friendship with each other. Through behaving in trusting and trustworthy ways, we co-create trust in our friendships. We promote trust communicatively through practicing respectful honesty with our friends. Recognizing these mutually achieved ethical qualities, we give special attention to our friends' needs and desires. Friendship is a conscientiously interested relationship. These practices contextualize each other in living ethically as friends.

Within limits these substantive ethical practices of personal friendships can provide models for political friendships. The recognition friends give to each other's distinctive potentials as concrete human beings, their ongoing achievement of edifying individuation, is a vital, guiding ideal for authentic justice. The conscientious interest in actual others developed through personal friendships and friendship networks can draw us out of narrow self-interest and into ethical involvement in broader political activity. We can be moved by the spaces for self- and other-actualization and recognition created within our personal friendships to seek broader domains of human freedom and dignity.

Political friendships also have significant ethical potentials. Voluntary participation is an ethical necessity for political friendship; we choose to embrace collective causes. Another vital practice involves citizens pursuing common goods in a spirit of good will despite our differences (Aristotle, 1980). In less than ideal worlds, treating fellow citizens respectfully as equals realizes ethical principles as well as political goals. Recognizing human dignity is both an ethical means and a worthwhile political aspiration. Political friends continually pursue knowledge about other citizens' circumstances and viewpoints to appreciate their identities, co-construct frames of reference, and coordinate activities. Political friends must work continuously to achieve and sustain shared trust because of its tenuous nature and constructive significance. Through respectful honesty in private, and notably in public settings, political friends work to accomplish trust in communicative practices. Political friendship can extend the conscientiously interested, other-regarding stance of all friendships to act on behalf of other people deserving just treatment. We can experience an ethical summons to extend the compass of our concern for friends to include formerly excluded others.

However, there are limits to the ethical potentials of political friendships in both private and public settings. Personal friendships can constitute exclusive retreats from the broader demands of politics. We may only befriend persons who resemble us and share our views.

We may enjoy our private comforts too much to become involved with disturbing social issues affecting those outside our small circle. In the political sphere excessive partiality toward our like-minded political friends may cloud and narrow our judgment. We may give our friends unfair advantages selfishly serving our own special interests. The unity of political friendship based on restricted identifications with similar friends too easily can foster insularity and sanctioned prejudices.

The size and demographic composition of our polity also can limit the viability of political friendship. Greater numbers of citizens produce proliferating bases for identification and coalitions (Burke, 1969). Pursuing the common good despite citizens' differences and participating in a spirit of good will are substantially challenged in polities involving sharply contrasting ideologies, structural inequalities, and multitudes of people. Sustained resentment is more likely than good will among social groups with asymmetrical power relations and resources. In volatile and fragmented circumstances, differentially suffering people must coordinate their responses to concrete injustices. Under these conditions feminists recommend vigilant partisanship to accomplish a contingently articulated solidarity (Disch, 1995). Instead of abstract commonalities, we evaluate our possibilities and choose sides because of tangible occurrences taking place in the world at definite moments. Viable political alliances recognize multiple worldviews on events affecting actors. We preserve sufficient distance between citizens for disputing a plurality of interests arising from diverse locations in working to address concrete problems and facilitate social justice. In situations of oppressively enforced differences achieving issue-driven alliances may be the best we can do.

The constructive political potentials of friendship necessarily are negotiated across a wide range of private and public circumstances. They vary considerably across four specific continua in their practices and accomplishments in light of the concrete sociocultural conditions under which they are attempted. *All of these endeavors constitute hopeful alternatives to hatred, violence, and attempting to annihilate others.* First, political friendships may seek more enduring common goods derived from shared lives and identities. The other pole of these activities may accomplish a temporarily shared space for concerted actions toward contingently held political goals for a purposely limited time. Second, the emotional tone of political friendship activities ranges from actively communicating good will in working together to consciously refraining from antagonism or aggression. Third, the space of friendship may include practices of mutual respect for the equality of participants. On the other hand, the activities may basically accomplish nonviolent political space to dispute meanings of concrete conditions of life. Fourth, political friendship endeavors may achieve varying degrees of shallow and deep trust (Putnam, 2000) in laboring together for political ends. The other pole involves wary recognition of consistencies between beneficial words and actions by others. How encompassing must the shared frames of reference of our political friendships be? Do these frames address our immediate circumstances or must they comprehend issues, events, and identities transcending the present moment? Can we conceivably bridge our differences or are our disparities too great? Friendship's ethical practices are always contingent achievements.

Human finitude constrains friendship's ethical compass just as human multiplicity expands and complicates it. We have difficulties getting outside ourselves. There are limits to our reflexivity and our empathy, our abilities to perceive ourselves and others clearly. In trying to reflect on our own selves, we find that we are changing every day and over time, revising our memories, forgetting more than we remember, even as we perform consequential actions in this present moment of reflection. The self we reflect upon is complex, contradictory, and constructed through numerous intersecting discourses across time and a maze of social contexts (Kahane, 1999). These intricacies also hamper our perceptions of others. How can we be so *certain* about the correctness of what we know about ourselves and others? Sometimes our friends can help us achieve understandings. But how open are we to their windows on the world?

*Collaborative learning about self and other is an ongoing ethical responsibility of friendship.* We must continue to learn about each other. Personal and political friends co-construct the grounds of our appraisals of each other as individuated persons and as participants in shared situations and moral visions. We question our premises for selecting differences that matter in recognizing our individuated identities. We examine the significant similarities and contrasts for constructing our collective identities. Yet we must be cautious about the potentials for self- and mutual deception in co-creating knowledge of ourselves and our circumstances (Annis, 1987). We must be free to question the effects of power differentials and material conditions on our perceptions and thoughts. We must contribute as equals in cross-examining our perceptions of the matters at hand. It is not necessary for the knowledge we co-construct to blend our perspectives perfectly or comprehensively. It *is* necessary for each of us to be able to address the grounds we invoke to establish our viewpoints. We must be free to comment on the process we are using to identify our agreements and differences, and how we are supporting our points (Burbules, 1992). We must listen carefully to the other and to ourselves in addressing and responding to our friend(s). Practicing dialogue and sharing our narratives facilitates co-produced knowledge of self and others.

Through these discursive activities we accomplish our involvement as participants and distance as individuated witnesses of our always needed activities of co-learning (Beiner, 1983; Kepnes, 1992). We engage in the dialectic of judgment and acceptance (Rawlins, 1992). We accept each other's narrated experiences and dialogical positions on that person's own terms, receptive to the new perspectives her or his words disclose. During other moments, we filter and evaluate these understandings through our distinctive worldviews as well as shared standards. How are our individual and collective identities implicated? We evaluate the applicability of our co-created understandings to our lives. Our co-learning may involve significant unlearning. We may need to relinquish ignorant, dispiriting, and destructive identifications and convictions. We discharge categorical descriptions of self and other that prevent us from being and recognizing who we actually are or can become. *We judge together and we judge each other in a spirit of compassionate objectivity.*

As friends we are humble in the face of our mutually recognized identities. The humble stance achieved in friendship respects each person's relational integrity and unique potential to make a difference in creating more humane worlds. *Humility involves the simultaneous awareness of our limits as individuals and our necessary participation in enlivening connections larger than our selves.* We accomplish our relational integrity without insularity.

The conjunctive freedoms living at the heart of friendship can summon us ethically to make responsive and responsible choices with our friends. Yet like the story of Hank and Barry told at the beginning of this book, friendships course between private and public expectations, loyalty to our friends versus duty to broader social covenants, upholding individual versus collective identities. *Moral action as friends demands "continuing thoughtfulness,"* which Koehn (1998) celebrates as "the most defensible ethical stance" (p. 161). On one hand, thoughtfulness requires careful, rational, principled appraisal of the alternatives posed by a given situation and their consequences for our broader community. At the same time, thoughtfulness requires caring regard for the specific contingencies and lived experiences conditioning our singular friend's actions. What concrete differences will our decision make for *this* individual? Our concern for our friend's well-being constitutes substantive partiality practiced in the context of impersonal community standards (M. Friedman, 1992). Practicing thoughtfulness continually involves both reasons of the heart and reasons of the mind (Bateson, 1972). Burke once observed, "Perhaps there is an evasion, a shirking of responsibility, in becoming certain too quickly" (1931/1968, p. 105). Acknowledging the complexity of human predicaments, friendship calls us thoughtfully to embrace our responsibilities and to make our choices.

In collaboratively learning and judging with others, we expand our ethical practices. Dialogues and storytelling with different people can reveal our biases, taken for granted standpoints, and oversights. These activities sharpen our perceptions of ourselves and others and the kinds of people we are capable of becoming (M. Friedman, 1992; Goering, 2003). Yet how diverse are our friends? Do we routinely encounter sufficiently different others to test and extend our viewpoints? Do we devote the effort to expand our comfort zones? Jane Addams spoke eloquently about the moral instruction provided by broader human encounters, "We know instinctively that if we grow contemptuous of our fellows, and consciously limit our intercourse to certain kinds of people whom we have previously decided to respect, we not only tremendously circumscribe our range of life, but limit the scope of our ethics" (quoted in Goering, 2003, pp. 404–405).

Where do we stand with the compass of friendship? We stand with other human beings in all our potentials, fallibilities, vulnerabilities, and multiplicities. We see friendship celebrated throughout history and around the globe at various times and in different ways because it tracks humankind's capacities for benevolence and cooperation (Brain, 1976). We see the good-hearted, responsive practices of friendship invoked in a variety of settings because it can bring out the best in people. We say friendship makes life worth living because of the joy, wisdom, and support our beloved personal friends bestow us. Yet we and our friends are not perfect and neither is friendship. As with our trusted friends, we often give friendship itself the benefit of the doubt as a human(e) ideal. In reality the compass of friendship offers contingent scope and guidance. Its world-enhancing qualities must be accomplished in every instance by human beings in conditional, concrete circumstances.

# References

Abbey, A. (1982). Sex differences in attributions for friendly behavior: Do males misperceive females' friendliness? *Journal of Personality and Social Psychology, 42,* 830–838.

Ackelsberg, M. A. (1983). "Sisters" or "comrades"? The politics of friends and families. In I. Diamond (Ed.), *Politics and public policy* (pp. 339–356). New York: Longman.

Adams, R. G., & Allan, G. (1998). *Placing friendship in context.* New York: Cambridge University Press.

Afifi, W. A., & Faulkner, S. L. (2000). On being "just friends": The frequency and impact of sexual activity in cross-sex friendships. *Journal of Social and Personal Relationships, 17,* 205–222.

Allan, G. A. (1979). *A sociology of friendship and kinship.* London: Allen and Unwin.

Allen, L. (2004). "Getting off" and "going out": Young people's conceptions of (hetero)sexual relationships. *Culture, Health & Sexuality, 6,* 463–481.

Annis, D. B. (1987). The meaning, value, and duties of friendship. *American Philosophical Quarterly, 24,* 349–356.

Arendt, H. (1958). *The human condition.* New York: Vintage Books.

Arendt, H. (1968). *Men in dark times.* New York: Harcourt Brace Jovanovich.

Aristotle. (1980). *The Nicomachean ethics* (D. Ross, Trans.). Oxford, UK: Oxford University Press.

Arnold, L. B. (1995). Through the narrow pass: Experiencing same-sex friendship in heterosexual(ist) settings. *Communication Studies, 46,* 234–244.

Arras, J. D. (1997). Nice story, but so what? Narrative and justification in ethics. In H. L. Nelson (Ed.), *Stories and their limits: Narrative approaches to ethics* (pp. 65–88). New York: Routledge.

Ashcraft, K. L., & Allen, B. J. (2003). The racial foundations of organizational communication. *Communication Theory, 13,* 5–38.

Bakhtin, M. M. (1981). *The dialogic imagination: Four essays.* Austin: University of Texas Press.

Bakhtin, M. M. (1990). *Art and answerability: Early philosophical works by M. M. Bakhtin* (M. Holquist & V. Liapunov, Eds.; V. Liapunov, Trans.). Austin: University of Texas Press.

Bakhtin, M. M. (1993). *Toward a philosophy of the act* (V. Liapunov & M. Holquist, Eds.; V. Liapunov, Trans.). Austin: University of Texas Press.

Barros, C. A. (1998). *Autobiography: Narrative of transformation.* Ann Arbor: University of Michigan Press.

Bateson, G. (1958). *Naven.* Stanford, CA: Stanford University Press.

Bateson, G. (1972). *Steps to an ecology of mind.* New York: Ballantine Books.

Bateson, G. (1979). *Mind and nature: A necessary unity.* New York: E. P. Dutton.

Beiner, R. (1983). *Political judgment.* Chicago: University of Chicago Press.

Benhabib, S. (1995). Feminism and postmodernism: An uneasy alliance. In S. Benhabib, J. Butler, D. Cornell, & N. Fraser (Eds.), *Feminist contentions: A philosophical exchange* (pp. 17–34). New York: Routledge.

Berger, P., & Luckman, T. (1966). *The social construction of reality.* Garden City, NY: Doubleday.

Berlin, I. (1969). *Four essays on liberty.* Oxford, UK: Oxford University Press.

Black, L. W. (2008). Deliberation, storytelling, and dialogic moments. *Communication Theory, 18,* 93–116.

Blum, L. A. (1980). *Friendship, altruism and morality.* London: Routledge & Kegan Paul.

Bochner, A. P. (1994). Perspectives on inquiry II: Theories and stories. In M. L. Knapp & G. R. Miller (Eds.), *Handbook of interpersonal communication* (2nd ed., pp. 21–41). Thousand Oaks, CA: Sage.

Bonilla-Silva, E., & Forman, T. A. (2000). "I'm not racist but . . .": Mapping white college students' racial ideology in the USA. *Discourse & Society, 11,* 50–85.

Booth, W. C. (1988). *The company we keep: An ethics of fiction.* Berkeley: University of California Press.

Brain, R. (1976). *Friends and lovers.* New York: Basic Books.

Bruner, J. (1996). *The culture of education.* Cambridge, MA: Harvard University Press.

Bruner, J. (2002). *Making stories: Law, literature, life.* Cambridge, MA: Harvard University Press.

Buber, M. (1937). *I and thou* (R. G. Smith, Trans.). Edinburgh: T. & T. Clark.

Buber, M. (1956). *The knowledge of man: A philosophy of the interhuman.* New York: Harper and Row.

Buber, M. (1957). Distance and relation. *Psychiatry, 20,* 97–104.

Buber, M. (1970). *I and thou* (W. Kaufmann, Trans.). New York: Touchstone.

Bukowski, W. M., & Sippola, L. K. (1996). Friendship and morality: (How) are they related? In W. M. Bukowski, A. F. Newcomb, & W. W. Hartup (Eds.), *The company they keep: Friendship in childhood and adolescence* (pp. 238–261). Cambridge, UK: Cambridge University Press.

Burbules, N. (1992). *Dialogue in teaching: Theory and practice.* New York: Teachers College Press.

Burke, K. (1966). *Language as symbolic action: Essays on life, literature, and method.* Berkeley: University of California Press.

Burke, K. (1968). *Counter-statement.* Berkeley: University of California Press. (Original work published 1931)

Burke, K. (1969). *A rhetoric of motives.* Berkeley: University of California Press.

Burrell, D., & Hauerwas, S. (1977). From system to story: An alternative pattern for rationality in ethics. In H. T. Engelhardt, Jr., & D. Callahan (Eds.), *Knowledge, value and belief* (pp. 11–152). New York: The Hastings Center.

Butler, J. (1990). *Gender trouble.* New York: Routledge.

Butler, J. (1995). Contingent foundations: Feminism and the question of "post-modernism." In S. Benhabib, J. Butler, D. Cornell, & N. Fraser (Eds.), *Feminist connections: A philosophical exchange* (pp. 35–57). New York: Routledge.

Carr, D. (1986). *Time, narrative, and history.* Bloomington: Indiana University Press.

Casey, J. (1979). Mandarins in a farther field. In *Testimony and Demeanor* (pp. 29–52). New York: Knopf.

Cissna, K. N., & Anderson, R. (2002). *Moments of meeting: Buber, Rogers, and the potential for public dialogue.* Albany: State University of New York Press.

Conlon, J. (1995). Why lovers can't be friends. In R. M. Stewart (Ed.), *Philosophical perspectives on sex and love* (pp. 295–299). New York: Oxford University Press.

Connell, R. W. (1993). The big picture: Masculinities in recent world history. *Theory and Society, 22,* 597–623.

Cooper, J. M. (1980). Aristotle on friendship. In A. O. Rorty (Ed.), *Essays on Aristotle's ethics* (pp. 301–340). Berkeley: University of California Press.

Crites, S. (1986). Storytime: Recollecting the past and projecting the future. In T. R. Sarbin (Ed.), *Narrative psychology: The storied nature of human conduct* (pp. 152–173). New York: Praeger.

De Andrade, L. L. (2000). Negotiating from the inside: Constructing racial and ethnic identity in qualitative research. *Journal of Contemporary Ethnography, 29,* 268–290.

DeMott, B. (1995). *The trouble with friendship: Why Americans can't think straight about race.* New York: Atlantic Monthly Press.

Deneen, P. J. (2001). Friendship and politics: Ancient and American. In P. D. Bathory & N. L. Schwartz (Eds.), *Friends and citizens: Essays in honor of Wilson Carey McWilliams* (pp. 47–66). New York: Rowman & Littlefield Publishers.

Dewey, J. (1988). Context and thought. In L. A. Hickman & T. M. Alexander (Eds.), *The essential Dewey: Vol. 1. Pragmatism, education and democracy* (pp. 206–216). Bloomington: Indiana University Press. (Original work published 1931)

Dill, B. T. (1983). Race, class, and gender: Prospects for an all-inclusive sister-hood. *Feminist Studies, 9,* 131–150.

Disch, L. J. (1995). On friendship in "dark times." In B. Honig (Ed.), *Feminist interpretations of Hannah Arendt* (pp. 285–311). University Park: Pennsylvania State University Press.

Du Bois, W. E. B. (1997). *The souls of black folk* (D. W. Blight & R. Gooding-Williams, Eds.). Boston: Bedford Books. (Original work published 1903)

Fisher, B., & Galler, R. (1988). Friendship and fairness: How disability affects friendship between women. In M. Fine & A. Asch (Eds.), *Women with disabilities: Essays in psychology, culture, and politics* (pp. 172–194). Philadelphia: Temple University Press.

Foss, S. K., & Griffin, C. L. (1995). Beyond persuasion: A proposal for an invitational rhetoric. *Communication Monographs, 62,* 2–18.

Foucault, M. (1970). *The order of things: An archaeology of the human sciences.* New York: Vintage Books.

Foucault, M. (1972). *The archaeology of knowledge and the discourse on language* (A. M. Sheridan Smith, Trans.). New York: Pantheon Press.

Frank, A. W. (1995). *The wounded storyteller: Body, illness, and ethics.* Chicago: University of Chicago Press.

Frank, A. W. (1997). Enacting illness stories: When, what, and why. In H. L. Nelson (Ed.), *Stories and their limits: Narrative approaches to ethics* (pp. 31–49). New York: Routledge.

Frank, A. (2002). Why study people's stories? The dialogical ethics of narrative analysis. *International Journal of Qualitative Methods, 1,* 1–20.

Frankenberg, R. (1993). *White women, race matters: The social construction of whiteness.* Minneapolis: University of Minnesota Press.

Fried, C. (1976). The lawyer as friend: The moral foundations of the lawyer–client relation. *The Yale Law Journal, 85,* 1060–1089.

Friedman, M. (1992). *What are friends for? Feminist perspectives on personal relationships and moral theory.* Ithaca, NY: Cornell University Press.

Friedman, S. (1995). Beyond white and other: Relationality and narratives of race in feminist discourse. *Signs, 21,* 1–49.

Gadamer, H. G. (1989). *Truth and method* (Rev. ed., J. Weinsheimer & D. G. Marshall, Trans.). New York: Continuum.

Gans, E. (1985). *The end of culture: Towards a generative anthropology.* Berkeley: University of California Press.

Gergen, M. M., & Gergen, K. J. (2006). Narratives in action. *Narrative Inquiry, 16,* 112–121.

Giddens, A. (1979). *Central problems in sociological theory: Action, structure and contradiction in social analysis.* Berkeley: University of California Press.

Goering, S. (2003). Choosing our friends: Moral partiality and the value of diversity. *Journal of Social Philosophy, 34,* 400–413.

Goffman, E. (1959). *The presentation of self in everyday life.* New York: Doubleday Anchor.

Granovetter, M. S. (1973). The strength of weak ties. *American Journal of Sociology, 78,* 1360–1380.

Greene, M. (1988). *The dialectic of freedom.* New York: Teachers College Press.

Greenfield, S. (1965). Love and marriage in modern America: A functional analysis. *The Sociological Quarterly, 6,* 361–377.

Grigoriou, T. (2004). *Friendship between gay men and heterosexual women: An interpretive phenomenological analysis.* London: London South Bank University.

Grunebaum, J. O. (2003). *Friendship: Liberty, equality, and utility.* Albany: State University of New York Press.

Gurevitch, Z. D. (1989). The power of not understanding: The meeting of conflicting identities. *Journal of Applied Behavioral Science, 25,* 161–171.

Haley, J. (1963). *Strategies of psychotherapy.* New York: Grune and Stratton.

Hall, R. L., & Fine, M. (2005). The stories we tell: The lives and friendship of two older black lesbians. *Psychology of Women Quarterly, 29,* 177–187.

Hansot, E. (2000). Civic friendship: An Aristotelian perspective. In L. Cuban & D. Shipps (Eds.), *Reconstructing the common good in education: Coping with intractable American dilemmas* (pp. 174–185). Stanford, CA: Stanford University Press.

Hastrup, K. (1990). The ethnographic present: A reinvention. *Cultural Anthropology, 5,* 45–61.

Henry, J. (1965). *Pathways to madness.* New York: Vintage Books.

Heron, M. (2004). *Deaths: Leading causes for 2004* [National Vital Statistics Reports No. 56(5)]. Hyattsville, MD: National Center for Health Statistics.

Hess, B. (1972). Friendship. In M. W. Riley, M. Johnson, & A. Foner (Eds.), *Aging and society: A sociology of age stratification* (Vol. 4, pp. 357–393). New York: Russell Sage Foundation.

Holquist, M. (1990). *Dialogism: Bakhtin and his world.* London: Routledge.

Hughes, M., Morrison, K., & Asada, K. J. K. (2005). What's love got to do with it? Exploring the impact of maintenance rules, love attitudes, and network support on friends with benefits relationships. *Western Journal of Communication, 69,* 49–66.

Hutter, H. (1978). *Politics as friendship.* Waterloo, Ontario: Wilfrid Laurier University Press.

Jackman, M. R., & Crane, M. (1986). "Some of my best friends are black . . .": Interracial friendship and whites' racial attitudes. *Public Opinion Quarterly, 50,* 459–486.

Jackson, R. L., & Hagen, P. L. (2001). The ethics of faculty–student friendships. *Teaching Philosophy, 24,* 1–18.

James, D. N. (1989). The friendship model: A reply to Illingworth. *Bioethics, 3,* 142–146.

James, W. (1991). *Pragmatism.* Amherst, NY: Prometheus Books.

Janis, I. (1972). *Victims of groupthink.* Boston: Houghton Mifflin Company.

Joseph, G. I., & Lewis, J. (1981). *Common differences: Conflicts in black and white perspectives.* Garden City, NY: Anchor Books.

Kahane, D. (1999). Diversity, solidarity and civic friendship. *The Journal of Political Philosophy, 7,* 267–286.

Kalmijn, M. (2002). Sex segregation of friendship networks: Individual and structural determinants of having cross-sex friends. *European Sociological Review, 18,* 101–117.

Kaplan, A. (1969). The life of dialogue. In J. D. Roslansky (Ed.), *Communication: A discussion at the Nobel conference* (pp. 87–108). Amsterdam: North-Holland.

Kaplan, M. (2005). Imagining citizenship as friendship in The Big Chill. *Quarterly Journal of Speech, 91,* 423–455.

Kennedy, T. M. (2004). Loading up the U-Haul: Traveling the spaces between friends and lovers. *Journal of Lesbian Studies, 8,* 44–55.

Kepnes, S. (1992). *The text as thou: Martin Buber's dialogical hermeneutics and narrative theology.* Bloomington: Indiana University Press.

Kermode, F. (1966). *The sense of an ending: Studies in the theory of fiction.* London: Oxford University Press.

Kermode, F. (1979). *The genesis of secrecy: On the interpretation of narrative.* Cambridge, MA: Harvard University Press.

Kirschner, C. (2004, November 15). The "hookup" defines the wild new world of sex on campus. *The Athens News,* p. 10.

Koehn, D. (1998). *Rethinking feminist ethics: Care, trust and empathy.* London: Routledge.

Krappmann, L. (1996). Amicitia, drujba, shin-yu, philia, freundschaft, friendship: On the cultural diversity of a human relationship. In W. M. Bukowski, A. F. Newcomb, & W. W. Hartup (Eds.), *The company they keep: Friendship in childhood and adolescence* (pp. 19–40). Cambridge, UK: Cambridge University Press.

Laing, R. D. (1968). *The politics of experience.* New York: Pantheon.

Laing, R. D. (1969). *Self and others.* Middlesex, UK: Penguin.

Laing, R. D. (1972). *The politics of the family.* New York: Vintage.

Lambert, T. A., Kahn, A. S., & Apple, K. J. (2003). Pluralistic ignorance and hooking up. *The Journal of Sex Research, 40,* 129–133.

Levinas, E. (1969). *Totality and infinity: An essay on exteriority* (A. Lingis, Trans.). Pittsburgh, PA: Duquesne University Press.

Lewis, C. S. (1960). *The four loves.* New York: Harcourt Brace & Company.

Lewis, R. A. (1978). Emotional intimacy among men. *Journal of Social Issues, 34,* 108–121.

Lindsey, K. (1981). *Friends as family: New kinds of families and what they could mean for you.* Boston: Beacon Press.

Lorde, A. (1984). *Sister outsider.* Trumansburg, NY: The Crossing Press Feminist Series.

Lunsford, A. A., & Ede, L. (1987). Collaboration and compromise: The fine art of writing with a friend. In T. Waldrep (Ed.), *Writers on writing* (pp. 121–127). New York: Random House.

MacIntyre, A. (1984). *After virtue: A study in moral theory* (2nd ed.). South Bend, IN: University of Notre Dame Press.

Maltz, D. N., & Borker, R. A. (1982). A cultural approach to male–female miscommunication. In J. Gumperz (Ed.), *Language and social identity* (pp. 196–216). Cambridge, UK: Cambridge University Press.

Mansbridge, J. J. (1975). The limits of friendship. In J. R. Pennock & J. W. Chapman (Eds.), *Participation in politics* (pp. 246–275). New York: Lieber-Atherton.

Marai, S. (2002). *Embers* (C. B. Janeway, Trans.). New York: Vintage. (Original work published 1942)

Martinez, J. (2000). *Phenomenology of Chicana experience and identity: Communication and transformation in praxis.* Lanham, MD: Rowman & Littlefield Publishers.

May, W. F. (1967). The sin against the friend: Betrayal. *Cross Currents, 17,* 158–170.

McCall, N. (1994). *Makes me wanna holler: A young black man in America.* New York: Random House.

McCullough, M. W. (1998*). Black and white women as friends: Building cross-race friendships.* Cresskill, NJ: Hampton Press.

McPhillips, K., Braun, V., & Gavey, N. (2001). Defining (hetero)sex: How imperative is the coital imperative? *Women's Studies International Forum, 24,* 229–240.

Mead, G. H. (1934). *Mind, self, and society.* Chicago: University of Chicago Press.

Meilander, G. C. (1981). *Friendship: A study in theological ethics.* Notre Dame, IN: University of Notre Dame Press.

Mills, J., & Clark, M. S. (1982). Exchange and communal relationships. In L. Wheeler (Ed.), *Review of personality and social psychology* (Vol. 3, pp. 121–144). Beverly Hills, CA: Sage.

Mink, L. O. (1970). History and fiction as modes of comprehension. *New Literary History, 1,* 541–558.

Monsour, M. (2002). *Women and men as friends: Relationships across the life span in the 21st century.* Mahwah, NJ: Lawrence Erlbaum.

Morin, S., & Garfinkle, E. M. (1978). Male homophobia. *Journal of Social Issues, 34,* 29–47.

Morrison, T. (1983). Recitatif. In A. Baraka & A. Baraka (Eds.), *Confirmation: An anthology of African American women* (pp. 243–261). New York: William Morrow & Company.

Morson, G. S., & Emerson, C. (1989). *Rethinking Bakhtin: Extensions and challenges.* Evanston, IL: Northwestern University Press.

Murphy, P. (1998). Friendship's eu-topia. *South Atlantic Quarterly, 97,* 169–185.

Naegele, K. D. (1958). Friendship and acquaintances: An exploration of some social distinctions. *Harvard Educational Review, 28,* 232–252.

Nardi, P. M. (1992). Sex, friendship, and gender roles among gay men. In P. M. Nardi (Ed.), *Men's friendships* (pp. 173–184). Newbury Park, CA: Sage.

Nardi, P. M. (1999). *Gay men's friendships: Invincible communities.* Chicago: University of Chicago Press.

Naylor, G. (1991). Etta Mae Johnson. In S. Konnelman (Ed.), *Women's friendships: A collection of short stories* (pp. 218–233). Norman: University of Oklahoma Press.

Newbold Chinas, B. (1993). *La Zandunga: Of fieldwork and friendship in southern Mexico.* Prospect Heights, IL: Waveland Press.

Nicholson, L. (1995). Introduction. In S. Benhabib, J. Butler, D. Cornell, & N. Fraser (Eds.), *Feminist connections: A philosophical exchange* (pp. 1–16). New York: Routledge.

Ohlemacher, S. (2007, November 13). Racial income gap gets wider: 3-decade study shows blacks slip farther behind. *The Columbus Dispatch,* pp. A1, A4.

Oliker, S. J. (1989). *Best friends and marriage: Exchange among women.* Berkeley: University of California Press.

Paine, R. (1969). In search of friendship: An exploratory analysis in "middle-class" culture. *Man, 4,* 505–524.

Pakaluk, M. (1994). Political friendship. In L. S. Rouner (Ed.), *The changing face of friendship* (pp. 197–182). Notre Dame, IN: University of Notre Dame Press.

Patchett, A. (2004). *Truth and beauty: A friendship.* New York: Perennial.

Paul, E. L., & Hayes, K. A. (2002). The casualties of "casual sex": A qualitative exploration of the phenomenology of college students' hookups. *Journal of Social and Personal Relationships, 19,* 639–661.

Paul, E. L., McManus, B., & Hayes, A. (2000). "Hookups": Characteristics and correlates of college students' spontaneous and anonymous sexual experiences. *The Journal of Sex Research, 37,* 76–88.

Peacock, B., Eyre, S. L., Crouse Quinn, S., & Kegeles, S. (2001). Delineating differences: Sub-communities in the San Francisco gay community. *Culture, Health & Sexuality, 3,* 183–201.

Peterson, E. E., & Langellier, K. M. (2006). The performance turn in narrative studies. *Narrative Inquiry, 16,* 173–180.

Pfuetze, P. (1954). *Self, society, and existence: Human nature and dialogue in the thought of George Herbert Mead and Martin Buber.* New York: Harper Torchbooks.

Putnam, R. D. (2000). *Bowling alone.* New York: Simon & Schuster.

Rake, J. M. (1970). Friendship: A fundamental description of its subjective dimension. *Humanitas, 6,* 161–176.

Rangell, L. (1963). On friendship. *Journal of the American Psychoanalytic Association, 11,* 3–54.

Rawlins, W. K. (1979). *A developmental and dialectical analysis of communication in friendship.* Paper presented at the annual meeting of the International Communication Association Convention, Philadelphia, PA.

Rawlins, W. K. (1982). Cross-sex friendship and the communicative management of sex-role expectations. *Communication Quarterly, 30,* 343–352.

Rawlins, W. K. (1983a). Individual responsibility in relational communication. In M. Mander (Ed.), *Communications in transition* (pp. 152–167). New York: Praeger.

Rawlins, W. K. (1983b). Negotiating close friendships: The dialectic of conjunctive freedoms. *Human Communication Research, 9,* 255–266.

Rawlins, W. K. (1983c). Openness as problematic in ongoing friendships: Two conversational dilemmas. *Communication Monographs, 50,* 1–13.

Rawlins, W. K. (1987). Gregory Bateson and the composition of human communication. *Research on Language and Social Interaction, 20,* 53–77.

Rawlins, W. K. (1989a). A dialectical analysis of the tensions, functions and strategic challenges of communication in young adult friendships. In J. A. Anderson (Ed.), *Communication Yearbook 12* (pp. 157–189). Newbury, CA: Sage.

Rawlins, W. K. (1989b). Cultural double agency and the pursuit of friendship. *Cultural Dynamics, 2,* 28–40.

Rawlins, W. K. (1992). *Friendship matters: Communication, dialectics, and the life course*. Hawthorne, NY: Aldine de Gruyter.

Rawlins, W. K. (1994). Being there and growing apart: Sustaining friendships during adulthood. In D. J. Canary & L. Stafford (Eds.), *Communication and relational maintenance* (pp. 275–294). San Diego, CA: Academic Press.

Rawlins, W. K. (1998a). Making meanings with friends. In R. L. Conville & E. Rogers (Eds.), *The meaning of "relationship" in interpersonal communication* (pp. 149–169). Westport, CT: Praeger Publishers.

Rawlins, W. K. (1998b). Writing about friendship matters: A case study in dialectical and dialogical inquiry. In B. Montgomery & L. Baxter (Eds.), *Dialectical Approaches to Studying Personal Relationships* (pp. 63–81). Mahwah, NJ: Lawrence Erlbaum.

Rawlins, W. K. (2000). Teaching as a mode of friendship. *Communication Theory, 10*, 5–26.

Rawlins, W. K. (2003). Hearing voices/learning questions. In R. P. Clair (Ed.), *Expressions of Ethnography* (pp. 119–125). Albany: State University of New York Press.

Rawlins, W. K. (2007). Living scholarship: A field report. *Communication Methods and Measures, 1*, 55–63.

Rawlins, W. K., & Rawlins, S. P. (2005). Advising as friendship. *NACADA Journal, 25*, 10–19.

Reeder, H. M. (1996). A critical look at gender difference in communication research. *Communication Studies, 47*, 318–330.

Reeder, H. M. (2000). "I like you . . . as a friend": The role of attraction in cross-sex friendship. *Journal of Social and Personal Relationships, 17*, 329–348.

Ricoeur, P. (1981). The narrative function. In J. B. Thompson (Ed. & Trans.), *Hermeneutics and the human sciences* (pp. 274–305). Cambridge, UK: Cambridge University Press.

Ricoeur, P. (1992). *Oneself as another* (K. Blamey, Trans.). Chicago: The University of Chicago Press.

Rommetveit, R. (1980). On "meanings" of acts and what is meant and made known by what is said in a pluralistic social world. In M. Brenner (Ed.), *The structure of action* (pp. 108–149). Oxford, UK: Basil Blackwell.

Rose, S. (2000). Heterosexism and the study of women's romantic and friend relationships. *Journal of Social Issues, 56*, 315–328.

Rosner, B., & Tubach, F. C. (with Tubach, P. S.). (2001). *An uncommon friendship*. Berkeley: University of California Press.

Rothleder, D. (1999). *The work of friendship: Rorty, his critics, and the project of solidarity*. Albany: State University of New York Press.

Rubin, L. B. (1985). *Just friends: The role of friendship in our lives*. New York: Harper and Row.

Ruesch, J., & Bateson, G. (1951). *Communication: The social matrix of psychiatry*. New York: Norton.

Sartre, J.-P. (1948). *Anti-Semite and Jew*. New York: Schocken Books.

Schutz, A. (1970). Interactional relationships. In H. R. Wagner (Ed.), *Alfred Schutz on phenomenology and social relations* (pp. 163–199). Chicago: University of Chicago Press.

Scott, E. K. (1998). Creating partnerships for change: Alliances and betrayals in the racial politics of two feminist organizations. *Gender & Society, 12,* 400–423.

Shifting attitudes: Survey results point to growing income-based division among blacks. (2007, November 21). *The Columbus Dispatch,* p. 10A.

Smith, A., & Nickerson, S. (1986). Women's interracial friendships. *Women's Studies Quarterly, 14,* 13–16.

Spence, L. D. (1978). *The politics of social knowledge.* University Park: Pennsylvania State University Press.

Stewart, J., & Zediker, K. (2000). Dialogue as tensional, ethical practice. *Southern Communication Journal, 65,* 224–242.

Suttles, G. D. (1970). Friendship as a social institution. In G. J. McCall, M. McCall, N. K. Denzin, G. D. Suttles, & S. Kurth (Eds.), *Social relationships* (pp. 95–135). Chicago: Aldine.

Swanson, J. A. (1992). *The public and private in Aristotle's philosophy.* Ithaca, NY: Cornell University Press.

Taylor, C. (1977). Interpretation and the sciences of man. In F. R. Dallmayr & T. A. McCarthy (Eds.), *Understanding and social inquiry* (pp. 101–131). Notre Dame, IN: University of Notre Dame Press.

Thomas, L. (1989). *Living morally: A psychology of moral character.* Philadelphia: Temple University Press.

Tillmann-Healy, L. M. (2001). *Between gay and straight: Understanding friendship across sexual orientation.* Walnut Creek, CA: Altamira Press.

Tillmann-Healy, L. M. (2003). Friendship as method. *Qualitative Inquiry, 9,* 729–749.

Todorov, T. (1984). *Mikhail Bakhtin: The dialogical principle.* Minneapolis: University of Minnesota Press.

Unger, R. (2000). Outsiders inside: Positive marginality and social change. *Journal of Social Issues, 56,* 163–179.

Vetere, V. A. (1982). The role of friendship in the development and maintenance of lesbian love relationships. *Journal of Homosexuality, 8,* 51–65.

Victor, B. (2003). *Army of roses: Inside the world of Palestinian women suicide bombers.* New York: St. Martin's Press.

Villard, K. L., & Whipple, L. J. (1976). *Beginnings in relational communication.* New York: John Wiley & Sons.

Walker, K. (1994). "I'm not friends the way she's friends": Ideological and behavioral constructions of masculinity in men's friendships. *Masculinities, 2,* 38–55.

Werking, K. J. (1997). *We're just good friends: Women and men in nonromantic relationships.* New York: The Guilford Press.

West, C., & Zimmerman, D. (1987). Doing gender. *Gender & Society, 1,* 125–151.

White, A. (2006). "You've got a friend": African American men's cross-sex feminist friendships and their influence on perceptions of masculinity and women. *Journal of Social and Personal Relationships, 23,* 523–542.

White, E. (1983). Paradise found: Gay men have discovered that there is friendship after sex. *Mother Jones*, 10–16.

Wiseman, J. P. (1986). Friendship: Bonds and binds in a voluntary relationship. *Journal of Social and Personal Relationships, 3,* 191–211.

Wittig, M. (1992). *The straight mind.* Boston: Beacon.

Wright, D. (1999). *Personal relationships: An interdisciplinary approach.* Mountain View, CA: Mayfield.

Wright, P. H. (1984). Self-referent motivation and the intrinsic quality of friendship. *Journal of Social and Personal Relationships, 1,* 115–130.

# Index

# About the Author

**William K. Rawlins** (PhD, Temple University) is Stocker Professor in the School of Communication Studies at Ohio University. His book, *Friendship Matters: Communication, Dialectics, and the Life Course,* was selected as an Outstanding Academic Book for 1993 by the editors of *Choice,* and received the Gerald R. Miller Book Award in 1994 from the Interpersonal and Small Group Interaction Division of the National Communication Association. In 2002 he received The Theory That Has Left a Legacy Award: "The Dialectical Perspective" from the Communication Theory Interest Group of the Central States Communication Association. Over the past 25 years, Professor Rawlins has published extensively about the unique challenges and dialectical tensions of communicating in friendships.

Bill teaches courses in communication in friendships across the life course, interpersonal and relational communication, communication theory, dialogue and experience, interpretive and ethnographic inquiry, communication and narrative, and Gregory Bateson and communication theory. While at Purdue University, he received the W. Charles Redding Award for Excellence in Teaching from the Department of Communication five times, the School of Liberal Arts Departmental Educational Excellence Award for 2000–2001, and the School of Liberal Arts Educational Excellence Award for 2002–2003.